WORDS AND WAYS
OF AMERICAN ENGLISH

WORDS AND WAYS
OF AMERICAN
ENGLISH

AN AUTHORITATIVE
ACCOUNT OF THE ORIGINS,
GROWTH AND PRESENT STATE OF
THE ENGLISH LANGUAGE IN AMERICA BY

THOMAS PYLES

ANDREW MELROSE
STRATFORD PLACE LONDON

Andrew Melrose Limited

London   Melbourne   Sydney   Auckland
Bombay   Cape Town   New York   Toronto

First published in Great Britain 1954

First published in 1952 *in U.S.A. by
Random House, Inc., and simul-
taneously in Canada by Random
House of Canada, Ltd. Copyright*
1952 *by Random House, Inc.*

*Set in eleven point Monotype Bembo
one point leaded*

*Printed in Great Britain
by The Anchor Press, Ltd.,
Tiptree, Essex*

To

KEMP MALONE

Contents

Preface

THE years that have elapsed since the end of the First World War—a relatively brief period in the history of our country since its first permanent settlement by English-speaking people—have witnessed the growth of a very lively interest in the study of American English. This has manifested itself most notably in H. L. Mencken's three substantial volumes devoted to what he prefers to call "the American language"; in the late George Philip Krapp's less bulky but still formidable two-volume work *The English Language in America*; in the monumental *Linguistic Atlas of New England*, which is but the first part of the projected *Linguistic Atlas of the United States and Canada*; in the four-volume *Dictionary of American English*; in M. M. Mathews's two-volume *Dictionary of Americanisms*; and in a good many valuable works of more limited scope, including a host of monographs, articles, word lists, glossaries, and notes which have appeared in *American Speech*, in *Dialect Notes* (the first volume of which appeared as long ago as 1890), and in the *Publications of the American Dialect Society*.

The present book, which owes much to all these works and to many others which must regrettably go unmentioned here, is an attempt to provide for the lay reader a brief yet adequate treatment of the English language as it has been and is spoken and written by Americans. The professional student of language will probably find little or nothing here with which he is not already familiar, although it is hoped that the presentation and interpretation of some of the material may strike him as fresh and perhaps controversial.

This book contains few of the impedimenta of scholarship. The temptation to use footnotes for documentation I have sternly and sometimes painfully resisted. I have no love for such unscientific terms as "flat" and "broad" *a* or "hard" and "soft" *g*, but they seem to have the virtue of being generally understood. I should have liked to use the alphabet of the International Phonetic Association to indicate pronunciation, but, for the sake of readers who are unfamiliar with them, I have refrained from using phonetic symbols. Consequently, no *eths* or *yoghs* will be found rearing their graceless, unloved head in the

9

pages which follow, and only once has an *e* been permitted to turn itself topsy-turvy to make a *schwa*.

In *The American Language* and the two supplements to that marvellously stimulating work, Mencken has dealt so fully and so well with the word stock of American English that any later writer must of necessity employ a good deal of his illustrative material. Indeed, there would seem to be little point in seeking out recherché examples simply because Mencken has used all the good ones. Nevertheless, although my debt to Mencken is tremendous in the chapters dealing with the American vocabulary, this book is quite independent of Mencken in its point of view as well as in its linguistic judgments.

I am indebted also to the Johns Hopkins Press for permission to use in somewhat modified form the greater part of my "Innocuous Linguistic Indecorum" (*Modern Language Notes*, January, 1949) as the concluding paragraphs of Chapter VI; to Professor Kemp Malone, of the Johns Hopkins University, and to Professor Allen Walker Read, of Columbia University, for many helpful suggestions; to Mr. Andrew Nelson Lytle, author and historian, for reading Chapter VI and discussing it with me, though it should be said in fairness to him that he is not in complete sympathy with my attitude toward what in the early part of the nineteenth century was thought of as the West; to Mr. G. Legman and Mr. Harold M. Cohen for putting me right on some Yiddish etymologies; to Mr. Jess Stein and Mr. Robert N. Linscott of Random House, for good advice and editorial aid; and to my wife for overseeing the whole job of writing this book with loving albeit stern eye and for exercising her sound critical sense. Finally, a word of appreciation should be said for those long-suffering students in the University of Florida who listened uncomplainingly to lectures ostensibly devoted to *Beowulf* and Chaucer which somehow managed to include long digressions on such apparently irrelevant matters as American pronunciation, the origin of *O.K.*, and linguistic geography.

T. P.

ONE

Early American Speech: Coinages, Adaptations, and Survivals

THE language of America, like America herself, has had a vigorous and interesting growth. We have seen to it, sometimes at the expense of our reputation for modesty, that all the world knows of America's political, economic, and cultural achievements, of her moral pre-eminence, of her technological genius—Yankee know-how, to describe it in native terms—in short, of America's contribution to civilization. This amazing development in less than three and a half centuries is mirrored to a large extent in the development of the American vocabulary. Such terms as *blue laws, sunbonnet, lightning rod, log cabin, almighty dollar, forty-niner, abolitionist, War between the States, dime novel, hash house, charley horse, linotype, Gideon Bible, Noble Experiment, G-man, hoodlum, New Deal, jeep, motel, ghost writer, baby sitter,* and *cybernetics* cannot fail to tell us something of the "American way of life" in all its fascinating and infinite variety, past and present. Moreover, American words, like the phenomena they name, have not stayed at home; indeed, some Americanisms, like O.K. and *telephone,* are known and used all over the world.

American English began as seventeenth-century British English. It was inevitable, however, that its subsequent development should diverge somewhat from that of British English, that a number of words, grammatical forms, and idioms lost in British English should survive in American English and, conversely, that American English should lose certain features of earlier British English which have been retained in England. It was equally inevitable that we should find new words, or adapt old words, to express concepts and to name institutions which arose in our New World, not to mention the more immediate task of finding verbal labels for topographical features and for flora and fauna which were new to English-speaking people.

By far the largest and most important group of early Americanisms are those coined from English metal. There is nothing characteristically American about the manner of their formation for the most part, although the circumstances that gave rise to many of them are peculiarly American. Some of them, whose use was not limited to exclusively American needs, have passed over into British English— usually after a good deal of objection on the part of outraged British commentators. Others have made the Atlantic crossing quietly and unobtrusively.

When the Reverend Dr. John Witherspoon invented the word *Americanism* in a paper published in the *Pennsylvania Journal and Weekly Advertiser* for May 9, 1781, he defined it as "an use of phrases or terms, or a combination of sentences, even among persons of rank and education, different from the use of the same terms or phrases, or the construction of similar sentences in Great Britain." His definition does not, of course, allow for the fact that "an use of phrases or terms, or a construction of sentences" may be at first characteristic of American usage and subsequently pass over into British usage or even become the common property of the entire English-speaking world. The definition of the *Oxford English Dictionary*, "a word or phrase peculiar to, or extending from, the United States," is somewhat more satisfactory if only because it covers more ground, though it does not by any means tell the whole story; it will, however, answer present needs well enough.

A discussion of the distinctive word stock of American English obviously could not be limited to words adopted in this country from other languages, along with those which have first come into use here, either as innovations, like George Eastman's *kodak* and Oliver Wendell Holmes's *anaesthesia* and *anaesthetic*, or as normal developments of the English language in this country, like *land office*. It must also include words or expressions used in America with meanings different from those they bear in England, a number in which an older English meaning has been retained, and even some which, without any change of meaning, are nevertheless much more applicable to American than to English life and hence more widely used and understood in this country than in England.

For features of the American landscape the colonists used such words as *run* "streamlet" and its synonym *branch, bluff, foothill, rapids, pond, barrens, bottoms, bottom land, neck, cliff, watergap, watershed, divide, clearing, hollow, swamp, underbrush,* and *creek.* Such words as *spinney, combe, fen, wold, copse, dell, heath,* and *moor,* all still familiar in British English, soon became more or less obsolete in America. Some of these early Americanisms are compounds, some are applications of individual English words to new uses by modifying their meanings, and some are words which were (and may still be) dialectal in England. *Bluff,* for example, was originally an adjective applied to the bows of a ship when presenting a nearly vertical front. Its meaning was later extended to describe a bank or cliff which resembled the bluff bows of a ship. In the latter part of the seventeenth century the word began to be used as a noun in American English. Although the American sense is now well established in British usage, *bluff* has the distinction of being, as H. L. Mencken points out in *The American Language* (4th ed., New York, 1936), the first Americanism to be sneered at by an Englishman, in this instance one Francis Moore, an adventurer who wrote a book called *A Voyage to Georgia, Begun in the Year 1735* in which, describing the infant city of Savannah, he referred to "the Bank of the River (which they in barbarous English call a *bluff*)." The noun *bluff* "pretense" and the verb *to bluff* "to put up a bold front" occur a good deal later; they may just possibly be derived from the earlier topographical uses. *Creek* in British English designates a small arm of the sea, whereas in American English it may mean any small stream. A *pond* in England is an artificial pool; in America, *pond* may also mean a small natural lake. It is not to be expected, of course, that all American adaptations should survive; some, like *bent* "bend of a river," have become quite obsolete.

Descriptive expressions for animals, birds, fishes, plants, and trees for which the colonists did not use the Indian words were formed of familiar English elements according to familiar English patterns. *Mockingbird, bullfrog, catfish, fox grape, garter snake, bluejay, ground hog, ground squirrel, ground pea, snap bean, barn swallow, muskrat, potato bug, canvasback, razorback, copperhead, peanut, rattlesnake, lightning bug, sweet potato, live oak, bluegrass, clingstone, slippery elm, black alder, eggplant, roasting ear,* and *popcorn* might just as readily have originated in England as here. The colonists chose to call the common swallow of North America and Europe a *barn swallow,* corresponding to British *chimney swallow*. The bird referred to in American usage as a *chimney swallow* is really a swift, and is indeed sometimes called a *chimney swift*. *Black alder* is one of many expressions of its type; there are about seventy composite names of plants, animals, birds, and fishes with *black* as one of their components, and almost as many with *blue*. The other words listed seem to require no special comment. *Bobolink, bobwhite, whippoorwill*, and *katydid* are imitative of the sounds made or supposed to be made by the creatures so named. Only rarely in the early days does one meet the pleasant fancifulness that inspired such words as *Johnny-jump-up*.

Frequently the colonists made an old word serve with slightly different meaning. The American red-breasted thrush, for example, was called a *robin*; the European bird which they had called a *robin* in Old England is somewhat smaller and has a yellowish-red breast. *Blackbird*, which in Europe denotes a wild bird allied to the thrushes, was applied in America to any of various birds having black plumage. A number of different brightly coloured birds not closely related to the orioles of Europe were nevertheless given that name in this country, for example, the *Baltimore oriole*. Similarly, the European partridge is not the same as its American namesake, or rather namesakes, for in New England *partridge* designates the ruffed grouse and in Virginia the bobwhite quail. *Corn* was applied here to an altogether different cereal and lost its older general meaning "grain." *Huckleberry* is a variant of *hurtleberry*, which is in turn an older form of *whortleberry* "bilberry"; but the American huckleberry is quite a different fruit. *Beech, hemlock, walnut*, and *laurel* also acquired new meanings in the colonies.

Freshet now usually has the same meaning in British as in American English, but the present British usage would seem to be the result of American contamination, for in the eighteenth century the word meant only a stream of fresh water. The element "flood" was the contribution of the colonists. Similarly, *barn* designated a building for storing grain (the word is historically a welded compound of two Old English words, *bere* "barley" and *ærn* "house"); in American English it came also to mean a place for housing stock, particularly cattle. References to the *lumber room* in British fiction may well puzzle those American readers who do not live in certain parts of the South, principally Virginia, where the term is still current. *Lumber*, a term for disused articles of furniture and other cumbrous material which took up space, was employed by the American colonists to designate roughly cut timber, a meaning which British English has gained while retaining the older meaning. The earlier sense survives in American English as a rule only in the derivative verb *to lumber* "to clutter."

In British English *store* usually means "warehouse" and in the plural designates a large commercial establishment selling different kinds of goods (what is called a *department store* in America), as opposed to smaller specialized establishments, which are known as *shops*: thus, "I buy most of our things at the stores," although *department store* is also now perfectly familiar in England. By the mid-eighteenth century *store* had come to be used in America for the type of establishment previously called a *shop*. *Hardware store*, first recorded in the latter part of the eighteenth century, would seem somewhat strange to an Englishman. He would probably know what *hardware* is, but in his own country he would buy nuts and bolts and spanners (in America, *wrenches*) at an *ironmongery*, an *ironmonger's shop*, or simply an *ironmonger's*. His wife, incidentally, would buy her cloth, linen, draperies, etc., at the *draper's* or *draper's shop*, not at the *dry goods store*, for *dry goods* has also changed its meaning in America; perhaps it would be more accurate to say that it has limited its meaning, for the term in British English includes nonliquid goods such as grain as well as cloth. Nowadays *shop* is coming back into wide American usage as a designation for a retail establishment selling a particular type of goods, as in *leather goods shop* and *dress shop*, particularly in the large cities. The word has in fact a certain "tone" when so used in America; one is likely to pay more in a *boot shop* than in a *shoe store* and may even obtain a superior grade of merchandise for one's money. Presumably a *shoppe* is even tonier and more expensive. Meanwhile, however, long before this comparatively recent development, *shop* had acquired the specialized meaning "place for doing work," as in *carpenter's shop*, *barber shop* (earlier *barber's shop*), *machine shop*, and *blacksmith shop* (earlier *blacksmith's shop*), while the word had all along been used in what is thought of as the British sense in the derivative verb *to shop*, as well as in such compounds as *shopgirl*, *shopworn*, and *shoplifter*.

In an American *store* one is waited on by a *clerk*; in an English *shop*, by a *shop assistant*. This American use of *clerk*, which is also used as a verb, as in *to clerk in a store*, dates from the eighteenth century. In British English a clerk (pronounced *clark*) remains a bookkeeper or an employee who copies documents; he works in a business office perched on a high stool like Bob Cratchit or at a desk in a law office, and as a rule has no personal dealings with customers or clients. The frequent statement in histories of English literature to the effect that Charles Lamb was a clerk in the East India House has doubtless confused many of our schoolboys. In his *Modern American Usage* (Oxford, 1935), H. W. Horwill tells of going to one of the desks in a Philadelphia hotel and inquiring whether it was the desk of the hotel clerk, absent-mindedly using his normal British pronunciation *clark*. "No," was the reply, "this is the Hotel Lafayette."

Rock has been widely used in American English since early in the eighteenth century as a synonym for *stone*. In British English, as in some varieties of American English, *rock* means "stone as a substance, a mass, or a very large stone"; one could not speak of "throwing rocks" in England, as American moppets do, without being thought to indulge in American "tall talk." Perhaps American verbal prudery was partially responsible for the original avoidance of *stone* in most sections of the country. The word retained the anatomical meaning it has in the twenty-third chapter of Deuteronomy until well into the nineteenth century, and Ozarkers still call a stallion a *stone-horse*, though not in the presence of their womenfolk. There must have been a time when the sexual meaning of the word was so much alive that it caused titters from the prurient even when used in its geological sense. Consequently it may have been avoided much as *ass* in the sense "donkey" as well as in its transferred sense "silly fellow" is avoided in American English today. Like *breast*, *stone* was doubtless felt to be particularly risqué in the plural number.

Balance in the sense "remainder" is an American development, as in "the balance of his money." Though it is listed in the *Oxford English Dictionary* with the label "commercial slang" to limit its British use, it may occur in American English in the most formal contexts. *Team*, in British English "a pair of horses," extended its meaning here to include the harness and the vehicle drawn. A plot of ground was called a *lot* in American English because as early as the seventeenth century lots were actually drawn to determine the apportioning (or *allotting*) of common lands.

Early in American English *to squat* acquired the specialized meaning "to occupy land without legal right," and it was not long before *squatter* was used to designate one who so occupied land and who frequently thus acquired his title to it. *Frontier* came early to take on a peculiarly American sense "the border of settled regions within a country." Previously the word had been used to designate a boundary between two countries, which is still its British English meaning.

New uses of words and new combinations reflect the physical, cultural, and social conditions of life in a new country, for example, *backwoods* and *backwoodsman*, *back country*, *backlog* "a large log at the back of the fireplace to keep the fire going," *log house*, *frame house*, *clapboard*, *buckshot*, *corncrib*, *corncob*, *corn bread* (and a good many other *corn-* combinations), *pine knot*, *blaze* "mark made on a tree," *salt lick*, *stamping ground*, *smokehouse*, *landslide*, *sinkhole*, *cold snap*, *prickly heat*, *bee* "meeting of neighbours to do certain work," *bundling* "method of courtship in which the participants lay in bed together with their clothes on," *shingle roof*, *sheet iron*, *spruce beer*, *eggnog*, *buckwheat cake*, *ice cream*, *land office*, *town meeting*, *statehouse*, *camp meeting*, *crazy quilt*, *rail fence*, *worm fence*, *snake fence*, *hired man* (and *girl*), *catboat*, and *schooner*. The origin of the last-named word is uncertain, but it is probably derived from a dialectal New England verb *to scoon* "to skim along."

England had had nothing which could appropriately be called a *backwoods* for a great many years; hence no term was ready to hand in the English language to designate areas lying beyond the more settled sections. The early settlers needed such a term, and they promptly formed one from familiar English elements. Because logs were widely used in this country for building as well as for heat and light, *log house* occurs as early as the seventeenth century, long before *log cabin*, which has seemed particularly American in the aroma of homespun saintliness which emanates from it because of its associations with Abraham Lincoln. Actually, *log cabin*, though recorded in the eighteenth century, came first to have valuable political connotations during the "Log Cabin Campaign" of General William Henry Harrison in 1840, a campaign which gave birth to the most successful of all Americanisms, *O.K.*, to be discussed in a later chapter. An Englishman might well be amazed by the recorded statement that "the cellar of our new house was dug by a bee in a single day," as would most present-day Americans, for the word in this sense is practically obsolete except when preceded by some modifying word such as *spelling*, *husking*, or *quilting*. The first *bee* in this sense, the origin of which is unknown, was a *spinning bee*. According to John Russell Bartlett's *Glossary of Words and Phrases Usually Regarded as Peculiar*

B

to the United States (1848), when a new settler arrived it was possible for the neighbouring farmers, by uniting their efforts in a *raising bee*, to build a log house for the newcomer in one day. There are still relics of such a pleasantly co-operative spirit in American life, even though the need for it is not so great as in pioneering days. The grimly humorous *lynching bee* also occurs, but not until well into the nineteenth century. *Blaze* "white spot on the face of a horse" was very early adapted in America to mean a similar though artificially produced mark on a tree for marking a boundary or indicating a path in a forest. The noun was later converted into a verb, as in *to blaze a trail*. Business concerning public lands was transacted in a *land office*, the term being recorded as early as the seventeenth century. *Land-office business* "bustling business" is much later, dating from the time when the West was opened up to homesteaders.

Bundling was no doubt one of the few joys in life allowed to the young in early New England, where the climate made its practice more common than elsewhere. The Reverend Samuel Peters in his *General History of Connecticut* (London, 1781) observed, as quoted by Bartlett, that "notwithstanding the great modesty of the females is such that it would be accounted the greatest rudeness for a gentleman to speak before a lady of a garter or leg, yet it is thought but a piece of civility to ask her to bundle." Another English clergyman, who travelled in New England in 1759–60, declared that, although the practice might at first "appear to be the effects of grossness of character, it will, upon deeper research, be found to proceed from simplicity and innocence." But youthful Puritan blood was frequently hot, and there is ample evidence that many abuses occurred. Consequently, Noah Webster virtuously refused to define the term in this sense in his dictionaries.

Other simple pleasures of early American life were *tarring and feathering* and *gouging*, the latter operation performed by twisting the forefinger in a lock of hair at the side and scooping out the eye with the thumbnail, which was allowed to grow long for that purpose. Although Captain Francis Grose in his *Classical Dictionary of the Vulgar Tongue* (London, 1785) calls gouging "a cruel practice used by the Bostonians in America," the art seems to have reached its highest stage of development at the hands (or, to be more specific, the thumbs) of the flatboat bullies who flourished on the Ohio and Mississippi Rivers in the early years of the nineteenth century, probably the greatest experts in mayhem this nation has ever known. These gallant heroes of American ballad, song, and story were, according to a commentator writing in 1822, "much given to drinking whiskey, fighting, and gouging, that is, they fight up and down, trying to put out each others [*sic*] eyes with their fingers and thumbs, and sometimes biting off each others noses or ears." Another horrified English observer of American mores, convinced that the human character could sink no lower than it had in the new country, declared that "no such practice would be endured by an English mob; no such disgraceful revenge ever entered the breast of a Creek, a Cherokee, or a Kickapoo Indian." *To gouge* later developed the metaphorical sense "to cheat," and was subsequently converted into a noun meaning "the act of cheating."

Shooting iron, to scalp, to tomahawk, rough-and-tumble, and *Lynch's law* also date from this early period. The honours for giving the last-named term to the world were long thought to be equally divided between two men, Colonel Charles Lynch (1736–96) of Bedford County, Virginia, and Captain William Lynch (1742–1820) of Pittsylvania County, Virginia. Evidence, however, pays little heed to the claims of superior rank and points incontrovertibly to the Captain. The careers of these two worthies are parallel in so many ways that each might well have been the father of *Lynch's law,* which in turn gave rise to *to lynch* and its derivatives; *Lynch's law* is now obsolete, being supplanted by *lynch law.* The Colonel and the Captain, who were no kin whatever to each other, were county magistrates during the latter years of the Revolutionary War, at a time when their counties were being harassed by Loyalists and by bands of armed robbers. Only the court at Williamsburg was authorized to try felonies in those days. Nevertheless, according to the tradition, or rather the traditions, alike in every respect except in the names of the counties (both in south-western Virginia) and the identity of the founder of lynching, both Colonel and Captain Lynch summarily tried and punished the rascally Loyalists and robbers. Incidentally, a third contender, a certain Mayor Lynch of Glasgow, was reported by the *Pall Mall Gazette* (as quoted in the New York *Tribune* of January 27, 1881) to have flourished around the end of the fifteenth century and to have hanged a criminal with his own hands on one occasion, but it is most likely that Mayor Lynch is a mere jealous interloper.

The terms thus far discussed have been for the most part redolent of homely, simple life, terms which might well have been, and probably were, coined by homely, simple people, who also originated such pleasingly homespun metaphors as *elbow room, to take to the woods*, and *to fly off the handle*. But there are also flossily sophisticated Americanisms, the self-conscious coinages of educated men, some of which ever so faintly foreshadow the verbal flamboyance of many of the Westernisms of the nineteenth century. Many of these are derivative forms, in contrast to the compounds which seem to have been favoured by the folk. *To advocate*, a conversion of the noun *advocate*, is now used freely in British English and was actually coming into use in England around the mid-eighteenth century. Both British and American purists belaboured it under the impression that it was an American coinage, as it may indeed have been, and hence barbarous; it was one of the words which Benjamin Franklin, whose attitude towards language was as prissy as any schoolmarm's, urged Noah Webster to use his authority in "reprobating," in a letter which Franklin wrote to the future lexicographer in 1789. Franklin was also opposed to *to improve* "to use," now archaic but never the Americanism that Franklin took it to be, along with *to notice, opposed to*, and *to progress*. *To notice* was certainly much more common in American than in British use in Franklin's day, though it is not of American origin. *To progress*, apparently an American retention of an older English usage, has passed into English use once more from America. The participial form *opposed* in the use Franklin disapproved of was actually new in his day. Less questionable as Americanisms than some of the words Franklin thought attributable to American linguistic depravity are *to locate* and *to legislate*, which appear to be back formations from *location* and *legislation* (or *legislator*), though the first is formed by analogy with other English verbs derived from Latin past participles in *-atus* such as *to exterminate, to illuminate*, and *to create*. A free-handed use of suffixes produced *to deputize, to Americanize, presidential, dutiable, customable*, and other similar derivatives.

Presidential, along with *congressional* and the flashily erudite *gubernatorial*, grew out of the distinctively American political organization. *Americanism* in the linguistic sense was, as we have seen, a coinage of Dr. Witherspoon, who seems also to be responsible for our somewhat pretentious use of Latin *campus*, previously *yard* (as still at Harvard). *Americanism* was shortly to develop another meaning, the one which it has in popular use today; perhaps it would be more accurate to say that it was independently recoined in the sense "American patriotism" —so used by Jefferson in 1797—and later, "a characteristic of the United States or its citizens." *To Americanize* also dates from the latter years of the eighteenth century.

Other contributions of the learned, or at least of men prominent in the early days of the Republic, include *to antagonize, to immigrate, to eventuate, to demoralize, constitutionality, to Anglify* (Franklin), and *Anglophobia* (Jefferson). When Jefferson used *to belittle* in his *Notes on Virginia* (written 1781–2), an English reviewer sneered, "It may be an elegant [word] in Virginia, and even perfectly intelligible; but for our part, all we can do is to *guess* at its meaning. For shame, Mr. Jefferson!" Jefferson had used the word in the sense "to make small," but by 1797 it had acquired its present figurative meaning "to disparage." It is now freely used in British English, though H. W. Fowler believed that it had only one meaning "that may pass uncensured," namely, "to dwarf by contrast," as in "a tower not so tall as to belittle the main building." Admitting that the word in the sense "disparage" had gained considerable currency in that form of the language of which he considered himself the guardian, Fowler declared in his *Modern English Usage* (Oxford, 1937) that "it is still felt by many to be an undesirable alien that should not be allowed to supplant the old-established words, of which we have a large supply suitable for various contexts and shades of meaning." This is certainly reminiscent of the attitude expressed by the English traveller, Captain Basil Hall, to Noah Webster when in answer to Webster's question, "If a word becomes universally current in America, where English is spoken, why should it not take its station in the language?" the doughty Captain replied, "Because there are enough words already." Horwill in his *Modern American Usage* states that *to antagonize* is in England "seldom used by good writers." In the sense "to oppose" it was frowned upon by Fowler, who felt that it produced "an effect of vulgar display," though he endorsed its use in the sense "to incur the hostility of, to expose oneself by one's action to the enmity of," declaring that "this sense probably comes also from America; but its usefulness is so obvious that we should welcome it." *To immigrate* with its derivatives seems very useful to many of us, despite the fact that a large proportion of our Southern and Southwestern population (those who pronounce *pen* exactly like *pin*) pronounce *to emigrate* and its derivatives in exactly the same way; but one sometimes wonders if the nice distinction is really worth bothering with, inasmuch as every immigrant must of necessity be an emigrant also. ("There are enough words already.") *Breadstuff* seems somehow unworthy of the man who, to use a Hollywoodism, gave us *Anglophobia* and *belittle*, but it appears nevertheless to have been first used by Jefferson in 1793. John Pickering suggests in his *Vocabulary or Collection of Words and Phrases which have been supposed to be peculiar to the United States of America* (1816) that the word made headway in American use because we lacked the general term *corn*, having used that word exclusively for *maize*. *Lengthy* is of seventeenth-century origin, but it was given widespread respectability in the latter years of the eighteenth century by such American magnificoes as John Adams, Jefferson, and Hamilton. It was for some time a particularly sharp thorn in the sides of British commentators, but is now freely used in England and usually listed in British dictionaries. Even H. W. Fowler issues no caveat against its use.

American English employs a small but highly interesting group of words and usages, sometimes regarded as Americanisms, which are actually nothing more than survivals from the British English of older days. It is no cause for wonder that some of the changes which have taken place in British English since the early days of our colonization have failed for one reason or another to be reflected in the language spoken and written in America. Some of these British fossils are encountered only in isolated rural and mountainous regions, where the British-influenced speechways of the coastal cities have never taken root; others are encountered in standard American English.

Isolated communities tend to be old-fashioned in speech as in other respects. The language of Iceland, for example, preserves many features which have been lost in the related Scandinavian languages; the English of rural Ireland is likewise archaic in many respects from the point of view of the British Standard. The most significant and progressive part of the whole American community, however, has never been isolated for long from the language or the cultural traditions of England, for Anglophobia, to use Jefferson's word for it, has never flourished among the genteel. While a number of older features of British English are preserved in American English, the importance of these must not be exaggerated, for American English has not only developed independently but has also shared in a great many of the developments in British English.

Our southern highlands, whose inhabitants are popularly supposed to speak a form of English practically identical with that spoken in the court of Queen Elizabeth, were not settled, as a matter of fact, until well into the eighteenth century. Consequently, southern mountain speech, while genuinely old-fashioned in many details, is not a survival of the language of Shakespeare, but rather a development of eighteenth-century English which is somewhat retarded as compared with the development which has taken place in less isolated regions. The ancestors of the mountain folk were old-fashioned people at the time they settled the Appalachians and subsequently the Ozarks, and their descendants have retained some forms of speech which had already become somewhat archaic in the more polite circles of eighteenth-century England and which, because they occur in the literature of the Elizabethan period, have been thought to be Elizabethan survivals.

Examination of the literature and the documentary records of seventeenth- and eighteenth-century America discloses a good many dialect words not hitherto recorded in English for the very reason that they were dialect words and therefore, from the point of view of English writers, unworthy to be used in literature. Some of these words, brought over here in the seventeenth and eighteenth centuries and recorded by men who were not primarily writers, have been preserved in American English. A second class of archaisms (from the point of view of the present British Standard) consists of words which were once a part of the standard language of England but have subsequently gone out of fashion and hence out of use there save in isolated rural areas.

Most of the words under consideration are still known in England, but are seldom used there at the present time. From the Englishman's point of view, they are archaic in the senses retained in America, for instance, *fall* for the season of the year which the speaker of contemporary standard British English calls *autumn*. In America we may occasionally write *autumn* but we customarily say *fall*. *Sick* used to be synonymous with *ill* in British as well as in American English, but the English have given it the specialized meaning "sick at the stomach, nauseated." Regurgitation is usually implied, as in "The dog was sick on the rug"; hence the word is considered not quite "nice." In America, however, it has retained its older, more general meaning, that which it has in Chaucer's "The hooly blisful martir for to seke, / That hem hath holpen whan that they were seeke" (To seek the holy, blissful martyr, who has helped them when they were sick) or in Shake-speare's "He is very sick, and would to bed" in *Henry V*. Illness to Americans denotes an extreme degree of indisposition; when one is ill, one is somewhat worse off than when merely sick. H. C. Wyld says of *sick* in his *Universal Dictionary* (London, 1932) that it is used predicatively in British English in the sense "ill" only in Biblical or archaic phrases such as *sick unto death, sick at heart,* and in a few collo-quial phrases such as *to fall sick*. Military usage is always likely to be highly conservative, and *sick* continues to appear in the British military usages *to go sick* and *to report sick*. *To be sick, to feel sick,* and *to look sick* are rarely used in England though still common and even usual in America. Attributively, however, the word survives in British use in *a sick man (dog, cow)* and in the phrase *the sick man of Europe,* denoting the old Turkish empire, as well as in *sick list* (military) and *sickbed*. The compounds *lovesick, homesick,* and *seasick* are common to British and American.

To *guess* in the senses "to suppose, to believe, to feel certain" is another American survival, no longer so common as it was when English authors began labelling their American characters by making them begin every speculation with "Wal, I guess" (alternating with "Wal, I calc'late" and "Wal, I reckon"). Chaucer uses the word in precisely the same way when the Knight informs the other pilgrims that Emilia's "yelow heer was broyded in a tresse/Bihynde hir bak, a yerde long, I gesse," as also when Chaucer himself says of the Squire, "Of twenty yeer of age he was, I gesse." Shakespeare also uses the construction, as in Escalus' "I guess not" in *Measure for Measure* and Talbot's "Better far, I guess, /That we do make our entrance several ways" in 1 *Henry VI*. Gilbert M. Tucker in his amusingly crotchety *American English* (New York, 1921) lists examples of the supposed American use of *to guess* occurring in British English as late as the nine-teenth century in novels of Anne and Emily Brontë and of Anthony Trollope, but that such uses of *to guess,* though readily understood, are merely sporadic in present standard British English cannot be gain-said. Wyld labels the usage "archaic or American," though his illus-trative example of the American use, "I guess we shall lose the train," is unfortunate, inasmuch as no American would be likely to say "lose the train" for "miss the train," and only the schooling-conscious would say *shall*.

To *loan* went out of use in British English in the eighteenth century, but is still in wide use in American English, though teachers and textbooks are of the opinion that we ought to use *to lend* instead and reserve *loan* as a noun. What is to be gained by so doing we are not told. *Homely* when used to describe a person had the same meaning "unattractive" for Shakespeare and Milton that it has for present-day Americans, but Englishmen now use it in the sense "simple," a meaning which it may have in American English only in reference to things, as in *homely fare*. What we should consider a *homely* girl would in England be called a *plain* girl, by an identical euphemistic process. It is highly unlikely that any woman would care to be considered homely or plain in either the British or the American senses of those terms, but to be plain is in America certainly preferable to being homely, and in England vice versa. *Well* was used attributively, as in *a well man*, in British English as late as the early eighteenth century, but is now archaic in this sense in British use; it is still very much alive in American English. *Slim* in the sense "small," as in a *slim chance* or *slim evidence*, has been obsolete in England for about as long as the attributive use of *well*. *To peek* went out of standard use in England at about the same time but has survived in America. *Drouth* "dry weather," still used in Scotland, has long been considered archaic in England. Despite the efforts of our native guardians of linguistic propriety to get us to use *drought* (rhyming with *out*), *drouth* is still a common form in America.

Shoat "weaned piglet" is no longer current in standard British English, though it has had an uninterrupted existence in America, at least in rural sections where people talk about pigs, which they usually call *hogs*—another survival, incidentally, for in England *pig* has come to mean "swine of any age," whereas rural American English uses *pig* in its earlier sense of "young swine." The American use of *shoat, pig*, and *hog* thus represents older English uses no longer surviving in England. *Pigsty* is perfectly well known but is not widely used by Americans. It may be employed figuratively, as in "The place was a regular pigsty," though even here *pigpen* would be more usual.

Trash with Iago's meaning in "Who steals my purse steals trash" is no longer common in British English, in which the usual term for refuse is *rubbish*; *trash* is used figuratively in the sense "worthless literary or artistic work." Iago's use of the same word to refer to a person has also survived in American English, particularly in the Southern phrase *poor white trash*, where it usually has the collective meaning "whites whose living standards are so low that even the Negroes look down upon them," but may be used of an individual, as in "He's just poor white trash." Incidentally, *cracker* as a designation for a Southern poor white person is also a survival of older British usage. It is listed in the sense "braggart" in the *Oxford English Dictionary* with a citation as early as 1509, but it seems to have become obsolete in England during the eighteenth century. The link between the American usage and the earlier British usage is supplied by M. M. Mathews in his *Dictionary of Americanisms* (University of Chicago Press, 1951) with the following citation, occurring in a letter written in 1766 by Gavin Cochrane to the Earl of Dartmouth: "I should explain to your Lordship what is meant by Crackers; a name they have got from being great boasters; they are a lawless set of rascalls on the frontiers of Virginia, Maryland, the Carolinas, and Georgia, who often change their places of abode." The word has extended its use to Florida, where it seems to mean simply a native, with no reference to social and economic status; at least, many Floridians seem to take particular pride in describing themselves as "just crackers," which is somewhat like the devotion of the Oklahoman to his nickname *Sooner*, originally applied to those who settled on the government land before it was legally opened to settlers and thereby gained an unfair advantage over those who did not "jump the gun." *Chore* "task, small job," a variant of *char* as in *charwoman*, has not been used in British English for a great many years but is still quite common in standard American use. When we speak of a *deck* of cards instead of a *pack*, we are using a word which in this sense has long been obsolete in British English, but which occurs in older literature, as in Shakespeare's "The king was slily fingered from the deck" (3 *Henry VI*). *Stock* "cattle" and *beef* for the animal while still on the hoof are survivals of older English usages, though British English uses *livestock* in the same sense as American *stock* (as opposed to *dead stock* "farm implements"). *After* in such phrases as *half after four* (instead of *half past four*) was formerly standard; it is now only dialectal in England though still common in America. Purists have long vociferated against *mad* in the meaning "angry," although the natural American use of the word in this sense is a survival of earlier English use. It is, as a matter of fact, still so used in colloquial standard British English. Teachers in this country have been so successful in their campaign against *mad* in this sense, however, that it is by now quite rare in formal contexts in American English.

Gotten as the past participle of *to get*, except in such phrases as *ill-gotten gains*, has long been archaic in England. It remains in common use in America by educated and uneducated speakers alike, despite the fact that many American writers of textbooks have placed the form in their *indices prohibitorum*, sometimes specifically, sometimes by implication in their failure to list it as the usual third principal part of *to get* in the senses "to receive, acquire, become," though the alternative participial form *got* is regularly used when the meaning of *to get* is "to have, possess."

Other archaic verb forms like *clumb* (rhyming with *come*) and *holp* (usually pronounced exactly like *hope*) as past tenses of *to climb* and *to help* survive only in nonstandard American English such as that spoken in the Appalachian area. The words cited, as well as others equally archaic, survive also in dialectal use in England. They are just as archaic from the point of view of standard American usage as from that of standard British.

In addition to the vocabulary items discussed, American English retains a number of pronunciations which have become archaic in standard British English. These will be treated in some detail in Chapters III and X.

It would be unfortunate if the numerous examples of English archaisms surviving in American English which have been cited here for their intrinsic interest should give any reader the impression that American English is simply archaic British English. After all, what one regards as archaic depends wholly upon where one happens to be standing. From an American point of view such words as *living* in the sense "benefice," *fortnight*, and *waistcoat*, along with many others freely used in British English, are as archaic as *fall* "season" and *deck* (of cards) are from a British point of view. The innovations which American English has introduced, to which attention has been given in the early part of this chapter, along with those which came later in the nineteenth and twentieth centuries, are much more impressive than the survivals. The conservatism of American English must be sought elsewhere than in its vocabulary and in such grammatical features as have been cited. Furthermore, an attitude which has been called conservative—the exaggerated respect for authority, practically any authority other than that of usage, which is so striking a characteristic of educated American English—is not really so; it is actually of comparatively recent growth, becoming predominant towards the latter part of the eighteenth century, when the schoolmaster's supposed linguistic omniscience was allowed to stultify the development of what might have been a "passing pleasing tongue" had it been left alone to develop in its own way.

TWO

Early American Speech: Adoptions from Foreign Tongues

BEFORE there was any permanent settlement of English-speaking folk in this land a number of Indian words had made their way into the language of England by way of Spanish or Portuguese—words from Nahuatl, the tongue of the Aztecs, who were the most highly advanced of the Indians that the Spanish found in Mexico, as well as from various Indian dialects spoken in Central and South America and the West Indies. Some of these words came in time to be current in all the languages of Europe.

The English language in those exuberant days of Elizabeth, of Raleigh, Drake, Hawkins, Bacon, Marlowe, Jonson, and Shakespeare, had been particularly receptive to augmentations of its already rich word stock from foreign sources—the so-called "inkhorn" terms from the classical languages, along with words from French, Spanish, Italian, and Portuguese. Words from the New World must have had all the charm of lush exoticisms in a period when the language was being enriched from so many nearby Continental sources, though they seem for the most part commonplace enough today—words like *potato*, *tomato*, *chocolate*, *cocoa*, *canoe*, *cannibal*, *barbecue*, *maize*, and *savannah*, which must have been known to the first Englishmen to come to these shores with any intention of staying. One of them, *maize*, was by a strange perversity of linguistic fate to be replaced by *corn* in the English of America. The British use *corn* in the sense "wheat," while retaining the older meaning of "grain," as in the "Corn Laws." Another of them, *cannibal*, a modification of *Caribal*

"Caribbean native," was used in slightly different form by Shakespeare in his play about the "vexed Bermoothes," for *Caliban*, if not
simply a metathetic form of *can(n)ibal*, is a variant of *Cariban*,
itself a variant of *Caribal*. *Barbecue*, while appearing first in British
English, is nevertheless much more familiar in America, and its use to
designate an outdoor social or political meeting at which animals are
roasted whole is exclusively American. But these words, while native
to the New World, must be distinguished from those which entered
the language of Englishmen who chose or were forced to transplant
themselves permanently in this strange and savage land.

The colonizers of this country were confronted with a land whose
topography, meteorological phenomena, trees, plants, birds, and
animals were frequently quite different from what they had known in
England. Inasmuch as an understanding of the principles of semantics
is not congenital, people generally are wont to ask when they see some
new object, "What is it?" and expect in answer to be told its name,
supposing then that they have learned something really significant
about it. This procedure, or something very similar to it, must have
been gone through a great many times in the early days of the colonization of America when Indians were friendly enough to be asked
and bright enough to divine what was being asked of them. Sometimes,
too, these first white Americans made up their own names for what
they saw, if there was no one to tell them the "true" names or if the
"true" names were too difficult for them to pronounce. As we have
seen in the preceding chapter, they frequently combined or modified
English words, as in *bullfrog* and *jimson weed* (originally *Jamestown
weed*); sometimes they made use of sound alone, as in *bobolink*.

The situation with regard to the American Indian languages, with
many tribes speaking apparently unrelated languages which are in turn
subdivided into dialects, is extremely complex. Fortunately it need
not concern us here, for to American English only one stock, the
Algonquian, is important. This huge group of tribes, comprising
among others the Arapaho, Blackfoot, Cheyenne, Cree, Delaware,
Fox, Micmac, Ojibwa (Chippewa), and Penobscot, formerly occupied
a larger area than any other North American Indian stock. It was they
whom the first English settlers in Virginia and Massachusetts came in
contact with.

As early as 1608 Captain John Smith in his *True Relation of . . .
Virginia Since the First Planting of That Collony* recorded *raccoon*, though

he did not spell it that way. He wrote it in various ways—for instance, *raugroughcun* and later, in his *General Historie of Virginia, New-England and the Summer Isles* of 1624, *rarowcun*—in his effort to reduce to symbols, which were, incidentally, ill-adapted to that purpose, what he heard or thought he heard from the Indians. It is highly unlikely, as a matter of fact, that a single English word of Indian origin would be immediately intelligible to an Indian today, for words have been clipped, like *squash* (the vegetable), which was originally *askutasquash*, folk-etymologized like *whiskey-John* "bluejay" from *wisketjan*, or in one way or another made to conform to English speechways.

Early Indian loan words naming creatures neglected by Adam are *opossum, moose, skunk, menhaden, terrapin, woodchuck,* and *caribou*. *Opossum* usually occurs in speech and often in writing in an aphetic form as *possum*, as does *raccoon* as *coon*. *Woodchuck* is a folk-etymologizing of Cree or Ojibwa *otchek* or *odjik*. Noah Webster was quite proud, by the way, of deriving *woodchuck* from an Avestan word meaning "pig" and made frequent reference to this acute etymological discovery in lectures and prefaces. *Caribou*, as the spelling of its final syllable indicates, comes to us by way of Canadian French; an Englishman would have been more likely to write *cariboo*. These words, all of Algonquian origin, designate creatures indigenous to North America. Ojibwa *chipmunk* would seem to belong to this group, though it was first recorded considerably later, in Cooper's *Deerslayer* (1841); it was almost certainly in use much earlier.

A good many native plants, vegetables, trees and shrubs bear names of Indian origin: *hickory, pecan, poke(weed), chinquapin, squash, persimmon,* and *catalpa,* all but one of which are Algonquian. That one, *catalpa,* is of Muskhogean origin. A good many Southern place names are of this linguistic stock, which includes Creek, Chickasaw, and Choctaw, but *catalpa* (with its variant *catawba*) and the topographical *bayou* (from Choctaw *bayuk* "stream," coming to us by way of Louisiana French) are the only widely known words other than place names taken from the languages of these Indians, who formerly occupied an area of our country including most of Georgia, Alabama, and Mississippi and parts of Tennessee, Kentucky, Louisiana, and Florida.

Other early borrowings from the Indians include words denoting foods, customs, relationships, or artifacts peculiar to the Indians at the time of borrowing: *hominy, succotash, johnnycake, pone, pemmican, moccasin, tomahawk, totem, wigwam, toboggan, powwow, mackinaw, caucus* (perhaps), *wampum, sachem, papoose,* and *squaw. Toboggan* and *mackinaw* are first recorded later than the others in this group, though their earliest use in English certainly goes back considerably beyond their first recording. Both entered English by way of Canadian French; the latter word has a half-French spelling, *Mackinac,* when used as a name for the strait, the island, and the town in Michigan. The first element of *johnnycake* is probably from *jonakin* or *jonikin,* apparently of Indian origin and meaning a thin griddle cake made of corn meal. *Johnnycake* was folk-etymologized to *journey cake,* which Noah Webster thought the original form; he assumed that it meant cake to eat when one went on a journey. It has also been suggested that the word is a corruption of *Shawnee cake,* a kind of cake supposed to have been eaten by the Shawnee Indians—an explanation which Mr. Mencken in *The American Language, Supplement One* (New York, 1945) considers "much more plausible" than any other. *Jonikin* (usually spelled *johnnikin*) is still used for a corn griddle cake in the eastern part of the Carolinas and on the Eastern Shore of Maryland.

As for *caucus,* somebody suggested a good many years ago that it was from a somewhat similar Algonquian word meaning "one who advises," and more recently efforts have been made to relate it to *cockarouse,* recorded by Captain John Smith in 1624 as *caucorouse* and designating an Indian chief in Virginia, later extended to designate an influential and wealthy white colonist. It is also possible that *caucus* is a variant form of *caulkers.* The learned John Pickering in his *Vocabulary* thought so, basing his belief on a statement in the *History of the Rise and Independence of the United States* (1788) by the Reverend William Gordon, who stated that in Boston "more than fifty years ago Mr. Samuel Adams's father and twenty others, one or two from the north end of town, where all the ship business is carried on, used to meet, make a *caucus,* and lay their plan for introducing certain persons into positions of trust and power." Pickering inferred from this reference to "the north end of town, where all the ship business is carried on" that it was "not improbable that *caucus* might be a corruption of *caulkers,* the word meeting being understood." The *Dictionary of American English* suggests the possibility that *caucus* may be the name of a long-forgotten neighbourhood in Boston called West-Corcus; indeed, the quotation given in support of this suggestion (from the Boston *Evening Post* of August 19, 1745) concerns a caucus-like meeting in that neighbourhood to "take into serious consideration the conduct of those reverend clergymen who have encouraged the itineration of Mr. George Whitefield," the Calvinistic Methodist evangelist. Another etymology of *caucus* with which Pickering flirted has recently come to light: among some of his old papers there occurs an explanation to the effect that it consisted of the initials of the names of six men—Cooper, Adams, Urann, Coulson, another Urann, and Symmes. Pickering states that he got this story from "B. Russell, who had it from Sam'l Adams and Paul Revere." The etymology has a familiar ring to it; it is precisely the sort upon which the dilettante etymologist dotes. Still another theory is that the American word is simply a borrowing of Latin *caucus* "drinking vessel," which may indicate a feature of the evening's entertainment in the early American gatherings.

All the other words in this last group save *johnnycake* have made the Atlantic crossing, and most of them are now about as familiar to the English as they are to us. In fact, all of them except *mackinaw* are listed in Wyld's *Universal Dictionary*; only *succotash* and *johnnycake* are labelled "U.S.A." The usual British pronunciation of *wigwam* rhymes with *big dam*, a pronunciation never heard in this country. *Pemmican*, the Indian name for dried meat pounded into paste, mixed with fat and dried fruits, and then compressed into cakes, has even acquired the figurative meaning in British English of "condensed statement." On the continent of Europe also, most of these words are quite well known as a result of literary transmission, for generations of European children have thrilled to the novels of James Fenimore Cooper, as well as of his European imitators.

Tammany as a political designation is a well-known Americanism of Indian origin. Tammany was a Delaware chief who flourished in the latter part of the seventeenth century and who was jocularly canonized as an American saint in 1771. His name was later used to designate a political club which ultimately grew into the present powerful Democratic organization in New York City. References to *Tammany* as the name of the club, which was founded in 1789, occur from 1790 onwards. The organization uses *the Wigwam* as a designation for Tammany Hall, *sachem* for a high official of the society, and *brave* (not of Indian origin, but long used to mean an Indian warrior) for a rank-and-file member.

A good many other words of Indian origin are included in the

Dictionary of American English, but most of them are not in wide current use: *tuckahoe* "edible part of a fungus found on roots of trees," which is also used to designate a poor white in Virginia and West Virginia, *carcajou* "wolverine," *manito* or *manitou* "a god," *quahog* or *quahaug* "hard clam," *sagamore* "chief," *samp* "corn porridge," *tamarack* "the American larch," *mugwump* "great man," and others considerably less familiar. *Mugwump,* though known much earlier, came into real prominence in the presidential campaign of 1884, when it was applied to those independent Republicans who, affecting an attitude of superiority, refused to support James G. Blaine as their party nominee. Nowadays the word is chiefly notable for the oft-recorded definition by a Congressional wag (would there were more of his kidney!) to the effect that a mugwump was one who always had his *mug* on one side of the fence and his *wump* on the other.

Some early Americanisms were translations or supposed translations of Indian words or phrases, for example, *paleface* (first used by James Fenimore Cooper), *war paint, warpath, firewater, pipe of peace, medicine man, Great Spirit, big chief, to scalp,* and *to bury the hatchet.* Frequently *Indian* was used in conjunction with another word, as in *Indian meal, Indian file, Indian summer,* and *Indian gift,* originally a gift for which one expected something of more value in return, but later a gift which the giver took back. *Indian giver* is first recorded, as far as we know, in Bartlett's *Glossary* of 1848, with the notation that "this term is applied by children to a child who, after having given away a thing, wishes it back again," though *Indian gift* occurs much earlier. The *Dictionary of American English* lists almost a hundred such combinations, though not all are early, for instance, *honest Injun,* which is not recorded until 1875. *Indian summer* is of special interest. By 1830 it had been used in British English (by Thomas De Quincey) in the figurative sense "declining years." That the term is still perfectly familiar in England in this slightly later sense is indicated by John Galsworthy's use of it as the title of a section of the *Forsyte Saga* dealing with the last years of Jolyon Forsyte. Although the English do not have occasion to use the expression in the meteorological sense that Americans have because the phenomenon it names is much less striking in Europe than here, it is nevertheless perfectly well understood in this sense. It has been suggested that Indian summer is so called because its occurrence was predicted by the Indians to the first batch of settlers, but there is no evidence that the term, which is documented only at a comparatively late date, was ever used by the earliest settlers. Other suggestions are that the Indians were responsible for lighting the brush fires common in the late autumn or early winter; that the period constituted a last chance before the final onset of cold weather for the Indians to harass and bedevil the white settlers; and that, because the early settlers thought of the Indians as false and fickle—an idea reflected in the term *Indian giver*—the sham summer weather was called *Indian summer*. The real origin of the term remains as hazy as the weather it designates.

Before passing on to other non-English influences it is interesting to note that British English borrowed *Mohawk*, which it usually spelled *mohock*, early in the eighteenth century to designate, according to the *Oxford English Dictionary*, "one of a class of aristocratic ruffians who infested the streets of London at night," but the term has only a historical interest today. It has never had any currency in American English save among professors of eighteenth-century English literature. The *Apache* of *Apache dance*, a rowdy, sexy dance performed by a pair of dancers attired as a Parisian gangster and his "moll," did not come to us directly from the well-known American aborigines of that name. It came instead by way of French, which borrowed the name of the Indian tribe, Gallicized its pronunciation, and used it to designate a Parisian street bully.

It is perhaps not surprising, considering the ultimate reduction of the American Indians to the status of a conquered people, that the Indian element in American English is no larger than it is. As a matter of fact, if we leave out of consideration place names, of which there are an overwhelming number—more than half of our states bear Indian names, and a large portion of our rivers, lakes, mountains, towns, and cities as well—the Indian influence on our vocabulary must be characterized as slight.

The Indian languages were not, however, the only non-European influence upon the English of America in colonial days. More than a year before the Pilgrims landed on Plymouth Rock in search of religious freedom, a group of people were against their will brought here from the west coast of Africa—principally from Senegal, Gambia, Sierra Leone, Liberia, the Gold Coast, Togo, Dahomey, Nigeria, and Angola—and forthwith sold into slavery. The traffic in Negro slaves continued until shortly before the Civil War, though slackening somewhat after 1808, when the Slave Trade Act went into effect.

A great majority of these Negroes were brought direct from Africa; some, however, had previously lived in the British West Indies, where they had picked up a bare working knowledge of English.

Most of the descendants of these transplanted Africans living in the South now speak conventional American English. Because of lack of social contacts with whites and lack of schooling, relics of older standard speech may occasionally be heard from them, such as the pronunciation *deef* for *deaf* and *obleege* for *oblige*. When a coloured charwoman with some embarrassment informed me that her small daughter had suffered an injury in her *grine*, she was not using an un-English, "darky" pronunciation, but merely saying *groin* in a manner which went out of fashion in more sophisticated usage years ago. There is, of course, no connection whatever between race and the ability to articulate given speech sounds, though it is popularly believed that the Southern Negro speaks as he does because of a peculiar conformation of speech organs, aided and abetted by indolence and stupidity. I was once gravely informed by a professor of government that the Negro does not have an *r* sound (my informant was of course referring only to *r* before a consonant sound and in final position) because the "letter *r*" did not exist in African languages—not one of which he had any acquaintance with, incidentally. When I presumed to disagree with his explanation, a corollary of which was that the speech of white Southerners was *r*-less because of the linguistic influence of Negro "mammies," and to point out that an Ohio-bred Negro has no difficulty whatsoever pronouncing *r* in all positions, he was grievously offended with me. The fact is that uneducated Negroes in the South by and large differ little in their speech from the uneducated whites. As for the presence of archaisms, they may also be heard from whites who have lived for a long time in cultural isolation, for instance the Southern mountain folk.

There are, however, communities of Negro Americans engaged largely in the cultivation of rice, cotton, and indigo along the coastal region of South Carolina and Georgia, both on the Sea Islands and on the mainland, who have lived in cultural and geographical isolation for many generations. Most of them have had little contact with whites; some, indeed, have seldom seen white people. These Negroes, numbering about a quarter of a million, speak a type of English which has been so heavily influenced by the African languages native to their remote ancestors that it is not readily intelligible to people, white or coloured, from other parts of the country. Their language, Gullah or Geechee, retains a good many African characteristics in its system of sounds, its syntax, its morphology, its vocabulary, its methods of forming words, and, most striking of all to one hearing it for the first time, its intonation. The word *Gullah* is probably either from *Gola*, the name of a Liberian tribe and its language, or from *Angola*. *Geechee*, also used in the up-country of South Carolina as a derisive nickname for a low-country white, particularly one living in the Charleston area, is probably derived from the name of another Liberian tribe and language.

It was very unlikely that Africans from the same tribe or language area would find themselves thrown together on a single plantation in sufficient numbers to enable them to maintain their native languages. The chances were all that they would be considerably dispersed upon their arrival at the various southern ports. Consequently, it became necessary for them to learn English as well as they could. It is not likely that anyone helped them to do so, unless there were proto-types of Mrs. Stowe's Little Eva gliding or floating about the plantations (for Little Eva seldom merely walked) in the seventeenth and eighteenth centuries. The only English many of them ever heard from native speakers was that of the illiterate or semiliterate white indentured servants with whom they worked in the fields or who were set over them as overseers. It was for them not simply a matter of translating word for word their native idioms into English. This cannot be done successfully even with related languages, where it may result in something intelligible if un-English, like *the bread is all*, a Pennsylvanian Germanism (though heard in other parts of the country) from German *das Brot ist alle*. It was for these Negroes a matter of acquiring a quite different linguistic psychology, a new attitude towards the phenomena of life as expressed by language. It is not surprising that their accomplishment fell considerably short of perfect. Their English was a sort of jargon or pidgin, which passed into use by their descendants as a native language. This type of so-called creolized language has been preserved largely in the speech of the Gullahs, Negroes who "stayed put" in a region in which they have always been far more numerous than whites and in which they have developed the only distinctive Negro speech in this country.

The principal importance of Gullah, aside from its intrinsic interest as a remarkable linguistic development, is that recent studies of it have been the means of identifying beyond doubt the African source of a number of words in Southern American English, a few of which have passed into other types of American English and one of which, *banjo*, if it is indeed of African origin, is part of the English language wherever it is spoken. Until Lorenzo Dow Turner began his investigations about twenty years ago, Gullah was traditionally regarded as "a quaint linguistic mongrel," to quote from one serious commentator; it was thought to be characterized by "intellectual indolence," "slovenly and careless," a debased form of the "peasant English" of poor whites, a sort of baby talk. One writer even went so far as to attribute its phonological characteristics to the "clumsy tongues," "flat noses," and "thick lips" of the Negroes who speak it.

Professor Turner's studies of Gullah, culminating in his *Africanisms in the Gullah Dialect* (Chicago, 1949), identify thousands of words in Gullah which have or may have African sources. Unlike earlier commentators, who assumed that many words which seemed strange to them were either nonsense words or mispronunciations of English words, Turner, himself of African descent, took the trouble to acquire a good working knowledge of West African languages. His studies and conclusions have made short shrift of some of the theories of previous writers, who assumed, for instance, that a Gullah word for "tooth" which sounded to them something like *bong* was merely a childish, clumsy-tongued, flat-nosed, thick-lipped mispronunciation of English *bone*, and that the Gullah word *det* or the expression *det rain* "a long, hard rain" was really *death rain*, which involved the further assumption that to the Gullahs a long, hard rain is an omen of death to come—as it were, folklore made to order. The fact that in the Wolof language, spoken in Senegal and Gambia, the word for "tooth" is very like *bong* (it is impossible to indicate the exact pronunciation of the un-English final sound of this word, a palatal nasal, without using phonetic symbols) and that in the same language the word for "long, hard rain" is *det* ought to dispose of the "baby talk" explanation for good and all—though of course it will not, for most people prefer "quaint" explanations of linguistic phenomena to the true ones.

From many Gullah informants, some of them bearing names which are a delight to contemplate—among them Saki Sweetwine, Prince Smith, Samuel Polite, Sanko Singleton, Balaam Walker, Scotia Washington, Shad Hall, and Paris Capers—Dr. Turner collected more than five thousand African words in the Gullah region. About four-fifths of these are now used only as personal names, but most of the remainder are everyday words in the speech of the Gullahs. Some of these words, doubtless the common possession of Negroes in all the slaveholding states, passed into the vocabulary of whites at what must have been a very early date.

How did words from the language of humble slaves get into the speech of their white masters? M. M. Mathews, who devotes the final chapter of his *Some Sources of Southernisms* (University, Ala., 1948) to Africanisms in the word stock of Southern American English, speculates with some reason that such words were transmitted by white children, who would not have resisted the influences of what their elders considered an inferior culture. Dr. Mathews cites his aged aunt's aversion to the "Negro word" *cooter* "turtle" and her regret that her brother, Mathews's father, had sullied the "purity" of his speech by ever using the word.

Actually, the African contribution is rather meagre. The remarkable thing is, considering the social and economic relationship of black to white, that there should have been any contribution. Many a white Southerner has imbedded in his vocabulary words whose African origin he probably never suspects. *Banjo* and *cooter* have already been cited. The first word has usually been considered as originating in a Negro mispronunciation of *bandore*, an English word of Spanish transmission denoting a musical instrument whose similarity to the banjo consisted mainly in the fact that it had strings to be plucked. According to Turner, the most probable source is Kimbundu, a language spoken in Angola, in which the word *mbanza* refers to an instrument very similar to the banjo. *Cooter* is very likely from *kuta*, a word appearing in two French West African languages, Bambara and Malinke, in which it has the same meaning as in the language of the Gullahs and in the English of many white Southerners.

Goober "peanut" is a modification of Kimbundu *nguba*, with similar forms occurring in Imbundu (also spoken in Angola) and Kongo (Belgian Congo and Angola). *Pinder*, with the same meaning, is from Kongo *mpinda*. Both these words are freely used in the South; the first has probably gained a limited national currency.

A number of gustatory and culinary terms of African origin testify to the skill of Negro cooks. Many of these, however, are local terms, like *cush* "corn meal stuffing" and *cala* "sweetened rice"—the latter term confined to the New Orleans area. *Gumbo* is confined to no locality or region, nor is *yam*, which is found also in British English and which is of Portuguese transmission; in Scotland it is used for the common white potato. If the word *yam* was brought to these shores by our early settlers, as it may have been, it is of course not to be regarded as belonging with the group of words under discussion; but there is no reason to insist that, because it occurs also in British English, we could not have got it independently. The same people from whom the Portuguese got the word were right here, and the word might well have entered the American vocabulary, as Dr. Mathews points out, from the language of the slaves. At the least, its use in American English would have been reinforced by their use of it. The word survives as an Africanism in the Gullah dialect (in the form *yambi*) to mean a red sweet potato, which is its usual meaning in Southern American English.

Buckra "white man" is also of African origin, appearing as *mbakara* in Efik and Ibibio, spoken in Southern Nigeria. Loss of the initial nasal sound in the word probably occurred in Negro speech before the word was transmitted to whites and is due to the influence of English on the speech of the Negroes. Simplification of the initial consonant combinations *mb-*, *mp-*, *nd-*, *nt-*, and *ng-*, which do not occur in this position in English, is frequent in the Gullah pronunciation of African words.

The great blue heron is frequently called *poor Joe* (or *po' Joe*) in those regions of the South in which the bird is found. There can be no doubt that this is the same word as Vai (Liberia and Sierra Leone) *pojo* "heron." It is likely that *chigger* and its variant *jigger*—the dictionaries give a spelling *chigoe* which suggests a pronunciation seldom if ever heard—are of African transmission as far as their use in American English is concerned, and perhaps of African origin as well. At any rate, *jiga* "flea" is found in a number of African languages spoken in Senegal, Gambia, Togo, Dahomey, and Northern and Southern Nigeria. The word got into British English probably by way of the British West Indies and has been thought to be of Carib origin. It is likely, however, that its use in American English is due independently to Negro transmission, regardless of its ultimate origin.

Pickaninny, which is probably used nowadays by whites more frequently than by Negroes, is of African transmission, but its source is Portuguese *pequenino* "very little." It is not impossible that the last part of the Portuguese word may have been identified by the Negroes with the Mende (Sierra Leone) word *nini* "female breast," *pequenino* being folk-etymologized into *pickaninny* after these Negroes acquired their English. The word is not exclusively American (the same is true of *buckra, jigger,* and others), though it is probably more commonly used here than elsewhere. It is, nevertheless, recorded in British English almost a century and a half earlier than in American English.

Hoodoo and its New Orleans variant *voodoo* are Africanisms. Both forms are in use by the Gullahs. They have, however, become somewhat differentiated in meaning, the latter usually referring to the cult which flourished in the West Indies and was later introduced into this country. *Hoodoo* is applied to a person or object that is thought to bring bad luck, *to hoodoo* consequently meaning "to bring bad luck to someone." Voodoo worship was introduced into Louisiana very early by slaves from the French colonies of Martinique, Guadeloupe, and Santo Domingo, where the cult—probably of African origin, as its name would indicate—raged furiously. It would seem to have grown rather slowly at first, but was a source of worry among the whites by 1782, when the Spanish governor of Louisiana prohibited further importation of Negroes from Martinique because slaves from there were thought to be "too much given to voudouism and make the lives of the citizens unsafe." Later, and partly for the same reason, a similar prohibition was extended to Negroes from Santo Domingo. After the American occupation, however, there were no such restrictions, and with the sudden influx of Negroes into Louisiana by way of New Orleans between 1806 and 1810, voodoo began to exert a strong influence upon the Louisiana Negroes. For a long time thereafter—until well after the Civil War, in fact—voodoo "queens" and "doctors" were persons of tremendous power and prestige among the Negroes, and even to some extent among the lower-class whites.

The most famous of the queens, who were priestesses of the cult and much more influential than the doctors who shared with them their powers of sorcery, was the remarkable Marie Laveau, a free mulatto of striking beauty in her younger years, who was by vocation a hairdresser and by avocation a procuress for white gentlemen. For more than forty years absolute ruler of the cult, she has remained a legend to this day. The visitor to New Orleans, if he is lucky, may still hear old Oscar "Papa" Celestin, a Robert Frost in ebony, sing *Marie Laveau,* an original composition which recounts some of the miracles performed by this celebrated "cunjer-lady."

Transmission into general use of African *zombi,* a word intimately associated with voodooism, is probably rather recent, though it must have been known to whites in certain areas of the South at an early date. Its present familiarity may well be credited to the cycle of "horror" films some years ago. The word originally designated the snake god which was the object of adoration in the voodoo cult. It later came to mean a supernatural force thought to restore corpses to life, and ultimately a corpse brought to life by means of this force. Recently it has been used, with an obvious appropriateness, to designate a mixed drink of (usually) rum and brandy.

Juke, which has come into general use among whites comparatively recently, mainly in the compounds *juke box* and *juke joint*, has been a part of the vocabulary of the Gullahs for a long time in the sense "disorderly," particularly in the combination *juke house*. Turner shows that the word is of African origin. In standard colloquial use its meaning has been considerably toned down, as has been that of *jazz*, which, though of unknown origin, is said to have been long used by Negroes, particularly in the New Orleans region. *Jazz* is very likely of African origin, though no African etymon has been found. These two words are included here because they have probably appeared in the English or creolized English speech of Negroes since pre-Revolutionary days, even though they may have been late in reaching the standard language. Their very nature would of course sufficiently explain the fact that they were not earlier transmitted to whites. *Jazz* as a verb is, as a matter of fact, sometimes used by whites, though only on a rather low social level, in the sexual sense which it seems originally to have had among the Negroes.

It is pleasant to be able to record that Professor Turner's researches in Gullah have cleared up the origin of *to tote*, long an etymological puzzle. Professor Turner found possible African sources in Kongo and Kikongo *tota* "to pick up," with related words in other West African languages meaning "to carry." The fact that *tote* is used in Gullah does not rule out the possibility of an unknown English source, for very many English words are used by the Gullahs. It is likely, however, that if the word is not of African origin, its use has been reinforced, at least in the South and particularly among the Gullahs, by the African words. Though it is usually thought of as a Southernism, *tote* is of fairly frequent occurrence in parts of New England; it has also been found in upstate New York, northern Michigan, and northern Minnesota, occurring alone and in the combinations *tote road, tote wagon, tote team,* and *tote sled.* There can be no doubt, however, that the dissemination of the word has been from the South.

Contacts with other colonizing peoples have also contributed to the American vocabulary. Relations between the English and the New Amsterdam Dutch were, it is true, never very friendly; nevertheless from the language of these Dutch settlers American English gained *coleslaw, cooky, cruller, boss, dope, hay barrack, spook, stoop* "porch," *poppycock* (from *pappekak* "soft dung"), *patroon* (which the Dutch had in turn taken from Latin *patronus*), *sleigh, scow, to snoop, bowery* "a farm" (but now more famous as the street name), *pit* "fruit stone," *boodle, Santa Claus, waffle,* and probably *Yankee.* In addition American English incorporated a number of geographical terms used in the region of the Hudson: *kill* "creek, stream, river," *dorp* "village," and *clove* "valley," which also appear in place names. Many of these Dutch words were not used by writers until well into the nineteenth century but we may be fairly sure that they occurred in English contexts much earlier; and we may be equally sure that many more Dutch words than are recorded were once in use. *Hay barrack* represents what English-speaking people did to Dutch *hooi-berg. Coleslaw* is from Dutch *koolsla* "cabbage salad"; folk etymology frequently converts it to *cold slaw. Dope* has acquired a good many slang uses, as in *to dope out, to get the dope on,* and *he's a dope* (i.e. a dolt). It seems to have begun its career in American English meaning simply a drug, later adding the connotation "narcotic." *Boss,* from *baas* "master," was a very useful word, for it allowed the American working man to enjoy the satisfying if purely verbal illusion that he had no master; only slaves had masters in early American democracy. *Father Christmas,* not *Santa Claus,* visits good English children on Christmas Eve. Our name for the jolly saint is from *Sante Klaas,* a Dutch dialect form of *Sant Nikolaas,* that is, "St. Nicholas"; it seems to have taken a long time catching on, and was probably not very common until the nineteenth century. In my childhood *Santa* was always pronounced *Santy* even by the most highly cultured; people nowadays have become much more conscious of spelling and many use a pronunciation which the spelling *Santa* seems to indicate to them.

The source of *Yankee* is uncertain, but the word is most probably from *Jan Kees* (a variant of *Jan Kaas,* which has been in Germany and Flanders a nickname of long standing for a Hollander), used by the

English to designate a Dutch pirate, a sense in which it apparently came also to be used in New York as an expression of the contempt in which the English held the Dutch. Because of the final -s, the name seems to have been misunderstood to be a plural; the form *Yankee* is thus what is known to linguists as a back formation, like *shay* from *chaise*. It should also be noted that *j* in Dutch has the sound of English *y*; hence the initial sound of the English form of the word. It is a little difficult to understand why the word was transferred from Dutchmen to people of English descent. Perhaps the shift in application was the result of the same type of humour involved in nicknaming the fattest boy in school "Skinny"—the *lucus a non lucendo* principle.

There are, however, many rival theories, for *Yankee* has presented a fascinating problem to etymologists, both professional and lay. One of them, that *Yankee* represents an Indian effort to pronounce the word *English*, is rendered improbable by the fact that the Indians had their own words for the whites; there is no evidence that they ever attempted to use the word *English*. Because Indian etymologies have always been popular, an alternative theory has been proposed, to the effect that *Yankee* was an Indian mispronunciation of *Anglais*; this is just as improbable as the preceding etymology, and for the same reason. Still another "Indian" derivation traces the word to *Yankos*, the name of an apparently mythical Indian tribe; no trace of their existence has ever been discovered. According to Washington Irving's *History of New York . . . by Diedrich Knickerbocker* (1809), the "simple aborigines" called the whites *yanokies*, "a waggish appellation since shortened into the familiar epithet of *Yankees*." Unfortunately for Irving's reputation as an etymologist, no trace of any such Indian word has ever come to light. A nonexistent "Cherokee" word has also been cited as an etymon. Non-Indian theories attempt to derive *Yankee* from Scots dialect words, from a word in the Lancashire dialect, and from numerous Dutch words.

The meaning of *Yankee* has been anything but static. By the mid-eighteenth century its use in this country to designate a New Englander seems to have been well established. During the Civil War Southerners were employing the term, usually derogatorily, for any Northerner, and it was not long before it acquired what was in the usage of many Southerners the inseparable prefix *dam*, as in *damyankee*.

Since the Revolutionary War the British have used the word to designate any American, with connotations no more derogatory than those of the word *American* itself as it is used by them. It is difficult to imagine any experience more painful to most deep Southerners than to be called *Yankees*; yet there is only sporadic evidence that G.I.s of Southern origin stationed in England during either World War ever objected very vigorously to the appellation. *Yank* is about as common in British colloquial usage as the unabbreviated form; the clipped form has never been very frequent in American use, though it was the title of a magazine distributed to American soldiers and occurs in a line of the World War I song *Over There* ("The Yanks are coming").

Despite the large number of Germans in this country long before the outbreak of the Revolution, few German words entered the American vocabulary until about the middle of the nineteenth century, when many new immigrants from Germany arrived. The first large groups of Germans came from the Palatinate; they arrived on Delaware Bay in the early years of the eighteenth century, and, finding that the good lands around Philadelphia were already taken by descendants of Penn's colonists, proceeded to settle the back country. Those who subsequently moved on to other parts with the Scotch-Irish soon abandoned their native language. Those who stayed on in Pennsylvania kept pretty much to themselves—on farms and in villages where they continued speaking their dialect of German, which was in time considerably influenced by English but which had no appreciable effect upon English outside the areas in which they were settled. *Sauerkraut* appears in British English as early as 1617, though neither the word nor the food it designates ever really caught on in England. It is most likely that it was borrowed independently in this country. Similarly, *noodle* is recorded in England before its first known appearance in America, but was probably reborrowed here.

It is not improbable that other words which entered American English through Pennsylvania German were known outside the immediate German settlement area before the nineteenth century, but most of them are of such a nature that we should not expect to find them recorded as early as the eighteenth century. Some of them, like *ponhaus* "scrapple," are not listed in modern abridged dictionaries, probably because lexicographers do not consider them "standard," despite the fact that they are known and used by many speakers of standard American English at the present day. *Rainworm* "earthworm" is used in settlements of German origin and is probably a translation of

Regenwurm. It occurs in the Pennsylvania German area and in the German settlements on the Yadkin in North Carolina, as well as in Nobleboro, Maine, which was settled from the Palatinate. Old English *regenwyrm* is doubtless the ancestor of the term as it occurs elsewhere, for instance, on Buzzards Bay in Massachusetts. *Sawbuck* is now widely disseminated but it originated in German and Dutch settlements from, respectively, *Sägebock* and *zaagbock.* The fact that each end of the rack on which wood is sawed is shaped like the letter X—the Roman symbol for ten—has given rise to the slang use of the term for a ten-dollar bill. *Woodbuck* is also heard over the entire German settlement area, obviously a partial translation of German *Holzbock. Hex* "a witch or the spell cast by a witch" and *to hex* "to cast a spell on" are fairly well known all over the country nowadays. *Ponhaus* (also occurring as *ponhoss, ponhorse, ponehoss,* and *pondhorse*) corresponds to standard German *Pfannhase;* it is current from the Pennsylvania German area proper westward to Ohio and is also well known in north-western Maryland and north-eastern West Virginia. Other gastronomical and culinary terms of Pennsylvania German origin are *sots* "yeast," *snits* (also *schnitz*) "dried apples; pieces of fruit cut for drying" (also used as a verb "to cut into pieces"), *fat-cakes* "doughnuts" (*fettkuche*), *fossnocks* (*fasnachskuche* "Shrovetide cakes"), *thick-milk* "curdled milk" (*dickemilich*), *smearcase* "cottage cheese" (*schmierkäs*), and possibly, but by no means certainly, *apple butter. Clook* "setting hen," with its less frequent variant *cluck,* is from Pennsylvania German *kluck* (standard German *Klucke*). According to Hans Kurath's *Word Geography of the Eastern United States* (Ann Arbor, 1949), "the derogatory phrase *dumb cluck* obviously contains this word." *Belsnickel* (or *Belschnickel*) was, and still is, the southern Pennsylvanian equivalent of *Santa Claus;* the last part of the name is an affectionate diminutive form of German *Nikolaus.* Another name of long standing for the unhappily commercialized saint who rewards good children at Christmas is *Kriss Kingle* (or *Kriss Kringle*); it is a modification of *Christkindl* "Christ child." *To dunk* "to dip (doughnuts usually) into coffee or milk" is from Pennsylvania German *dunken* "to dip," corresponding to standard German *tunken.* It has not really been widely current for more than about twenty years, although it spread very rapidly once it caught on. There is no usage label for the word in the *American College Dictionary,* so that it is apparently considered standard American English nowadays. *Dunker* (or *Dunkard*) is the popular name of a member of the German Baptist Brethren, a pietistic sect which practises baptism by immersion, that is, by dunking.

From French explorers and colonizers American English acquired, usually by way of the Canadian border, such words as *prairie, bateau, voyageur, chowder, buccaneer, carryall* (vehicle), *levee, calumet,* and perhaps *gopher. Chowder* is a modification of *chaudière*"cauldron." Although it is recorded first in England, *buccaneer* should probably be regarded as an Americanism by virtue of its many American historical associations; it is ultimately a Carib word, but comes to English by way of French *boucanier. Carryall* is a folk-etymologizing of *cariole. Gopher* is most likely from *gaufre* "honeycomb," in reference to the animal's burrowing habits. *Prairie* is of frequent occurrence in American English, alone and in a number of compounds such as *prairie dog, prairie wolf* "coyote," and *prairie schooner* "small covered wagon." The word is now perfectly familiar in British English also. *Levee* is a derivative of French *lever* "to raise." Its use to designate an embankment for preventing the overflow of a river is largely confined to the South, as is also its later sense "landing place for vessels." *Calumet,* ultimately a derivative of Latin *calamus* "reed," was the word used by the French explorers for the ceremonial tobacco pipe of the Indians.

A number of Spanish words, such as *mosquito* "little fly," *negro* "black" (an adjective which was soon converted into a noun), *peccadillo* "little sin," *armada* "armed (naval) forces" (originally a past participle), and *alligator* (from *el lagarto* "the lizard"), along with Nahuatl words adopted by the Spanish, such as those cited at the beginning of this chapter, entered the English language as early as the sixteenth century. These words, though some of them are more frequently used in this country than in England, should be distinguished from words taken from Spanish by English-speaking people settled on this continent. Such words are very numerous at a later date but very rare before the nineteenth century. *Calaboose* "jail" is a modification of Spanish *calabozo,* used chiefly in the southern states; it is recorded first in the latter years of the eighteenth century. *Cockroach* (as *cacarootch*) first appears in the *General Historie* of Captain John Smith, who refers to it in a somewhat ambiguous passage as "a certaine India Bug, called by the Spaniards a *Cacarootch,* the which creeping into Chests they [that is, the "cacarootches"] eat and defile with their ill-sented dung." The word used by Smith is a modification of Spanish *cucaracha* "wood louse," or possibly a variant form of it. It was later folk-etymologized to *cockroach* (just as Latin *asparagus* is converted by some speakers into *sparrow grass*) and subsequently clipped to *roach* in this country, American verbal prudery perhaps playing some part in the elimination of the first element of what deceptively appeared to be a compound of *cock* and *roach*. *Key* "reef or low island" from Spanish *cayo* was in English use before it was recorded in America, but its use is now mainly confined to this country, particularly to Florida. *Key West* is a modification of *Cayo Hueso* "bone key." The form *cay*, rhyming with *day*, is now more usual in British English than *key*. *Stevedore*, from Spanish *estívador*, occurs first in the form *stowadore* by association with English *to stow*.

THREE

Some Characteristics
of American English
and Their Backgrounds

O u r early settlers were not for the most part illiterate peasants speaking local dialects, but Englishmen of the upper-lower and lower-middle classes, with the prejudices and intolerances, linguistic as well as religious and economic, which are frequently attendant upon those stations in life. Though there were some dialect speakers among them, the greater part spoke the common speech of the regions to which they were native. This had been greatly influenced by the literary standard which had arisen in London and had come to be accepted in most parts of England, at least as a standard written language, by the latter part of the fifteenth century. But in their pronunciation and in their vocabularies they retained characteristics of the regions and even of the localities whence they sprang, for common speech is inevitably based upon folk speech.

About two-thirds of the earliest settlers around Massachusetts Bay hailed from the south-eastern counties of England—many from East Anglia, which was the principal centre of Puritanism in England. With them came families from Yorkshire, Lancashire, and even farther north, with more than a sprinkling of West Countrymen. It is not of course suggested that these folk from the north and the west of England were immediately upon their arrival on these shores to adapt their regional usage to that of south-eastern England, but it is certain that a basically south-eastern English type of speech was to prevail in Massachusetts.

From the small settlements around Massachusetts Bay, colonists spread throughout New England and into the Middle Atlantic states.

Eastern New Jersey was early dominated by them, and, after the
Revolution, a large number of settlers migrated westward from
Connecticut into New York, where the Dutch had never actually been
very numerous, and into northern Pennsylvania, the Western Reserve
on Lake Erie, and ultimately the Great Lakes area. New Englanders
not many generations removed from transplanted Old Englanders
carried westward with them their customs, their beliefs, their language
and their place names. Hundreds of places throughout the Middle West
were settled by families from western New England—mostly farming
people, for eastern New England had in the meantime become largely
mercantile and industrial. In the course of their migrations, these folk
from western New England—using a development of an early type of
Massachusetts Bay speech—mingled with the predominantly Scotch-
Irish folk from Pennsylvania, from Kentucky, and from West Virginia
who were in the great westward tide which followed the opening up
of the Old Northwest Territory.

The middle colonies, with the exception of the southern sections
of Maryland and Delaware, were settled by people whose speech was
native to the north and, to some extent, the west of England. Pennsylvania was originally planned as a refuge for Quakers, some of whom
also settled on the Delaware in western New Jersey. Since their sect
had arisen in the north of England and found most of its early converts
there and in the west, a large proportion of Penn's colonists probably
came from these regions. The Society of Friends had not in the late
seventeenth century acquired the intellectual and social prestige that
it has in our own day. The speech of Penn's protégés, who were for the
most part simple folk who had never been near a university and had
had no contact with high life, obviously had a good many characteristics peculiar to the north and west of England, with pious overtones
from the King James Bible.

Maryland was settled originally by English Roman Catholics, but
all Trinitarian Christians were made to feel welcome in the colony.
As a result of this enlightened policy—enlightened for those days, at
any rate—it was soon swarming with Protestants. The northern and
north-western sections were later settled from Pennsylvania, and these
sections are linguistically, and to a large extent culturally, quite distinct
from the earlier settlement areas of the state.

The Scotch-Irish who, beginning about 1720, settled the back
country were mostly descendants of lowland Scotsmen who had only

a few generations earlier settled the north-eastern part of Ireland. They were Calvinists, not to be confused with the Catholic Irish who emigrated to this country in the following century. The fortunes of these Scotsmen in their Ulster home had been consistently bad; they had been the victims of flint-hearted landlords, drought, sheep rot, and epidemics of smallpox. The New World must have seemed a haven of hope to them, as also to the Germans who were arriving at about the same time, Protestant pietists from the Palatinate who had suffered religious, political, and economic persecution in their homeland.

These Germans, whose influence on our language has been principally confined to the sphere of vocabulary—and even here it has been small—settled in the valleys of the Lehigh and the Susquehanna. In a few of the communities of this region "Pennsylvania Dutch" (or what might more accurately be called Pennsylvania German) may still be heard. Benjamin Franklin computed that the Germans comprised a third of the population of Pennsylvania in about 1750. Many of these, and most of their descendants, were to acquire the northern English speech of their Scotch-Irish neighbours.

Linguistic geography has made clear the direct relationship of dialect areas to settlement areas, as well as to trade areas and culture areas. In his *Word Geography of the Eastern United States* Professor Kurath has demonstrated the existence of a speech area, the Midland, separating the North from the South—an area which on the coast stretches only from the southern half of New Jersey to midway through Delaware. Its boundaries, which are those of the Pennsylvania settlement area, expand considerably as one travels inland: the northern boundary, bisecting New Jersey, swings to the north-west and runs along the northern part of Pennsylvania; the southern boundary, bisecting Delaware, goes through northern Maryland and turns south-westward to run along the crest of the Blue Ridge in Virginia. This concept of a Midland speech area separating North from South fits the historical facts better than the older concept of American English as comprising New England (sometimes called Eastern), Southern, and a so-called General American.

Many of the Scotch-Irish and some Palatinate Germans as well pushed into the hinterlands of the South Atlantic states in the half-century preceding the Revolution. The speech of the upper Potomac and the Shenandoah valleys, of West Virginia, and of the western

Carolinas consequently has many features in common with that of the upper Ohio Valley, the Susquehanna Valley, and the Delaware Valley —all together constituting the Midland, though it is quite possible that, after further examination and evaluation of the data, what is now designated the South Midland (the southern Appalachians and the Blue Ridge south of the James River) may have to be regarded as a subarea of the South.

Throughout this whole vast Midland area the *r* sound is retained in *farm, board, beard, door, father,* and the like, as in northern British English, though it has considerably weakened. In the levelling-out process which apparently occurred as a result of the frequent intermingling of different elements in our population, the trilled *r*'s of the Scotch-Irish seem in a few generations to have toned down to the sound at present heard in the Midland and its western and southwestern extensions as well as in its north-western settlement area. It may well be that the present Midland *r* in such words is at the same stage as the *r* which must previously have existed in eastern New England and the coastal South and which was subsequently lost, probably under British influence. In any case, it is only a slightly less obvious means of differentiation from present-day eastern New England and tidewater Southern speech than the trilled *r* would be.

The Midland is also set off from other regions by its use of certain words, usually having to do with the house and farm and invariably simple and homely. It is, in fact, more sharply differentiated from the North in this respect than in pronunciation; for instance, Northern *pail* and *faucet* are in the Midland *bucket* and *spicket* (*spigot*) respectively (as also in the South). *Skillet* is primarily a regional word of the Midland, though it has spread elsewhere; in the North and a large part of the coastal South the utensil is usually called a *spider*, though the trade term *frying pan* may be heard in towns and cities all over the country. Midland cows are called by shouting *sook* or *sookie*; in the North the call is *boss, co-boss, come boss, co,* or *coaf*; in the South it is *co-wench, co-inch,* or *co-ee*. The construction *I want in* (or *out* or *off*) is, according to the records of the *Linguistic Atlas of the United States and Canada,* in frequent use in the Midland area, though avoided by educated speakers. This construction is not a Pennsylvania Germanism, as has been supposed, though its agreement with German *ich will 'rein* may have aided somewhat in its preservation in German settlement areas; it occurs in older English and was presumably transmitted to this country in the northern English speech of the Scotch-Irish, who subsequently carried it with them in their western migrations.

To turn now to the settlement history of the South, the Virginia settlers were a motley group of royalists, roisterers, blackguards, indentured servants, Commonwealth soldiers, Puritans, and, painful as it is to contemplate, a good many transported criminals. Defoe's Moll Flanders, "twelve year a whore, five times a wife (whereof once to her own brother), twelve year a thief, eight year a transported felon in Virginia," is a fictitious character, but she probably did not altogether lack real-life counterparts in the colony. Although people from all the counties south of Yorkshire were well represented among them, more than half of the colonists were from the southern part of England, with London quite well represented. As in the Massachusetts Bay colony, a type of speech basically south-eastern English was to prevail here.

The dissemination of the speech of the South Atlantic settlements was similar to that of New England. Although there had been a good many Puritans among its earliest settlers, the coastal South suffered less from the Calvinistic *mythos* than had New England. Perhaps the softer climate helped to mitigate the Puritan harshness; perhaps the more productive soil; perhaps the arrival of large numbers of Cavalier immigrants fleeing the military dictatorship of Cromwell. In any case, by the early years of the eighteenth century the plantation system had come into being in the Southern coastal areas, and with it an attitude towards living unlike anything ever known before or since in this country. Even when allowances are made for romancing, it remains the most charming form of life that our country has ever known. Nevertheless, the tidewater Southerners did some colonizing. Obviously, not all could be fortunate enough to live the gracious life of the plantations. Shortly after the middle of the eighteenth century a large number of emigrants from Virginia and the Carolinas joined Oglethorpe's colonists in Georgia. In the early years of the nineteenth century sons of planters from Virginia and the Carolinas carried their Southern speech to the cotton lands of the Gulf States.

In the lands beyond the Appalachians to the south, other migrations were taking place. Virginians, Marylanders, Pennsylvanians, and North Carolinians settled in large numbers in Kentucky. Scotch-Irish from the southern mountain country joined the French in Louisiana;

some of them pushed westward from the Appalachians to the Ozarks; some got as far west as eastern Texas.

The Atlantic coastal area, extending from Maine to Georgia and occupied at the time of the first Federal Census in 1790 by ninety-five per cent of our total population of about four million, thus formed the mould from which have come all types of American speech. Its speechways were, as we have seen, to be carried westward to the lands beyond the Alleghenies and the Appalachians, and there transplanted. New varieties of English which were blendings of the usages of western New England, the large Pennsylvania settlement area, and the coastal South, were to be developed in the course of that great westward migration which plays so important a part in American history.

Although there is evidence that the speech of the north and west of England was sufficiently noticeable to be used as a shibboleth in the colonial period, features of it have made their way into American English, and it has undoubtedly modified American speech considerably. But it should be constantly borne in mind that many, if not most, of the settlers from the north and the west of England did not speak local dialects, but rather regional variants of the London Standard, retaining unconsciously no doubt certain phonological features and word usages characteristic of their native regions. Many indentured servants were, incidentally, men of sufficient education to be employed as schoolmasters. Perhaps some among the great number of Scottish and Irish teachers who "have had no inconsiderable influence in the Middle States, upon our pronunciation and language," according to John Pickering in the *American Quarterly Review* for September, 1828, had been or were indentured.

Specific evidence is of course lacking as to the number of speakers of local dialects among our earliest settlers. There probably were not very many of them, despite the existence of a good many dialect words in unsophisticated American speech. In its grammatical forms and even in its pronunciation, the educated speech we use today resembles an older form of the English Standard to such an extent that we must conclude that those who did speak peasant dialects were persons of little prestige in the New World and consequently that their speech had little influence upon the development of American English other than to contribute a number of dialectal expressions to its vocabulary.

Patterns for the linguistically ambitious were furnished by the usage of the cities which sprang up along the coast and at the heads of navigation on rivers—notably Boston, New York, Philadelphia, Richmond, and Charleston. These cities, which are of great significance in the development of American English, were not only important centres of trade, but also seats of culture and fashion. By the rest of the country they were regarded much as London is regarded by the rest of England. From their bustling ports ships plied to England bearing the produce of the colonies and bringing back new goods and new settlers. Though immigration from England slackened somewhat after the middle of the seventeenth century, it never ceased altogether during the entire colonial period. It is likely that many of the later immigrants were people of a higher social and cultural level than the earlier settlers and that they brought with them the latest fashions in speech as in clothes.

In refinement and éclat, the cities set the tone for the back country. Language is an important part of the cultural and social equipment of a people, and these centres of wealth and high life became the mould of fashion linguistically as well as otherwise for their hinterlands. Consequently, the more or less localized expressions of the inland were in large part to give way to the usage of the cities. This must in turn have been much affected by the changing usage of England, as indicated by the fact that American English reflects so many of the changes which took place in British English during our colonial period— changes such as the replacement of the *ay* sound in words like *sea, peak, leap,* and the like, by the *ee* sound which they have in standard British and American English at present. Similarly, words with *oi, oy,* such as *boil, join, poison, hoist, boy,* have had an identical development in British and American English. In the seventeenth and early eighteenth centuries these words were pronounced approximately as *bile, jine, pizen, hist* (rhyming with *iced*), and *bye*—pronunciations which survive in the speech of folk who live far from the centres of linguistic fashion. Towards the end of the eighteenth century this pronunciation gave way to that now usual in England and America alike. Except for the usage of simple people living in isolated regions, who have lacked any contact with British English since long before the sound shift took place, American English has here again chosen the same variant as British English.

On the other hand, changes which occurred in standard British English during the eighteenth century, such as the loss of preconsonantal and final *r* and the shift from "flat" to "broad" *a* in certain words, are not reflected in American English away from the Atlantic coast. Except for eastern New England and the coastal South, which seem to have followed the British practice, the *r* sound is regularly retained in American English. The British treatment of *a*, sometimes written *au*, before certain consonants and consonant combinations, as in *after, staff, ask, grasp, grass, path, past, command, aunt, dance*, and *half*, has likewise had no effect upon the natural speech of Americans outside eastern New England, eastern Virginia, and the Charleston area. All these words had the flat *a* in standard British English until the latter part of the eighteenth century, the broad *a* beloved of Anglophile Americans being up to that time considered low.

Evidence of this sort leads Professor Eilert Ekwall to conclude, in his *American and British Pronunciation* (Upsala, 1946), that "educated American pronunciation on the whole remains at the stage which British pronunciation had reached about the time of the Revolution, while modern British pronunciation has left that stage far behind." It is an attractive theory. Certainly there can be no doubt that for many details it holds true. There is ample evidence that American English preserves a good many pronunciations which were current in standard British English in the latter years of the eighteenth century. Although Ekwall is concerned only with pronunciation, his theory finds some support in vocabulary, for our use of many words can also be said to be about the same as British usage at the time of the Revolution.

Even though we are not able to determine its extent with perfect accuracy, we cannot doubt the existence of this influence from the mother country, an influence which continued throughout the colonial period. Nor can there be any reasonable doubt that it must be reckoned among the factors which have brought about the present homogeneity of American English.

There were also at work, in New England at least, such uniformizing agencies as the compulsory schools, with their spellers by Dilworth, Fenning, and later the famous blue-backed spelling book of Noah Webster and the Grammar of Lindley Murray, and the churches, with their interminable but literate sermons. The Yankee farmers and artisans whose usage Webster frequently preferred to that of what he smugly referred to as "the gay and fashionable world" were for the most part able to read, though certainly not much given to *belles lettres*. There can be no doubt that the comparatively high degree of literacy which prevailed among them has been an important factor in the development of American English.

In the Southern seaports speech was modelled to a large extent upon that of London, for ties with the mother country were even stronger in the South than in New England. The same was true of the speech of the planters. In the countryside, although a successful small farmer might and sometimes did rise into the plantation caste, the plantation system frequently had the effect of forcing those who were not at the top of the social and economic scale into what amounted to cultural isolation. As a consequence of this isolation, local differences in the speech of marginal farmers and poor whites had little chance of blending into a broader regional usage; hence the great diversity of local usages in the South. Such usages are preserved to this day in the speech of the descendants of those who did not acquire the cultured regional speech of the planter class: some of them are thriving business and professional men, prosperous farmers, and holders of public office; many others are simple folk still, whose social contacts have been almost exclusively with others of the same kidney—in the crossroads store and the nearest clapboarded evangelical tabernacle, with an occasional trip to the county seat.

In the Midland, social differences were hardly noticeable. From the very beginning Philadelphians had a culture of their own, not dependent upon London. Away from Philadelphia, the Scotch-Irish and the Palatinate Germans who had settled the back country of the Midland were also not much interested in the fashions, linguistic or otherwise, of London. The Scotch-Irish with a certain amount of justice blamed most of their woes on England, which they certainly had no reason to love. As for the Germans, there was absolutely no reason why they should have had any regard for the London Standard, even if they knew of it. In this great Midland area, less class-conscious and hence more democratic than either eastern New England or the tidewater South, there were no distinctly marked social dialects. Instead, there was the common speech of a sturdy middle class which, on the educated level, was to evolve into a new type of speech, different in many of its details from that of both the North and the South.

The comparative lack of class dialects in the United States is certainly to be attributed to the theoretical and to some extent actual classlessness of American society. American English has no such marked class variants as distinguish the speech of Mayfair from that of

Limehouse. This is not to say that all types of speech are socially acceptable or even that all types which are socially acceptable have equal prestige values. In the single state of South Carolina the absence of preconsonantal and final *r* is indicative of higher social position than its presence, because *r*-lessness is characteristic of the speech of the plantation caste who occupied the tidewater region of that state, particularly those living in the Charleston area. It is true, however, despite the prestige sometimes associated with the speech of Boston and the tidewater South, that we have no single standard stemming from the usage of a particular section, nothing at all comparable to the Southern English Standard, a form of speech which is to some extent geographical but nowadays to a considerably larger extent social. In actual fact the Midwesterner is likely to be as proud of his *r*'s as the Bostonian is of his *r*-lessness. A Southwesterner whose oil wells have "come in" may send his daughter to a finishing school in Virginia and complain that he is not getting his money's worth if she fails to acquire what is popularly thought of as a "Southern accent." So long as she can manage to insert an occasional *you-all* and *sho' 'nough* into her conversation, she may with impunity fall down on her *r*'s from time to time, for the fact would hardly be noticed. As an embellishment of Western and Southwestern American womanhood, a "Southern accent," or something vaguely resembling one, is all well and good. But the chances are all that the old man will send his sons to the state university, where they will not be subjected to linguistic influences other than those current in the educated speech of the region.

To say that American speech is uniform is thus not the same as saying that the speech of any one section of the country is precisely the same as that of any other section; such a claim could not be made even for individuals of the same cultural background in the same section of the country. Indeed, the distinctive speech areas of the original English settlements extending along the Atlantic seaboard from Maine to Georgia—a relatively small section of our present nation, but extremely significant from a linguistic point of view as the matrix whence sprang all types of American English—are a refutation of any such notion.

Nevertheless, practically all who have written knowingly upon the subject have noted that American English is characterized by a high degree of uniformity. It is well to remember, however, that the conception of uniformity in speech must be to a large extent relative; that is, much depends upon who is doing the observing. He who looks for differences will surely find them, and very interesting and significant differences they are. The danger lies in not seeing the woods for the trees—in losing sight of the larger unity of American English by becoming absorbed in a mass of details. The linguistically unsophisticated, for instance, are prone to be so intolerant of deviations from their own usage as to exaggerate the frequency of their occurrence.

It cannot be denied, of course, that a person with even one good ear is able to identify the speech of the tidewater Southerner, the eastern New Englander, and the New Yorker, and to distinguish these types of speech from that of the Middle West. Furthermore, on a more or less unsophisticated level, the usage of words pertaining largely to the farm and the home—words such as the synonymous *andirons*, *hand irons*, *fire dogs*, *dogs*, and *dog irons*, all used in the eastern United States—varies from region to region. Even on a sophisticated level there is some variation in word usage. For instance, what in other parts of the country is called a *sidewalk* was and may still be called in my native section of Maryland a *pavement*, and what is elsewhere called a *pavement* was in our usage the *street* if in town and the *road* if in the country. Whether the road was paved or not, it would never have been called a *pavement*; pavements were in towns and cities and were for the use of pedestrians only. Consequently, I step from the pavement to the street; speakers from other sections step from the sidewalk to the pavement. No serious problem has thus far resulted from the ambiguity.

The study of the historical, sociological, and geographical distribution and background of such differences is fascinating and rewarding. It should not, however, obscure the picture of an essentially homogeneous American English, which no one cognizant of the far more prominent and significant regional and dialectal differences in French, in Spanish, in Italian, in German, and even in British English could ever fail to recognize. Such matters as the different treatment of postvocalic *r* in Boston and Omaha, while they are of major significance to the student of American English, have never really been significant so far as intelligibility is concerned, and no serious misunderstanding is likely to arise even when the context fails to make immediately clear that when a man from Maine speaks of *curd cheese* he means what is elsewhere designated variously as *sour-milk cheese*, *Dutch cheese*, *pot cheese*, *smearcase*, *clabber cheese*, and *cottage cheese*, revealing as the study of such differentiae may be. The fact that the last-named term, the trade name, is understood by all who have been to school and are thus able to read advertisements is a further instance of the uniformizing tendency.

Nevertheless, regional and even local usages are still with us, on various cultural levels ranging from educated or cultivated speech, where they are rarest, through common speech to the folk speech heard in more or less isolated localities. In a civilization such as ours, however, the local usages of folk speech give way rapidly, as in the past they gave way slowly but steadily, to regional common speech— the speech of the independent farmer, the skilled craftsman, the shopkeeper, the man in the street, spiritual descendants all of Noah Webster's American yeoman. This regional common speech in its turn is influenced and may be in a generation superseded by educated or cultivated speech, to some extent regional also but tending to be national. A very simple illustration is provided by the tendency of a word like *waiter*, the Southern folk term for an attendant at a wedding, to be supplanted, as consolidated schools, the radio, and the automobile continue to increase rural sophistication, by the regional *groomsman*. This regional word, current in parts of the South in both common and cultivated speech, may in its turn be supplanted by the national terms *usher* and *best man*.

Local and regional variations are most noticeable on the Atlantic seaboard because of the comparative isolation of communities from each other in colonial times. Nevertheless, there can be little doubt that from a geographical point of view American English is characterized by an even greater degree of uniformity at present than it had in 1781, when Dr. Witherspoon remarked upon this quality, which he attributed to the fact that "being . . . unsettled, and moving frequently from place to place, they [Americans] are not so liable to local peculiarities either in accent or phraseology." To this day, one of the characteristics which foreign observers note about us is the fact that we do not "stay put." On the contrary, we like to be "on the go"; a not inconsiderable part of our population is on wheels the year round, in cars and trailers.

In addition, such mass entertainment as is provided in our present age of enlightenment by the motion pictures, the radio, and television has been on the whole a uniformizing influence. "Artists" in all these media have striven to achieve a type of American speech unmarked by local, regional, or class peculiarities. The stress which radio lays upon "diction"—the network announcers are popularly believed to be highly trained specialists in speech—must certainly have had some effect upon American English. It is as yet impossible to define this influence, but it is a fact that specific pronunciations of the more highly paid announcers are frequently cited as authoritative by those who listen to them. In time the announcer may come to usurp some of the authority of the schoolmarm and her textbooks. His criteria of excellence are, however, essentially the same as those of the schools, which have by and large been a most potent standardizing influence. The origin and nature of that influence will be discussed in some detail in subsequent chapters.

FOUR

Linguistic Nationalism
and the Schoolmaster

ANY study of the development of the English language in the modern period must take into consideration the influence of the prescriptive grammarians who came into fullness of power in the eighteenth century. In England and America this influence differed only in degree. In a review of early instalments of the *Dictionary of American English* (*Kenyon Review*, Spring, 1940), Harold Whitehall states that the older, aristocratic type of speech survives principally in tidewater Virginia and a few other parts of our South, and that it has completely disappeared in England, where the careless elegance of cultivated eighteenth-century speech has been supplanted by the tortured precision prescribed by the grammarians who served as arbiters of language for the "new men" created by the Industrial Revolution —sons of the bourgeoisie who were more or less suddenly elevated to positions of prominence and affluence by the change from an agricultural to an industrial economy and who needed a linguistic Emily Post to lean upon.

But Professor Whitehall's view is one which would seem to be somewhat at variance with many facts which might be set forth: for instance, the disregard for schoolbook grammar shown by such representative English writers as Cardinal Newman, who wrote in the most formal of contexts that a gentleman's great concern is "to make every one at their ease and at home" (*The Idea of a University*), thereby exposing his ignorance of the important fact, according to practically any textbook, that a plural personal pronoun should not be used to refer to a singular indefinite pronoun like *everyone*; or Dean Church, the eminent Victorian divine, who wrote, "I think if I was beginning again, I should begin with a serious study of Paracelsus" (*Life and Letters*), and thus showed his unawareness that the subjunctive is required in *if* clauses in which the condition is contrary to the truth—that is, he ought to have written, according to the best authorities, "I think if I *were* beginning again . . ."; or Lytton Strachey, who apparently did not possess the elementary knowledge that "*lay, laid, laid* is a transitive verb (takes an object)" when he wrote in his *Books and Characters* of "manuscripts which had long laid hidden." These are not isolated examples. Many more could be cited to show that, according to the standards of linguistic propriety as taught in our schools, the most reputable authors would fail even a high-school course in American English usage.

On the other hand, pronunciations based upon spelling rather than upon oral tradition are a certain indication of the influence of the schools; and these, though they are indeed becoming increasingly common in British English, are according to the most reliable observers much more frequent in American English. M. B. Ruud tells in *American Speech* (October, 1925) of trying the traditional pronunciation of *Theobald* (indicated by Alexander Pope's spelling *Tibbald*) on a London bus conductor, who looked perfectly blank until *Theobald's Road* was pronounced as spelled. This is not really surprising, for the traditional pronunciation is decidedly old-fashioned nowadays. Of Ruud's report that in Oxford he heard a shop assistant pronounce Magdalen College as spelled, we can only say that in this instance a little learning presumed to alter the cultivated usage of centuries, as it frequently does. It is highly doubtful, however, that *Magdalen* will be widely pronounced otherwise than as *maudlin* for a long time to come by Englishmen or, for that matter, by Americans who are at all familiar with British usage. To this horrible example may be added *Harwich* as spelled (instead of rhyming with *carriage*), heard from the lips of an English businessman in the boat train from that port. But such pronunciations are highly exceptional. It is nevertheless true that sometimes two pronunciations, particularly for place names, may be widely current in British English, as with *Shrewsbury*, the first syllable of which rhymes with *those* in the speech of those connected with Shrewsbury School and of the landed gentry, though outsiders and people living in the town rhyme it with *news*. A better-known example, one which in the past has doubtless taken many a visiting American tourist off his feet, is *Cirencester*, called *sisiter* by the gentry, but given four syllables by the tradespeople who live in the town, just as the spelling seems to indicate to them.

There can be no question that a good many spelling pronunciations are to be heard in British English and that the tendency to pronounce as spelled is gaining ground at the expense of tradition. Of the words cited, however, only the spelling pronunciation for *Theobald* is as prevalent in cultivated British usage as are the spelling pronunciations of *Berkshire, Greenwich* (except for Greenwich Village in New York, which is prevailingly *grennitch*), *Birmingham, Anthony,* and *almond* in American usage. These words are in British English pronounced as if spelled *barksher, grinnidge* (or *grennidge*), *birming'em, antony,* and *ahmond.* (In case the reader uses the same pronunciation for *almond* as is here indicated, it should be explained that many very literate Americans, particularly New Englanders, pronounce the first syllable exactly like the name *Al.*)

After all, the "new man" of the late eighteenth and early nineteenth century sent his sons to good schools where they were taught traditional pronunciation by men who, if not quite gentlemen themselves, made a career of teaching young gentlemen and those who aspired to be young gentlemen. Nevertheless, there can be no denying that the careless, aristocratic speech heard in eighteenth-century English drawing-rooms has been to some extent supplanted by the stilted and unnatural language recommended by schoolmasters and lexicographers to whom the Industrial Revolution gave a new lease on life. No one had paid much attention to them before. Now they saw their way to power of a sort, for the "new men," uncertain of their linguistic as of their ballroom deportment, required such recipes for "good speech" as the schoolmasters and lexicographers, to whom gullibility was bread and butter, were ready and willing to prescribe. Not many of the prescriptivists really knew the speech of the older aristocracy; those who did know it hated it because they had been snubbed by those who spoke it; furthermore, they quite sincerely disapproved of its lack of regularity and of conformity to standards which they, like Dean Swift's spider, had spun out of their own guts. Authoritarianism, self-confident in its very ignorance of linguistic change, took over the job of regulating language. It has done that job well, and its ultimate success is to be seen in the development of American English from about the time of the Revolutionary War to the present day.

The linguistic authoritarianism of the schoolmaster and of the schoolmarm who supplanted him has been at one and the same time an important cause of linguistic change and an agency for maintaining uniformity in American English: change from an older, traditional standard to one based largely upon the written representation of the language and the perpetuation of the newer, more "literate" standard, as when Norwich, Connecticut, named from the city in England, changed its pronunciation from the traditional one rhyming with *porridge* (as in the nursery rhyme about the "man from Norwich" who "ate some porridge") to its present supposedly more "educated," more "reasonable," more "logical" pronunciation rhyming with *or witch*.

As early as 1647 a law of the Puritan church ordered that every Massachusetts township of fifty or more householders should "appoint one within their town to teach all such children as shall resort to him to write and read" and every town of a hundred families or householders had to set up a grammar school, "the master thereof being able to instruct youth, so far as they may be fitted, for the university." Similar laws were enacted when men from Massachusetts colonized other parts of New England. By the latter half of the seventeenth century, jurisdiction passed to the state, and the school ceased to be the church school and became the district school. In addition to these lower schools, academies and colleges came into being, and in time Harvard and Yale universities.

The southern colonies and those in the middle states were somewhat less zealous in their attitude towards learning than the more highminded Yankees. In the South, as Noah Webster pointed out in his *Essays* of 1790, gentlemen of property sometimes employed tutors for their children. These tutors were not considered gentlemen and were hence "excluded from genteel company," though grammar masters, who could teach Latin, were regarded more highly. James Fenimore Cooper commented in his *Notions of the Americans* (1828) that "the gentlemen of the middle and southern states, before the revolution, were very generally educated in England."

The relationship that the New Englanders saw between the church and the school (which were usually side by side in New England towns) was essentially that established by the Protestant reformers whom they followed in their religious philosophy. The New Englander's attitude of extreme adulation towards book-learning was in time to be typical of the "American way." Today practically everyone is convinced of the great value of schooling, despite a rather appalling lack

E

of evidence that men are any more honourable in their dealings with their fellows or any more devout in their relationship to their God than were the illiterates of earlier days. There is, nevertheless, the possibility that lives are made richer by the ability to read the comic books (with some lip-movement, of course), although the question is perhaps debatable.

But the influence of schooling upon the development of American English is not debatable; it is, on the contrary, very apparent to any observer of American linguistic practice, much of which has been acquired from the evangelistic efforts of teachers to regularize and uniformize our language. It was not until the second half of the eighteenth century, however, that the notion arose of making English subject to a universal grammar which was assumed to govern all language. A corollary to this notion is that there is an absolute distinction between right and wrong language—a concept which appealed greatly to Americans, whose attitude towards life has ever been characterized by moral earnestness. The need for an unwavering line setting off right from wrong was just as urgent in the sphere of language as in that of morals. It is little wonder, when one considers the social, moral, and economic background of the most influential of our earliest settlers, that the linguistic earnestness of the prescriptive grammarians should have met with such enthusiasm and sympathy on these shores. If Noah Webster had not been born, we should have had to invent him.

In the eighteenth century the time was especially ripe for policing the language. The exuberant and colourful qualities of Renaissance English best known to us in the works of Shakespeare and his contemporaries had gradually to give way under the belabouring of the schoolmaster's rod. Those who chose to concern themselves with "refining, ascertaining, and fixing" were in the ascendant and could promulgate their theory of linguistic corruption and their belief, held by many to this day, that language is founded upon the same principles as logic. Reason, analogy (frequently drawn from Latin grammar), and what they conceived to be the "logic" of language were their guiding principles. Usage was not a safe guide; indeed, it was no guide at all, for it was believed that unless language was regulated, brought to order, it would inevitably become hopelessly corrupt. Dryden, Swift, and Pope, as well as many others of almost comparable intellectual calibre, were convinced that, unless something was done to arrest linguistic change, their writings would not be understood in a few generations. Swift voiced a common complaint in his *Proposal for Correcting, Improving and Ascertaining the English Tongue* (1712), when he asked, "How then shall any man, who hath a genius for history equal to the best of the ancients, be able to undertake such a work with spirit and cheerfulness, when he considers that he will be read with pleasure but a very few years, and in an age or two shall hardly be understood without an interpreter?"

In the absence of a regulative academy, Dr. Johnson's *Dictionary* (1755) answered what was felt to be a real need for authority. As Johnson himself declared, his chief intent was "to preserve the purity, and ascertain the meaning of our English idiom." But, though he prefixed a *Grammar of the English Language* to the *Dictionary*, his heart was really not in syntax. His genius was rather for definition. Sentence structure and idiom actually concerned him but little, perhaps because, as he himself said, "our Language has so little inflection that its Construction neither requires nor admits many rules."

The second half of the eighteenth century saw the rise of a tribe of linguistic dictators who lacked Johnson's good judgment and his powers of accurate observation. The rules which Johnson quite rightly thought unnecessary were the breath of life to those remarkably energetic but linguistically ignorant men who have succeeded to a very large extent in laying upon the English tongue shackles conjured up in their own brains. One of the most prestigious of these was Robert Lowth, whose *Short Introduction to English Grammar* was published in 1762. Lowth, a clergyman who was later to become Bishop of London, was highly conscious of what seemed to him to be the deplorable state of anarchy attained by the English language. He had, moreover, a self-confident, pontifical manner which doubtless contributed a great deal to his rise in the hierarchy of his church and which certainly convinced people that he knew all the answers. Usage concerned him not at all. Many of the "errors" which he cited were taken from the most reputable English authors. He was in fact praised by one of his admirers, William Ward, for showing "the grammatic Inaccuracies that have escaped the Pens of our most distinguished writers" and by another, Thomas Sheridan, father of the dramatist, for having proved "that some of our most celebrated writers, and such as have hitherto passed for our English classics, have been guilty of great solecisms, inaccuracies, and even grammatical improprieties, in many places of their most finished works" (Preface to his *Dictionary*, 1780). Lowth frankly stated his aims—"to lay down rules" and "to judge of every phrase and form of construction, whether it be right or not." His guiding principles were drawn from "universal grammar," whose common principles were applicable to any particular language. He is largely responsible for the still widely current belief in the absoluteness of grammatical rules, which to him were as inflexible as the laws of nature itself.

Lowth's attitude towards language was altogether to the taste of his day, and he had many followers who, like him, exercised themselves over such matters as the use of *lie* and *lay*, *who* and *whom*, *between* and *among*, *would rather* instead of *had rather*, *different from* instead of *different than* or *different to*, and the proscribing of *it is me*. Lowth's condemnation of *you was* has deprived us of the useful distinction which our eighteenth-century ancestors made between this form for the singular and *you were* for the plural. It was he who formulated the rule condemning the double negative: "two Negatives in English destroy one another, or are equivalent to an Affirmative." Of course it is not true, but it has nevertheless prevailed. Because it seemed to him illogical, he outlawed the use of the superlative degree when one of two was referred to, so that we now feel it necessary to say "the younger of the two" but "the youngest of the three." We must therefore assume, if we believe in the good Bishop's principles, that the incomparable Jane was grievously at fault when she described Emma Woodhouse as "the youngest of the two daughters of a most affectionate, indulgent father," but it is to be suspected that only an unmitigated booby would refuse to proceed in his reading of *Emma* because of Miss Austen's "faulty grammar." The *shall-will* rules were formulated by a mathematician-cum-grammarian named John Wallis more than a century before the appearance of Lowth's book, in his *Grammatica Linguae Anglicanae* (1653), but Lowth and his followers perpetuated them; the complexity of these rules, their "reasonableness," and their utter lack of justification in the facts of normal usage have appealed greatly to teachers ever since.

Lowth's disciple, Lindley Murray, a Pennsylvania-born Quaker who retired from a lucrative law practice and moved to England at the age of thirty-one, gave the complicated rules supposed to govern the correct use of language their widest currency in his *Grammar of the English Language* (1795). This Grammar in its original form went through fifty editions: the work was revised in 1816, and an abridgment of this revision went through no fewer than 120 editions of 10,000 copies each. Murray was in many respects the epitome of eighteenth-century attitudes toward language. He and Noah Webster, also a child of the Age of Reason, have probably had more to do with the direction and regulation of the English language than any other individual figures. Both, it should be noted for what it is worth, were Americans.

There were, it is true, dissenters, the most prominent being the brilliant Joseph Priestley, schoolmaster, chemist, and nonconformist divine, who at the age of twenty-eight wrote the *Rudiments of English Grammar* (1761), and George Campbell, whose *Philosophy of Rhetoric* appeared in 1776. Both these men recognized that language was, to use Campbell's own words, "purely a species of fashion" and that usage was the highest law, but even they thought there was need of control—a need filled by the principle of analogy.

It is not likely that many people of consequence amended their natural, normal use of language because of the prescriptions of Lowth and his followers. Many of the old order were probably not in the least disturbed by Lowth's charge that "the English Language, as it is spoken by the politest part of the nation, and as it stands in the writings of our most approved authors, often offends against every part of grammar" (Preface to the *Grammar*). But many others, caught in the intellectual currents of the latter half of the eighteenth century, must have approved his contention that English was "easily reducible to a System of rules"; such an attitude was much more comfortable than to believe it "in its nature irregular and capricious." What seemed linguistic anarchy was deplored not only by schoolmasters; even Lord Chesterfield called for "good order and authority" in language and advocated, in a letter published in 1754, that "we must have recourse to the old Roman expedient in times of confusion, and chuse a dictator."

America, with its ideologically classless society and its idealistically highfalutin notions of equality, was particularly receptive to such ideas. One of the implications of prescriptive grammar is that anyone may talk and write as well as anyone else provided he follows the prescriptions laid down by the authority. Good usage was no longer the prerogative of a hereditary aristocracy; the grammarians had put it within the reach of every man.

The flagpole, somewhat warped and considerably shrunken, became the schoolmaster's rod when the spirit of nationalism which followed the American Revolution intensified the desirability of having a uniform linguistic standard for our newborn nation. Perhaps the often-repeated insistence upon the importance of a uniform language was due in part to a fear of disunity which was quite natural in a young nation, particularly a federation of states such as our young nation was. In any case, it became a patriotic duty to follow the precepts of those who knew what language ought to be. The schoolmaster saw his chance, and he was not slow to take advantage of it.

There were, it is true, a number of proposals for an academy, but none of them ever came to much of anything, and the authority of the schoolmaster was thus never seriously threatened. As early as January, 1774, a writer in the *Royal American Magazine* who signed himself "An American," being convinced that the greatest perfection of the English language is "perhaps reserved for this Land of light and freedom," had advocated the formation of such an institution, to be styled "The American Society of Language," for ensuring this worthy desideratum. The Society, according to the proposal, would publish annually "some observations upon the language and from year to year, correct, enrich, and refine it, until perfection stops their progress and ends their labour." In a burst of glowing patriotism, "An American" predicted that "our rising posterity . . . may far surpass all the sons of science who have shone in past ages, may light up the world with new ideas bright as the sun."

Six years after the proposal of "An American," John Adams wrote a letter from Amsterdam to the "President of Congress" in which he made a similar proposal, so similar in fact that G. P. Krapp in *The English Language in America* (New York, 1925) conjectures that the author of the earlier communication was also Adams. Be that as it may, Adams expressed the hope that "the honour of forming the first public institution for refining, correcting, and ascertaining the English language is reserved for congress" and expressed his conviction that "it will have a happy effect upon the union of the States to have a public standard for all persons in every part of the continent to appeal to, both for the signification and pronunciation of the language."

In 1788 a group of young linguistic idealists banded themselves together as the Philological Society of New York. Their purpose, according to Noah Webster, who has been called the "monarch" and who was certainly the prime mover of the Society, was that of "ascertaining and improving the American tongue." Webster cannily saw to it that the Society acted as a pressure group for the promotion of his *American Spelling Book*, which Josiah Hoffman, its president, recommended in a letter dated July 4, 1788, because among its other virtues it would promote uniformity in pronunciation, "an object very desirable in a federal republic." Never one to let an opportunity slide, Webster printed this letter in subsequent editions of the *Spelling Book*. Shortly after the future lexicographer's removal from New York to Boston early in the following year, this worthy organization seems to have folded up.

The unsuccessful projectors of a bill introduced in Congress in 1806 providing for the incorporation of a national academy which had for one of its purposes the regulation of the English language were later, in 1820, to organize in New York an American Academy of Language and Belles Lettres, with John Quincy Adams as president. One of its objectives was "to promote the purity and uniformity of the English language." It was not concerned with the "Federal English" of the linguistic patriots; in fact it disapproved of such Americanisms as *lengthy*, *to tote*, and *to approbate*. Thomas Jefferson, whose patronage was sought, would have none of it, though he was elected an honorary member after refusing the honorary presidency. He was quite cognizant of the foolishness and futility of any attempt, no matter how well-intentioned it might be, to fix the language, for, as he expressed himself in a letter written January 27, 1821, to the Academy's secretary, "Judicious neology can alone give strength and copiousness to language, and enable it to be the vehicle of new ideas." Webster was not in sympathy with the Academy's methods, for good business reasons: he was already engaged in the writing of his *American Dictionary of the English Language*, which he believed would furnish a much more authoritative standard than the pronouncements of any academy.

Dr. Johnson had long before pooh-poohed the idea of such an academy for Englishmen in the Preface to his *Dictionary* and expressed the hope that "the spirit of English liberty will hinder or destroy" any institution which might attempt to shackle the linguistic libertarianism which had in the past been so marked a characteristic of British English. Of Swift's *Proposal* of 1712, Johnson later remarked that "every man would have been willing, and many would have been proud to disobey" the decrees of such a body as Swift proposed. He was of course speaking of Englishmen only.

Although little or nothing has come of these or of subsequent proposals for an American academy, many of our citizens feel a real need of some organized body with authority to tell us how we should speak our language. Teachers and writers of textbooks on "correct" English would of course constitute an overwhelming majority of any such body. It is highly doubtful that linguists would be allowed any part in its august deliberations. For one thing, they are more concerned with observing and recording than with recommending and legislating; for another, they are far too "liberal," although as a matter of fact their point of view is essentially conservative, going back as it does to a tradition far more ancient than that of public education. Linguists take for their criteria the usage of those who are generally acknowledged, even by the schoolmasters themselves, to be the best writers and speakers. Paradoxically enough, from the point of view of the schoolmasters, these same writers and speakers sometimes use very "bad" English indeed, as in the examples cited earlier.

No, it would never do to have linguists as members of such an academy as has been proposed. They "have no standards"; they are altogether too likely to believe that good English is that which accomplishes the job of communication with accuracy and grace—the English of effective writers and speakers, not to be achieved merely by the avoidance of "grammatical errors" and sometimes none the less effective for an occasional occurrence of these "errors." On the other hand, it is quite generally believed that schoolteachers, professors of English, and authors of handbooks of the English language do have standards: they know what language ought to be, in contrast to the benighted linguists, who are content to know only what it is; they are indeed the real academicians. Even without an academy, these proponents of an ideal language have supplied the American need to be told how to speak and write. They have come to be regarded with an awe amounting almost to superstition: they are, in the American scheme of things, mahatmas.

The Declaration of Independence and the rebellion against the mother country caused a great surge of linguistic and cultural patriotism. The general idea of the superpatriots was to improve upon English, as Adams had it in mind to do when he proposed "the first public institution for refining, correcting, improving, and ascertaining the English language"—to restore to it something of its supposed pristine purity, to render it more orderly, more correct. This is really where the schoolmaster came in, for many believed he could provide a means of arriving at a uniform national standard. To many, however, "pure English" continued to mean simply British English, of which American English was held to be a debased form, so that any type of speech which deviated from the British Standard was impure. This opinion was held by American and English commentators alike. An outstanding exception was that sturdy linguistic patriot Noah Webster, who regarded American English as in no sense inferior to British English; both were, as a matter of fact, in a state of decay. In a letter to Thomas Dawes, written from New Haven in 1809, he declared that in the "few alterations . . . which I propose [in the *Dictionary* of 1806], I am guided by fixed principles of etymology, and endeavour only to call back the language to the purity of former times."

Dr. Witherspoon felt that the eminent authors of his own day wrote with greater purity than "those of the first character in former times." He was a little vague, however, about what constituted purity; apparently it was in his opinion largely a matter of "taste, propriety, and accuracy." Of Americanisms he declared that "It does not follow from a man's using these, that he is ignorant, or his discourse upon the whole inelegant; nay, it does not follow in every case that the terms or phrases used are worse in themselves, but merely that they are of American and not of English growth." Despite this liberal profession, he found absolutely nothing that he could approve in what he considered characteristically American usage. It must therefore be assumed that the purity to which he referred was a characteristic of the style of English writers of his own day. Witherspoon was a member of the Continental Congress and one of the signers (the only clergyman among them) of the Declaration of Independence, but he had none of Noah Webster's passion for linguistic independence. In the Essay prefixed to his *Vocabulary*, John Pickering stated his conviction that every American should give his attention to "the preservation of the *English language* in its purity throughout the United States." He grimly anticipated that a time might arrive when Americans "shall no longer be able to understand the works of Milton, Pope, Swift, Addison," etc., "without the aid of a translation" and quoted with implicit approval the British reviewer of John Marshall's *Life of Washington* who in 1808 wrote that "the *common speech* of the United

States has departed very considerably from the standard adopted in England, and in this case it is not to be expected that *writers*, however cautious, will maintain a strict purity," along with another commentator's reference to "*that torrent of barbarous phraseology*, with which the *American* writers threaten to destroy the purity of the English language."

Despite sporadic classroom recommendation of such pronunciations as *diction'ry, eyether,* and *nyether,* American standards seem to have won the day quite completely in this country. We have achieved in effect a national language, partly the result of independent development, but largely attributable to conscious regulation and direction. "Pure English" is no longer British English, which by prevailing American school standards would have to be adjudged somewhat reckless and sloppy. Of course, it is actually seldom so adjudged, because of a complex of factors, among them vestigial linguistic Anglophilia, unfamiliarity, inaccurate observation, the "quaintness" of its intonation to American ears, and the personal glamour of British actors and actresses well known in this country. Nevertheless, most of us think it better to "talk American." There is very little tendency on the part of Americans to imitate British speech. When we speak of "good English" or "correct English" we mean English according to the standards inculcated in the classrooms, the dictionaries, and the handbooks of usage.

The tendency towards regulation, the desire to make what appear to be exceptions conform to what seems to be the rule, has always been an important factor in linguistic development. It is the degree of regulation which is characteristic of American English, for, quite apart from the desirability of a national language, the very idea of regulation, with its assumption of a universal standard and an unwavering distinction between right and wrong in language as in morals, appealed especially to our somewhat self-righteous nation. Furthermore, in the person of Noah Webster, we were blessed by the presence of a schoolmaster of almost unlimited energy for the publicizing of the authoritarian point of view, a pedagogue *par excellence* who was more than willing to assume the mantles of Dr. Johnson, Bishop Lowth, and even of Joseph Priestley—for linguistic disciplinarian though he was, he recognized the power of usage as did Priestley, and, like Priestley, he believed that usage might be directed and irregularity corrected by analogy, the guiding linguistic principle of the eighteenth century.

FIVE

Noah Webster,
Man and Symbol

NOAH WEBSTER, whose name is known all over the English-speaking world—"according to Webster" is as familiar a recommendation as "according to Hoyle"—was a Connecticut Yankee whose father, a thrifty and industrious farmer, ultimately rose to the rank and dignities of a Calvinist deacon. It is worthy of note, to show the superior moral background of our great American schoolmaster, that the senior Webster, also named Noah, once served as one of a committee appointed to reprimand a harassed pastor for tippling. The younger Noah grew up with all the tiresome virtues. He was possessed of almost unlimited determination and an infinite capacity for taking pains. He rose early, worked hard, took healthful exercise, was strictly temperate, led the church choir on Sundays, and, full of years, honours, and virtues, lived to the venerable age of eighty-five. The lovable qualities which we detect in the great English lexicographer, even despite the frequent waspishness of Boswell's portrayal—the bohemianism, the fondness for late hours and conviviality, the endearing eccentricities, the prejudices (so often justified), the very human passionateness, the brilliant talk, the warmth of the transcendent smile which every so often lighted up his ugly, pitted face—all these were absent in the Great Cham of the American language, who had none of the vast personal charm which is so striking a characteristic of Dr. Johnson. Webster was smug, self-assured, and pugnacious in his pedantry as in his Puritanism and his patriotism: the dour, thin-lipped, jut-jawed righteousness of his later portraits seems always to have been characteristic of him. It is difficult to think of him as ever having been young; the report of the mild foppishness of his college days surprises the chronicler when he comes upon it.

75

But there was the stuff of greatness in him. Furthermore, he possessed the capacity to work twice as long and hard as other men without getting tired. His moral earnestness drove him to toil indefatigably for the greater glory of God, of his beloved country, and of Noah Webster. In many respects this Yankee schoolmaster is a far more appropriate symbol of our young nation than is either the cosmopolite printer-philosopher Franklin or the squirish-minded Washington.

Webster was born just outside Hartford in 1758. As a youth he did military service of a sort in the war for national independence when his state guard regiment set out for Saratoga too late for the battle. The stirring times during which he passed his formative years left their mark, for throughout his life in all his manifold undertakings, linguistic and otherwise, he was actuated by an extreme form of patriotism which frequently manifested itself in Anglophobia, and sometimes bordered very narrowly on chauvinism.

Upon his graduation from Yale, he hankered after the law. The state of the family finances made it impossible for him to prepare himself for the bar immediately. Like many another American father since his day, Deacon Webster had impoverished himself and his family in order to give his son an education; like many another ambitious young man, Noah Webster, Jun., got himself a post as schoolmaster and read law whenever he could find the time for it.

It is not to be supposed that his heart was not in his teaching, however, for it was during this period, in 1779 and 1780, that he began to see very clearly the defects of the American educational system. Education was already a sort of bourgeois fetish in America, but actually we were doing very little about it except talk. Methods were antiquated, textbooks equally so and—even worse, from the point of view of an American nationalist—imported from England. School buildings which had been primitive to begin with were run-down and out of repair. Those who presided over the youth of the land were frequently uncouth louts who had themselves received only a smattering of learning, but who could wield a wicked lash over shrinking youthful posteriors.

With Webster, to see a fault was to do something about it. What he saw most clearly was not the frightful inadequacy of what in modern educational jargon is called the "plant." Nor did the ignorance of the teachers worry him unduly. Armed with proper textbooks, even doltish teachers could not go wrong. The proper textbooks would be

quite naturally American textbooks. It is true that there were no
American textbooks yet, but that was a defect which could be remedied
by Noah Webster, Jun. Moreover, the writing of textbooks could be
a very lucrative business, and money was what Webster needed badly.

The idea had been conceived, but its gestation and birth were
deferred until Webster had qualified as a lawyer. He passed the bar
examinations in his native Hartford and was admitted to practice.
Thereafter, until he was made an honorary Doctor of Laws—the
democratic equivalent of the accolade—he was Noah Webster, Jun.,
Esq., which looked well on the title pages of his earlier books. Fortunately for American youth, few clients came to consult him, and he
was forced for the time being to turn again to teaching.

Thenceforth, in the midst of a long life so active and so manifold
in its activities that it would have worn out most men, he found time
to write a series of grammatical and lexicographical works for the
express purpose of correcting, regulating, and guiding the language of
his country. Patriotism imbued all his writings, patriotism which
manifested itself in many ways, and not least in his concern with
uniformizing the language of his fellow Americans, for, as he believed,
"a national language is a band of national union."

His petition for copyright for his textbooks declared that they
would aid in correcting and unifying the language, for they were
calculated "to reform the abuses and corruption which, to an unhappy
degree, tincture the conversation of the polite part of the Americans
. . . and especially to render the pronunciation . . . accurate and uniform
by demolishing those obvious distinctions of provincial dialects which
are the subject of reciprocal ridicule in different states." A familiar
American pedagogical principle may be observed here in the assumption that Noah Webster, a New England farm boy who had been to
college, in some mysterious way knew better how the language
"ought" to be than the "polite part" of our population—an attitude
similar to that of Bishop Lowth, who thought that our greatest writers
wrote bad English.

The spelling book which appeared in 1783 was the first of a series
of three volumes somewhat pompously called *A Grammatical Institute
of the English Language*, a title probably suggested, not altogether
inappropriately, by Calvin's *Institutes*. The other two volumes,
published in 1784 and 1785, were respectively a grammar and a reader.
In the Preface to the first volume Webster emphasized in a character-

istically heavy-handed fashion the moral, religious, and patriotic value of the book and of those to come. Actually, the title of this first volume of the *Grammatical Institute* said nothing about spelling, but simply stated that, in addition to "Comprising an easy, concise, and systematic Method of Education, Designed for the Use of English Schools in America," it contained "a new and accurate Standard of Pronunciation." It is significant in view of a very important characteristic of American pronunciation, its frequent reliance upon spelling, that the first American work purporting to deal with pronunciation was actually a speller. In 1788 the book appeared under the title *The American Spelling Book* ("containing an easy Standard of Pronunciation"). This edition and all subsequent ones appeared within blue paper covers, whence the familiar term "blue-back speller." In 1829 the title became *The Elementary Spelling Book*.

The *American Spelling Book* must surely be among the best sellers of all times. It has been estimated that a hundred million copies of it were sold before it was finally supplanted, and this figure seems quite reasonable. Unfortunately Webster, who was extremely good at the promotion of his books and who obviously wanted to profit materially by them, was not a very good man of business. Royalties would have made him a rich man, but he sold rights for the sale of this book for comparatively trifling sums of money and was frequently taken advantage of by unscrupulous booksellers. Even so, the greater part of his income for the rest of his life came from the many editions of the speller.

In the *Spelling Book*, for which he devised a system of numerical notation to indicate pronunciation, Webster first promulgated the standard of "general custom" to which he was to pay lip service throughout his life. He had nothing but a sneer for the pronunciation of the "polite part" of American society, which for a long time sneered at him in return. He consoled himself with the belief that "it is always better to be *vulgarly* right than *politely* wrong." When he declared that the standard of propriety should be set by the most enlightened members of the various communities, he of course meant sober and godly people like himself, not people distinguished by social brilliance, of whose usage he very frequently disapproved. It is to be noted that, while recognizing that usage varied somewhat from community to community, he believed that a national standard was most desirable and that such a standard could be inculcated by schooling. Actually his distrust of usage was so great that he regretted that "the pronunciation of our language, tho' the most important and difficult part of grammar, is left to parents and nurses—to ignorance and caprice—to custom, accident or nothing. Nay, to something worse, to coxcombs, who have a share in directing the *polite part* of pronunciation, which of course is as vicious as that of any other class of people."

It should be said that Webster was sometimes willing to accept actual usage, so long as it did not seem to him to be decadently fashionable usage. "Where people differ in opinion and practice," however, "analogy should always decide the controversy," for he was convinced, like any philosopher of the Age of Reason, that "if we examine the structure of any language, we shall find a certain principle of analogy running through the whole." Nevertheless, it was usage rather than analogy which was responsible for his sanctioning *it is me*, *who is she married to*, and *them horses*, though he thought the last expression analogical as well as established by usage. Amazingly enough he justified *them horses* by the analogy of "our parent language, the German" [*sic*] and proceeded to expose an ignorance of German which would disgrace a freshman in his explanation that *in dem Himmel* meant "in them heavens." Webster thought, of course, that in his endorsement of *them horses* he was bringing the language back to its "purity and original simplicity." He believed that he had shown that such expressions were by no means innovations, which he liked no better than any other linguistic authoritarian likes them.

Webster was not really liberal in his linguistic point of view, as some have thought him to be. It is true that he disapproved of all previous writers upon language, as well as those contemporary with him who dared claim any authority. But it was not authority that he objected to; he made his own pronouncements, which were frequently wrong, in the most authoritative manner. What he objected to was the authority of others. His occasional acceptance of the usage of the yokelry—the yeomanry, to use his own term—does not even remotely resemble the modern doctrine of usage, which has never assumed that the usage of yokels was socially acceptable save among yokels; his attempted elevation of the bumpkin as arbiter was patently only a means of expressing his contempt for the "gay and fashionable world," whose grace and luxury he envied, but for which he had no gift. Actually, he usually recorded New England usage—frequently without knowing that he was doing so, for he was not an expert observer of speech habits; however, even when he knew of a variant more generally used than the New England pronunciation, the latter was the one most likely to receive his recommendation, though he certainly did not approve of all types of New England speech, such as the "drawling, nasal manner of speaking" and the pronunciations *marcy* for *mercy* and *kiow* for *cow*. Nevertheless, he did set himself firmly against local usage in the *Spelling Book* when he declared that "general custom must be the rule of speaking, and every deviation from this must be wrong. The dialect of one State is as ridiculous as that of another; each is authorized by local custom; and neither is supported by any superior excellence."

Webster actually understood very little of the historical development of language. His guiding principle, as has been said, was analogy. "To renounce a practice confessedly regular for one confessedly anomalous . . . would hardly be consistent with the dignity of lexicography," he said in his "Essay on a Reformed Method of Spelling." "When we have principle on our side, let us adhere to it." He was actuated by the belief that he had such principle on his side in his lifelong insistence that *deaf* should be spoken with the vowel sound of *leaf* and *sheaf*. The pronunciation *def* he considered "evidently a corruption." As an old man he was still sticking to his guns in regard to this word and commented to Captain Basil Hall, an English naval officer who called upon him to pay his respects, "Your way of pronouncing *deaf* is *def*—ours, as if it were written *deef*; and as this is the correct mode from which you have departed, I shall adhere to the American way."

Webster's speller, under its various titles, is a much more important book than its small size and generally modest appearance would indicate. The modesty is purely superficial, it must be said; there is little humility in the widely praised flag-waving Preface or in Webster's claims of superiority over the predecessors from whom he lifted a great deal of material, so much in fact that Professor (later President) Samuel Stanhope Smith of Princeton, who examined the manuscript in 1782, referred to it as "a plan of reforming the spelling book of Mr. Dilworth" [the *New Guide to the English Tongue*, called "the nurse of us all" by Joel Barlow, but characterized by Webster in advertising his own book as "one half . . . totally useless, and the other half, defective and erroneous"], "associating with it an abridgment of Mr. Lowth's Grammar." Incidentally, much was also lifted from Fenning's *Universal*

Spelling Book, the principal competitor of Dilworth's *New Guide* until both were supplanted by Webster's book.

Webster did not depart from conventional English spelling in the early editions of his *Spelling Book*. Those changes for which he was responsible and which to this day differentiate American from British spelling were not advocated until much later, in his *Compendious Dictionary* of 1806, after he had perceived that the more radical changes proposed in his *Dissertations* of 1789 would never be acceptable. In 1783 he specifically condemned leaving the *u* out of the *-our* words (*labour, honour*, etc.) and considered that those who omit it do so because of a "rage for singularity." Few innovations or departures from British usage as established by Johnson were introduced into the speller until comparatively late editions.

Aside from the patriotic, moral, and religious precepts which its homely fables and maxims inculcated and the patent fact that for a number of generations it taught the American people how to spell, it is likely that the *Spelling Book* has also influenced American pronunciation. Much of the self-conscious carefulness of educated American pronunciation may be attributable to Webster's principles, which changed speech from a social and traditional accomplishment into an intellectual chore. As James Fenimore Cooper in his *Notions of the Americans* remarked of the typical New Englander, "He has a theoretical knowledge of the language, without its practice," that is, he tended to substitute analogy for tradition and felt that in so doing he had effected an improvement: "It is vain to tell a man who has his book before him, that *cham* spells *chame*, as in *chamber*, or *an, ane*, as in *angel*; or *dan, dane*, as in *danger*. He replies by asking what sound is produced by *an, dan*, and *cham*. I believe it would be found . . . that a great number of their peculiar sounds are introduced through their spelling books."

But the influence of the old blue-back speller was not confined to classes of words such as those Cooper mentions. Rather it was a habit of mind, an attitude towards language, which Webster inculcated, along with the notion that American pronunciation should be uniform. He was not one to deny himself credit where he thought credit was due, declaring on a flyleaf of the *Elementary Spelling Book* of 1843 that "in the early years of our independence much was done to promote this object [of a uniform national language] by Webster's Spelling Book . . . and the effects of the general use of Webster's Book for more than thirty years, are visible at this day, in the remarkable uniformity of pronunciation among the citizens of the United States." Speaking well depended upon how diligently one had learned one's lessons out of Webster's book, not upon anything so meretricious as caste. The articulation of speech became a test both of one's intelligence and of one's patriotism.

The careful pronunciation of educated, that is, socially acceptable, American English evinces itself not only in a general deference to spelling as a guide, but also in an attitude towards syllables, no longer necessarily conscious, which has tended to preserve their full values. The secondary accent in American English on the next to the last syllable of long words in -ary, -ory, -ery (secretary, explanatory, cemetery) was also characteristic of British English in the seventeenth and eighteenth centuries. This syllable has lost its accent in British English and has at the most a "murmur vowel"; more often, words of this type show complete loss of the syllable in question. American retention of both the syllable and its stress is not of course to be attributed to Webster, but is probably only an instance of American linguistic conservatism. What is certain is that the habit of mind instilled by Websterian teaching would vigorously have resisted any tendency in American English towards a reduction or loss such as that which has occurred in British English. An altogether literal attitude towards language, instilled by four generations of schoolteachers armed with one or another of the many editions of Webster's speller (there were more than three hundred before 1829) is at least partially responsible for the distinct articulation of all syllables in that type of pronunciation upon which educated American speakers pride themselves.

In the early days spelling was frequently taught by having the pupils read aloud, all together, letter by letter and syllable by syllable. Then all books were closed save that of the master, who, with his little blue-backed volume in hand, proceeded to give out words for spelling. The pupils spelled as they had read, letter by letter and syllable by syllable, thus: o,r—or; d,i—di; n,a—na; r,y—ry; ordinary. Occasionally the pupils (they were usually "scholars" in those days) were permitted to choose sides in order to introduce a spirit of group competition. He who misspelled had to take his seat; the master's purpose was to "spell down" the pupils. The winning side was that which had the member who could survive the onslaught upon his orthographical powers longest. Thus was born the spelling bee, a peculiarly American institution, and thus was encouraged that careful and deliberate pronunciation, highly conscious of the supposed value of syllables, which has been cited as typical of American speech on the educated level.

In 1785, Webster began the composition of a series of lectures which became the basis of his *Dissertations on the English Language*, published in 1789, as well as of his *Collection of Essays and Fugitiv [sic] Writings* (1790). Significantly, one of his objects in these lectures was "to point out and reconcile, on established principles, the most material differences of pronunciation and use of words in the United States; to check the errors and abuses which the fashion of another country is palming upon us for propriety." The lectures were given before audiences "generally small, but always respectable," in about twenty of the larger towns between Williamsburg, Virginia, and Portsmouth, New Hampshire. It is saddening to record that only six auditors made up his audience in Williamsburg. Of this indifference to plain patriotic duty on the part of the Virginians, Webster self-righteously wrote: "I am a stranger and a Yankee, tho' well introduced; the Virginians have little money and great pride, contempt of northern men, and great fondness for dissipated life. They do not understand Grammar." (Alas for the South!) Later, when informed in Annapolis that "few white men in Maryland or Virginia could even write their own names," he was struck anew with the baseness of our Southern states and was moved to inscribe in his diary, "O New England! how superior are thy inhabitants in morals, literature, civility, and industry!"

The *Dissertations* are a fascinating farrago of the soundest linguistic common sense and the most egregious poppycock. (Webster himself described the book as "full of criticisms, which some will call good sense and others nonsense.") Some of the ideas and attitudes expressed are those typical of the eighteenth century, though it must be said in all fairness both to Webster and the eighteenth century that they are still widely held by teachers, even on the college level; others anticipate the doctrine of usage of modern linguistic science.

In this work, bristling with linguistic patriotism and dedicated to Benjamin Franklin, Webster proposed an American standard, a "Federal English," independent of the British. "Several circumstances," he declared, "render a future separation of the American tongue from the English necessary and unavoidable." For one thing, "as an independent nation, our honor requires us to have a system of our own, in language as well as government." England should not be our standard, "for the taste of her writers is already corrupted, and her language on the decline." Later he singled out for attack, among others, Gibbon ("It is difficult to comprehend his meaning and the chain of his ideas. ... The mind of the reader is constantly dazzled by a glare of ornament, or charmed from the subject by the music of the language") and Johnson, who perhaps had it coming to him for having declared in 1769 that the American colonists were "a race of convicts, and ought to be thankful for any thing we allow them short of hanging" ("His style is ... an intolerable composition of Latinity, affected smoothness, scholastic accuracy, and roundness of periods"). Furthermore, England was at "too great a distance to be our model, and to instruct us in the principles of our own tongue." Webster, on the other hand, was readily available to do the job.

Webster was quite right in pointing out that "numerous local causes, such as a new country, new combinations of ideas in arts and sciences, and some intercourse with tribes wholly unknown in Europe, will introduce new words into the American tongue." But this was, after all, a pretty safe prediction. Somewhat less accurate was his belief, which he modified later in his career, that "these causes will produce, in a course of time, a language in North America as different from the future language of England as the Modern Dutch, Danish, and Swedish are from the German, or from one another: like remote branches of a tree springing from the same stock, or rays of light shot from the same center, and diverging from each other in proportion to their distance from the point of separation." In a fine burst of patriotism, he concluded that "we have therefore the fairest opportunity of establishing a national language and of giving it uniformity and perspicuity, in North America, that ever presented itself to mankind." "Let us then seize the present moment," he pleaded, "and establish a national language, as well as a national government." The cultured and the well-washed in this country had considerably more to lose by Webster's proposed severance of cultural and linguistic ties with the mother country than had the eighteenth-century common man—the American yeoman, as Webster called him—for whom the idea seems to have had some appeal. Though not in the least dependent upon England, this American yeoman was by no means uneducated. He did not allow his reason to be dazed by such frivolous writers as Gibbon and Johnson, but he read the Bible and the very best sermons. He, directed along the paths of analogy by Noah Webster, was to determine the standards of American speech rather than those who constituted "the polite part" of society, certainly rather than those doubtless immoral British play actors, Thomas Sheridan, whose *General Dictionary of the English Language* had appeared in 1780, and John Walker, whose *Critical Pronouncing Dictionary and Expositor of the English Language* (1791) was considered by many as a sure guide to the most fashionable type of pronunciation, and hence a means of acquiring social distinction.

Consequently, Webster's proposals met with a rather cool reception in the larger centres of population, particularly in Boston and its environs, which remained somewhat suspicious of the Connecticut schoolmaster who insisted upon saying *heerd* and *deef* for *heard* and *deaf*, and defended such locutions as *them horses* and *you was*. He in his turn had no great love for city people, and always idealized the simple virtues of rural life: the phrase "this wicked world" occurs a number of times in his writings and refers not to the skulduggery of rustics but to the sophistication of urban dwellers.

Only three years after the publication of the first part of the *Grammatical Institute*, Webster's mind had buzzed with plans for spelling reform, and he was now all for "expunging the superfluous letters," a procedure which he had opposed in that work. The results of his lucubrations were given to the world in an Appendix to his *Dissertations*. As early as 1768 Benjamin Franklin had worked out an elaborate scheme of phonetic spelling, but when Webster had heard of it from Dr. Franklin in 1786 he was unsympathetic, mainly because it required six new characters. Nevertheless, the younger man's passion for tinkering with language had been fired, and he immediately went to work on a scheme of his own—naturally a better scheme than that of the self-educated Franklin, whose lack of erudition the Yale-bred Webster referred to somewhat smugly in his 64-page *Letter to the Honorable John Pickering* (1817). He had discussed his plan with various members of the Congress with a view to the enacting of a law requiring its use. It is surprising that no such law was ever introduced, for the desire to regulate custom by law seems always to have appealed to Americans. It is likely that the idea of spelling reform appealed not only to Webster's desire to manipulate, but also to his intensely patriotic feelings. He declared, in fact, that "a capital advantage of this reform in these States would be that it would make a difference between the English orthography and the American. . . . I am confident that such an event is an object of vast political importance."

The plan to reform American spelling as outlined at the end of the *Dissertations* and blunderingly exemplified in the preface and two of the essays in his *Collection of Essays and Fugitiv Writings* drew down a storm of wrath and scorn upon Webster's unruly republican thatch (a physical characteristic not even hinted at in the serene, idealized portrait by a modern artist used as a frontispiece in some of the dictionaries bearing his name). Conventional spelling is very dear to the hearts of most people, who, while believing it to be chaotic (which it is not) and difficult (which it certainly is), yet resist stoutly, as if it were a moral obligation, any effort to change it. After a while, Webster's enthusiasm for such extreme measures as he had advocated was to abate. Much ridicule and vituperation had greeted his proposals; also he was never able to exemplify his own reforms with any consistency. Perhaps he came to lack faith in them himself.

The next ten years of Webster's life were spent in a whirl of earnest and purposeful activity—patriotic, educational, political, editorial, and scientific. In 1800 he announced to the world that he "had in hand a Dictionary of the American Language, a work long since projected, but which other occupations have delayed till this time." There were "considerable differences between the American and English language" which had arisen as a result of "new circumstances, new modes of life, new laws, new ideas of various kinds. . . . The differences in the language of the two countries will continue to multiply, and render it necessary that we should have *Dictionaries* of the *American Language*."

In the preface to his first lexicographical work, *A Compendious Dictionary of the English Language* (1806), Webster announced that his intention had been to compile a dictionary "which shall exhibit a far more correct state of the language than any work of this kind." Having given up some of his more fantastic spelling reforms, he now predicted that, because of printing, mutual intercourse would continue to exist between English-speaking peoples; "but those terms in Great Britain which express local ideas only will be lost in the dialects of India and America, while local circumstances among the descendants of the English in their new settlements will originate new words or give to old words new significations which will never be received or generally known in Great Britain." He was furthermore convinced that "in each of the countries peopled by Englishmen, a distinct dialect of the language will gradually be formed, the principal of which will be that of the United States."

Unfortunately for his commercial success, Webster was still riding his reformed spelling hobby, though he had indeed slackened his pace somewhat, and many who would have welcomed the *Compendious Dictionary* for patriotic reasons were wary of such spellings as *tung, fether, crum, soop, porpess* (for *porpoise*), *wimmen, ake, soe* (for *sew*), *sut* (for *soot*), *groop, cag* (for *keg*), and *iland*. Such spellings as *draft, favor*, and *theater*, for *draught, favour*, and *theatre* must have looked equally offensive at the time, but these have become established in American spelling. Curtailment of *axe* to *ax* has also become standard in America, but in Webster's day it must have seemed as strange as *medicin* and *definit* do to us.

In this dictionary Webster recommended a good many pronunciations which were either old-fashioned or plebeian (some were both) by 1806, though most of them are in our own day still current: his spellings *sut* and *cag* indicate such pronunciations. He favoured the pronunciations *ax* for *ask*, *lecter* for *lecture*, *nater* for *nature*, and *figger* for *figure* (which last is, ironically, now the usual British pronunciation, though Walker in 1791 called it "coarse"). That his judgments were in part a rationalization of his hatred of fashionable and would-be fashionable people living in cities is indicated by his comment in the *Dissertations* that "there are many people, and perhaps most of them in the capital towns, that have learned a few commonplace words, such as *forchin, nachur, virchue*, and half a dozen others, which they repeat on all occasions." As late as the *Elementary Spelling Book* of 1843, he gave *gesture* and *jester* as homophones. The *yu* sound of *u* was not the "true sound" under any circumstances, and he rejected it in *mute, pure, beauty, few, volume, value, tenure* (which last two he equated with *valley* and *tenor*). One cannot but wonder how he knew what the "true sound" was. In any case, there can be no doubt that the pronunciation recorded by Walker—that which is now current in these words—was by and large more typical of American educated usage in Webster's day than Webster's own. But Webster was amazingly stiff-necked in such matters and, it is to be suspected, recommended many pronunciations of the "American yeoman" simply because they were *not* fashionable: "A man of great soul," he declared in the *Dissertations*, "would sooner imitate the virtues of a cottage than the vices of a court; and would deem it more honorable to gain one useful idea from the humble laborer, than to copy the vicious pronunciation of a splendid court, or become an adept in the licentious principles of a Rochester and a Littleton"—which shows how easy it is to confuse language with morality.

In the *Compendious Dictionary*, and in a somewhat condensed form of that work published in 1807 as *A Dictionary of the English Language compiled for the use of common schools in the United States*, in which he made a play for the favour of the "common people," including "the great body of farmers and mechanics," Webster stated that, despite his conviction that the irregularity of our spelling needed attention, he had come to the conclusion that "no great changes should be made at once, nor should any change be made which violates established principles, creates great inconvenience, or obliterates the radicals of the language."

The more sweeping proposals, not all of which were new, called for (1) dropping of final *k* after *c* in words of more than one syllable (*physic, music* for older *physick, musick*, etc.; *cassoc, hammoc, demoniac*, etc.), though Webster seems to have slipped up with *almanack, traffick, frolick*, and *havock*; (2) uniform use of *-or* for *-our* in words of more than one syllable (*honor, favor*, etc.); (3) uniform use of *-er* for *-re* in *theater, meter*, and the like; (4) *-se* for *-ce* in *defense, offense, pretense*, but not in *fence*. The last three of these reforms have come to be characteristic of American spelling, though *glamour* and *Saviour* (with reference to Christ) occur as exceptions to the second proposal. The *-ck* is retained in modern spelling after *o* (but not in *havoc*, the one word of this class in which Webster neglected to drop the *k*); after *a* the reduction regularly occurs (but not in *arrack*). This treatment of the *k* is now characteristic of American and British practice alike, though *almanack* occurs occasionally as a British spelling. Among the other more sensible proposals, Webster's recommendation of *-in, -iv, -it* for *-ine, -ive, -ite* in *feminine, fugitive, definite*, and the like did not catch on. Equally unsuccessful was *f* for *ph* in *phantom* and the like, *oo* for *ou* in *group* and the like, *ou* for *ow* in *crowd* and the like, and the simplification of *ea* to *e* in *bread, steady, feather*, and the like.

The innovations in spelling offended many; others objected to the dictionaries because new words, frequently local terms, had been added. Adding anything to what Johnson had recorded as the body of the English language was painting the lily. Webster attempted to meet this objection by one of his frequent vicious attacks upon Johnson and, in the manner of Bishop Lowth, pointed out somewhat irrelevantly in a 25-page pamphlet addressed to Dr. David Ramsay "respecting the Errors of Johnson's Dictionary" (1807) that Johnson frequently chose illustrations from authors who did not write "pure" English. The later British commentator who said "there are enough words already" was quite representative of conservative linguistic opinion of the time, for it was widely held that the English language was complete in itself. New words were by virtue of their very novelty "impurities" and "colloquial barbarisms." Such an attitude towards language is not altogether archaic today.

The years between the publication of the *Compendious Dictionary* and 1825 were largely devoted to the preparation of *An American Dictionary of the English Language*, though the indefatigable Webster found time to engage in political activities, give pious but unsought advice to President-elect Madison, and become a founder of Amherst College. Unlike the earlier lexicographical work, which provided only spelling, pronunciation, and definition, this was to be an etymological dictionary, and Webster early set about to prepare himself for the great task—in his opinion not merely to set down a record of the language, but "to search for truth, to proscribe error, and repress anomaly." Even with such exalted ideals, however, it was necessary to have some information at hand, and he set about to prepare a synopsis of the supposed affinities of the twenty-three languages, not to mention "the early dialects of English and German," which he is supposed to have learned.

Moving about a specially constructed semicircular desk, thumbing grammars and dictionaries, noting similarities and supposed correspondences of consonants and letting the vowels fall where they may, is not the same thing as buckling down and actually learning languages. Webster might have saved himself a great deal of time if he had taken the trouble to find out what keener-minded and better informed men had discovered instead of pursuing such feckless tasks as trying to prove, in line with his belief in the divine origin of language, that "Chaldee" (Biblical Aramaic) was the parent of all languages. He did not bother to learn Sanskrit, the study of which in the late eighteenth century gave rise to the Indo-Egyptian hypothesis, namely the now universal assumption of a common ancestor for most of the languages spoken in Europe and the Americas, as well as some spoken in Asia, the Indic and the Iranian. Why the discoveries of Sir William Jones were not better known to him—Jones had written forty years before the publication of the *American Dictionary*—it is impossible to say. The foundations of modern linguistic science had been soundly laid by such scholars as Jones, Jacob Grimm, Franz Bopp, and Friedrich von Schlegel. But Webster was too busy "mastering" languages—according to his own claims, German, Dutch, Swedish, Danish, Anglo-Saxon, Gothic, Welsh, Armoric (Breton), "Hyberne" (Irish), Ethiopic, Persian, Hebrew, Samaritan, Chaldaic, Syriac, Arabic, Greek, Latin, Italian, Spanish, French, Portuguese, and Russian—to familiarize himself with the important and exciting discoveries which others had made and which were by no means unknown in this country. James Gates Percival, the poet, who read proof on the *American Dictionary*, was quite familiar with them, but Webster would not listen to the young man's remonstrances. Those "Chaldee" etymologies were very dear to his heart.

In 1824 Webster set out for France and England to visit libraries. Though he was thrilled by the sight of so many volumes, he saw in both countries much to disapprove of, much to convince him of the superiority of his native New England. Like many another American visitor since his day, he was disappointed in the University of Cambridge because its buildings were so old: he declared with patriotic pride that they looked "very heavy, cold, and gloomy to an American accustomed to the new public buildings in our country." It was here in decadent old England, ironically enough, that he finished writing his great dictionary.

The *American Dictionary of the English Language* burst upon the world in 1828 in two large quarto volumes—bulkier than any dictionary ever before printed. Seventy thousand words were defined, admirably for the most part, with spelling, pronunciation, and etymology indicated. To it was prefixed "an introductory dissertation on the origin, history and connections of the languages of Western Asia and of Europe, and a concise grammar of the English language." Webster had modified some of his earlier views about the desirability of emphasizing the differences in British and American usage, for by 1828 he seems to have been convinced that the language of America was essentially the same as that of England and that it was "desirable to perpetuate that sameness" rather than to point out the differences as he had done in his *Dissertations* of 1789. Actually, he had come to think that there were not many local terms in use in this country.

Although it is dwarfed by its lineal descendant, the 1934 *New International* (popularly *Webster's Unabridged*) with its more than

550,000 words, the *American Dictionary of the English Language* was a tremendous accomplishment compared with any previous lexicographical work: the *Compendious Dictionary* of 1806, the largest in the country, had listed a mere 28,000 words with pronunciations and definitions but no etymologies. The aging lexicographer no longer had to content himself with an *Esq.* on the title page; five years earlier, in 1823, Yale had conferred upon him the degree LL.D. *honoris causa*, and he was proud to pin this well-earned merit badge to his name.

As an etymologist Webster was something less than adequate. As has already been pointed out, he chose to ignore (perhaps because of an inability to read German, one of those twenty-three languages he is reported to have "mastered") the really significant work which had been done in linguistics in his day, preferring the tower of Babel explanation of the origin of individual tongues to the scientific methods of the Indo-Europeanists. Furthermore, he does not seem really to have learned languages at all well. Charlton Laird in his "Etymology, Anglo-Saxon, and Noah Webster" (*American Speech*, February, 1946) concludes that Webster's knowledge of Anglo-Saxon (Old English) was inferior to that of Thomas Jefferson, who claimed to be no better than an amateur. Professor Laird has examined four works in Old English which Webster presented to Yale in 1837, presumably the only ones in this older form of our language that he owned. From marginal notes in Webster's hand—the sort, according to Laird, which "one would expect from a beginning graduate student"—it is obvious that Webster's ignorance of Old English was deplorable as compared with what was well known by British scholars in his day. In the light of such facts, it is difficult not to question his proficiency in some of the other languages which he "mastered" in the course of a myriad half-circuits around his famous desk. In any case, subsequent editors have without comment excised by the basketful Webster's etymological "boners."

But if his etymologies are frequently worse than worthless, there can be no doubt that Webster was superb in definition, though even here his personal bias is frequently evident. In the *Compendious Dictionary* he had defined *Federalist* as "a friend to the Constitution of the U. States," paralleling Johnson's definition of a Tory as "one who adheres to the ancient constitution of the state, and the apostolical hierarchy of the Church of England, opposed to a Whig." The *American Dictionary* also contains a good many nonobjective definitions and illustrations designed to support Webster's political and moral predilections and to uphold the Calvinistic department of the Christian religion. But such definitions are, after all, exceptional, just as are the oft-quoted crotchety definitions of Johnson. For the most part, the reader is struck with admiration and must perforce agree with Sir James Murray, the great editor of the *Oxford English Dictionary*, that Webster was "a born definer of words."

The spelling changes which Webster advocated most vigorously in the *American Dictionary* he had also advocated in the dictionaries of 1806 and 1807. Before Webster, both Lowth and Walker had recommended one *l* in *traveller, jeweller,* and the like, but Webster is probably responsible for the general American practice of not doubling final *l* when adding a suffix unless the word in its primary form is stressed on the final syllable: thus *travel—traveled, traveling, traveler* (but *excel— excelled, excelling*). The British practice is always to double final *l*: thus *travelled, travelling, traveller.* Also to be attributed to Webster's precept and practice is the ending *-ize* instead of *-ise* in such words as *baptize, civilize, organize* (but not in *advertise, devise, surprise,* and a number of others). Although the American distinction of *-ize* and *-ise,* which is also observed by the London *Times* and preferred by the *Oxford English Dictionary,* is, for reasons which it is unnecessary to go into here, etymologically sound, it seems hardly worth making. The simpler practice followed by most English printers of using *-ise* consistently has much to commend it.

As for pronunciation, Webster's recommendation in the *American Dictionary* is probably largely responsible for *schedule* with the same initial sounds as *school* and of *lieutenant* with the first syllable as *loot;* pronunciation as *leftenant* was formerly current here as it still is in England. Though not altogether a matter of pronunciation, since variant forms are involved, *aluminum* was his choice for the name of the metal which in England is called *aluminium* with the principal stress on the third syllable. Both forms were at one time current in England. American English has settled upon the *aluminum* form ever since its inclusion in the *American Dictionary* of Noah Webster.

But Webster was not always so successful in having his own way. He thought, for instance, that the noun *wound* should be pronounced exactly like the past tense of *wind,* though admitting that *woond* was "the fashionable pronunciation" (no recommendation from his point of view!). Nevertheless, pronounciation as *woond* has prevailed, though it is doubtful that it would have done so had subsequent editions of the *Dictionary* continued to recommend *wownd*, such is the supreme confidence of our people in the authority of the lexicographer. Webster also disapproved of the insertion of a *y* sound after the initial consonant in such words as *car*, *garden*, and *girl* (polite British pronunciations in the eighteenth century), but such pronunciations are still occasionally to be heard in cultivated Virginia speech. He frequently had to capitulate, as in his previous recommendation of the pronunciation *heerd* for *heard*, though he was still adamant in his objection to *def* for *deaf*.

The *American Dictionary* and to a lesser extent the *Compendious* were the first dictionaries to list, as he had boasted in the preface to the earlier work, words which were "either new in the United States or, what is more usual, English words [which] have received a new sense." Local words and words having to do with American religious and political life, with American commerce and finance, were included and defined in both dictionaries, as were also some New England rural colloquialisms. He had already, in the *Compendious*, admitted some new words peculiar to the United States and English words in new senses, citing in his preface *to fourfold*, *dutiable*, *to girdle* (trees), and *to gin* (cotton), among others, and he had been harshly criticized for doing so. Fortunately not much daunted by adverse criticism, in the *American Dictionary* he also included Americanisms (though, strangely enough, omitting *prairie*, *Indian summer*, *pecan*, *paleface*, *pone*, and *platform* "body of political principles") and even provincialisms if of New England, such as *clever* "good-natured" and *to spell* "to relieve someone at work." "Such local terms exist," he had declared in a letter written in 1809, "and will exist, in spite of lexicographers and critics. Is this *my* fault? And if local terms exist, why not explain them? . . . How are such words to be understood without the aid of a dictionary?"

In the *American Dictionary* Webster took pride in his use of illustrative quotations from the works of American writers, many of them now passed into merciful oblivion. Jefferson, whose politics Webster abhorred, is conspicuously absent. Along with the rustic piety of some of the definitions and illustrations, this use of American writings is actually the principal justification for the use of *American* in the title, for despite all his high-sounding talk about an American language, Webster really had little conception of the differences between American and British English in his day, as is indicated by his remark to Captain Basil Hall in the very year of publication of the *American Dictionary* that he believed "there were not fifty words in all which were used in America and not in England." Localisms, words peculiar to America, and English words used in a special sense by us do not actually loom very large in Webster's great dictionary.

The *American Dictionary* did not pile up much of a profit for Webster, who had been forced to borrow money to cover the printer's bill when his publisher had been unable to raise the necessary funds. He therefore conceived the idea of a less expensive abridgment, securing Joseph Emerson Worcester, a lexicographer who had just prepared a combined edition of Johnson's *English Dictionary* and Walker's *Pronouncing Dictionary*, to do the job. This abridgment appeared in 1829. In 1830 Worcester published a dictionary of his own, the *Comprehensive Pronouncing Dictionary of the English Language*, the plans for which he had already made before accepting employment with Webster. This book furnished Webster's only serious competition until the publication of the *Century Dictionary* in 1891. Many preferred Worcester's dictionary because it did not tinker much with conventional spelling (later editions accepted the Websterian simplification of *-our* to *-or*) and it recorded the pronunciation of ladies and gentlemen, not of farmers and artisans as Webster had sometimes (perhaps unwittingly) done. In 1846 a larger edition of Worcester's dictionary was published under the title *A Universal and Critical Dictionary of the English Language*, an abridgment of this work appearing in 1850.

In the English edition of the *Universal and Critical Dictionary*, published ten years after Webster's death, Worcester's publisher made the egregious blunder of having on the title page, "Compiled from the Materials of Noah Webster, LL.D., by Joseph E. Worcester." This set off a furious "War of the Dictionaries," the ammunition being a series of pamphlets issued by the rival publishers. The excitement lasted through the '60s, with Boston and Harvard throwing their influence to the side of Worcester, but Webster was ultimately to prevail in these rarefied circles as he had elsewhere among the plain people.

In 1841, when he was eighty-three years of age and only two years removed from his eternal reward, Webster, who had mortgaged his house in Hartford to pay the expenses of publication, brought out a second edition of the *American Dictionary*. At his death, G. and C. Merriam of Springfield, Mass., made arrangements with the Webster heirs to insure their rights to publish revisions of this edition. For

the edition of 1864, the Merriams employed Dr. C. A. F. Mahn, a
German scholar, to overhaul the etymologies completely. This edition
was not a one-man job, but the product of a distinguished group of
editors, as all subsequent editions have been. The *New International*
(it appeared first under this title in 1909; the edition of 1890 was
Webster's International Dictionary), shows few signs of the hand of old
Noah.

The *American Dictionary* was not the only great work of Webster's
old age. Indeed, his energy was so boundless that this sketch limited to
his purely linguistic activities is altogether inadequate as a measure of
the man. What he must have considered the crowning glory of his
career was his corrected, sterilized, and bowdlerized version of the
King James Bible, which he published in 1833. He had long been
troubled by the bad grammar of the English Bible, such as its use of
his for *its*, as in "If the salt have lost his savor, wherewith shall it be
salted?" (it is not surprising that *its*, which appears first in writing in
1594, was not used in 1611 by linguistically conservative theologians)
and its frequent misuse of *shall* and *will*. Even more serious was its use
of indecent and obscene language, its "many words and phrases . . .
so offensive, especially to females, as to create a reluctance in young
persons to attend bible classes and schools, in which they are required
to read passages which cannot be repeated without a blush." In order
to protect American youth, especially "females," he employed in his
version such euphemisms as *to nourish* for *to give suck*, *breast* for *teat*,
peculiar members for *stones* (testicles), and *to go astray* for *to go a-whoring*.
Womb was one of the "dirty" words he expunged; it must indeed have
troubled him somewhat to utter the word *woman*, inasmuch as he
seriously believed it to be derived from *womb* and *man*.

It is surely a most cruel irony that this Puritan Pico della Mirandola,
this Connecticut Crichton, inspired with an overweening love for his
native land which manifested itself not only in the desire to reform and
regularize its language, but also in a dozen other ways, should have
become a shadowy figure in our own day—the pale reflection of a
great modern dictionary which is his in name only. Quite aside from
his lexicographical labours, Noah Webster would occupy a position of
some importance in the early history of our nation as patriot, political
writer, polemicist, experimental scientist, editor, theologian, economist,
lawyer, and legislator. But all through his long and bustling life, in all
his manifold activities, he was pre-eminently the schoolmaster, the

flagellator anorum of his countrymen, his sole object, in his own words, "to enlighten and benefit his fellow-citizens." He thought of himself, with uncharacteristic modesty, as the Prompter, "the man who in plays sits behind the scenes, looks over the rehearser, and with a moderate voice corrects him when wrong, or assists his recollection when he forgets the next sentence." He wanted "to whip vice and folly out of the country." He remains an appropriate symbol of much that has been considered good in American life.

It has been remarked that Webster may have taught us how to spell but taught us nothing else. With this it is difficult to agree. Webster was certainly one of the most influential commentators upon language who ever lived. More than any other single person, he shaped the course of American English, for he supplied us with the schoolmaster's authority which we needed for linguistic self-confidence. He was largely responsible for the dissemination in this country of an attitude toward language which prevails to this day, even among the rank and file of our people—an attitude which, while it is by no means exclusively American, is yet notably so. He tried to teach us many other things as well as how to speak and write our native language; but the solid virtues of industry and thrift for which he stood have been to a large extent discredited in the land he loved so well. Bitterest irony of all, children are no longer taught how to spell. There is a cruel appositeness in the fact that *demoralize* is Noah Webster's only contribution to the American vocabulary.

The editors of *Webster's Biographical Dictionary* (Springfield, Mass., 1943), with which he of course had nothing to do, find it necessary to append to this great and good man's biographical sketch the injunction "Do not confuse Noah Webster with Daniel Webster." *Sic transit gloria mundi.*

SIX

Some Stylistic Characteristics: Tall Talk, Turgidity, and Taboo

FOR some years after the Revolution there was no national literature worthy of the name and in language British fashion continued to hold sway. A genuinely indigenous American spirit was not to make itself manifest until well into the nineteenth century—not, in fact, until the reverberations of the amazing westward thrust began to be heard in the land. This new spirit, completely uncolonial, self-confident, daring, pushing, uncouth, obsessed with the notions of greatness and strength, was quite unlike anything that had been known before. Its incarnation was a new folk hero, Andrew Jackson, compared to whom such men as Washington, Adams, and Jefferson must have seemed as moonlight unto sunlight and as water unto wine. He was the pioneer *par excellence*, the Bayard of the backwoods, the rough diamond, the epitome of the noble, free soul. For a new America had indeed come into being beyond the Alleghenies, an America of wilderness, mountains, rivers, plains, and mining camps—an America whose voice was strident and whose words were wild and whirling. Vulgar it was, perhaps, but it was at least vigorous and virile.

Rodomontade and turgidity, born of a new expansiveness of spirit and nourished by backwoods braggadocio, were rampant in the American speech of the first half of the nineteenth century, particularly in what was then called our West, the area south of the Ohio River and

G

west of the Allegheny Mountains—the "dark and bloody hunting ground" of American romance. Although the "tall talk" was somewhat toned down after the Civil War, it remains a minor characteristic of American English to this day, and the leaping, shouting, boastingly rhapsodical backwoodsman, the self-styled "half hoss, half alligator, and a touch of the airthquake," the "yaller flower of the forest," who spoke it—or is supposed to have done so, for one suspects, despite ample evidence of his reality, that he was to some extent a literary convention—is still popularly regarded as having been a sort of beau ideal of American manhood.

The heroes who pushed the frontier constantly westward were rough men, with gargantuan appetites and little refinement, men who did prodigiously hard physical labour. They are epitomized in such folk characters as Paul Bunyan, Ben Hardin (Davy Crockett's mythical companion who had taken mermaids for concubines), and Mike Fink. Their idea of play was the rough-and-tumble brawl, in which they brought to perfection the manly arts of biting, butting, scratching, and gouging. Their ways of life were indeed not modest; neither were their opinions of themselves; neither was their language. "I can lick my weight in wildcats" was a favourite boast—and the expression has become a part of the national speech. They were proud to boast of animal ancestry or upbringing: "I'm a child of the snapping-turtle"; "I was raised with the alligators and weaned on panther's milk." They could "wrastle a buffalo and chaw the ear off a grizzly" or "outrun, outjump, outshoot, throw down, drag out, and lick" any other man in the country. Cooper's Paul Hover in *The Prairie* (1827) is such a one. "If a bear crosses my path," he brags, "he is soon a mere ghost of Bruin. . . . As for the buffalo, I have killed more beef . . . than the largest butcher in all Kentuck." In answer to the question "Is your hand true and your look quick?" this preposterous ass, whom the reader is expected to regard as a noble fellow and a true-blue American, replies: "The first is like a steel trap, and the last nimbler than buckshot. I wish it was hot noon now . . . and that there was an acre or two of your white swans or of black feathered ducks going south, over our heads; you or Ellen here might have set your heart on the finest in the flock, and my character against a horn of powder, that the bird would be hanging head downwards in five minutes and that too with a single ball." Cooper had not, it is obvious, mastered the grammatical minutiae of frontier speech, but the spirit is there. Davy Crockett tells in his *Life* of a "smart, active young fellow of the steamboat and alligator breed" of whom Crockett inquired (the question was of a sort which caused no surprise at the time and place) "whether he was a rhinoceros or a hyena." "Neither the one nor the t'other, Colonel," said this remarkable person, "but a whole menagerie in myself. I'm shaggy as a bear, wolfish about the head, active as a cougar, and can grin like a hyena, until the bark will curl off a gum log. There's a sprinkling of all sorts in me, from the lion down to the skunk [a sprinkling of the skunk?]; and before the war is over, you'll pronounce me an entire zoological institute, or I miss a figure in my calculation. I promise to swallow Santa Anna without gagging, if you will only skewer back his ears, and grease his head a little." Such exuberance could hardly be confined to language; this amazing, if somewhat nauseating, breed of "roaring boys" had a whole repertoire of physical stunts: they crowed, they neighed, they roared, they made prodigious leaps and cracked their heels together in mid-air. It is indeed a wonder that any sensible person ever took them seriously. That they were admired is, however, obvious, and to this day Dan'l Boone, Davy Crockett, and "Old Hickory" Jackson are far more sympathetic characters to most Americans than the Adamses, the Lees, or even the self-made Franklin.

The race of putative supermen who inhabited the West were reported to use an almost incredible lingo. Whether their talk was actually as represented by literary observers I shall not attempt to answer. But enough of the "tall" words have at any rate survived— for instance, *rapscallionly, rambunctious, to hornswoggle, cahoots, to cavort,* and such elegant expressions as *to go the whole hog, root hog or die, slick as goose grease, to pick a crow with someone, to kick the bucket*—to lead one to believe that at least some of the others—for instance, *conbobberation, helliferocious, mollagausauger, to puckerstopple,* and *peedoodles*—were actually in use and seem unbelievably outlandish today only because of their unfamiliarity. And there can be no doubt that the rough-hewn, stout-hearted, straight-shooting characters in buckskin who gave utterance to these verbal delicacies were regarded, perhaps somewhat wishfully, by merchants and their bookkeepers in the East as typical of the American spirit. The Revolutionary worthies must have seemed an altogether different breed, anaemic by comparison, and only a few degrees above Englishmen. Even today some of these "tall" words, words like *bodacious, to absquatulate, cattywampus, slantindicular, grandi-*

ferous, ring-tailed roarer, to exflunctify, to exflunctificate, to hornswoggle, to honeyfogle, blustiferous, monstracious, monstropolous, to obflisticate, sockdologer, to sumtotalize, and *teetotaciously* are popularly regarded as picturesque and admirably American.

The "tall talk" of the backwoods, moving ever westward with the frontier, left unmistakable traces in the writings of Mark Twain, John Hay, Bret Harte, and a good many smaller fry. Strangely, there is really very little of it in Walt Whitman, who expressed his admiration for what he called "strong and beautiful words . . . tangible and clean-lived, all having texture and beauty," although he neither tells us what words he had in mind nor does he make much use of "tall" words in his poetry; there are, of course, some individual novelties, but these must be considered Whitmanisms rather than Americanisms. In general his diction, unlike his subject matter, hardly differs from that of the salon coteries for which he professed such wholesome American contempt. In his "American Primer," which was not published until 1904, when it appeared in the April issue of the *Atlantic Monthly,* he declared that "the appetite of the people of These States, in popular speeches and writings, is for unhemmed latitude, coarseness, directness, live epithets, expletives, words of opprobrium, resistance," informing us that "I have pleasure in the use, on fit occasions, of—*traitor, coward, liar, shyster, skulk, doughface, trickster, mean cuss, backslider, thief, impotent, lickspittle,*" a number of which are, it will be noted, standard English words. His own coinages are usally epicene affairs, linguistic cream puffs like *to eclaircise, to imperturbe, to effuse, affetuoso, poemet,* and *civilizee.* As far as literary men of the nineteenth century other than those mentioned are concerned, "tall talk" seems to have had little effect; but the psychology which gave birth to this somewhat naïve love of orotund exaggeration has had a continuous life.

There can be little doubt that the political and patriotic oratory which thrived between the War of 1812 and the Civil War was a development in part of the talk of the frontier. There is little flamboyant boasting in the speeches or the writings of the founding fathers of the Republic, whose models in prose were Addison, Pope, Swift, Goldsmith, Hume, and to some extent Johnson, and whose thinking was coloured by the rationalism of eighteenth-century Enlightenment. We have Webster's word for it that the common people of the period of the Revolution, and for a long time thereafter, read the Bible and volumes of elevating sermons—at least in Connecticut.

After the War of 1812, unbridled eloquence, expansiveness, a fine flux of words, particularly long, mouth-filling words, came to be passionately admired in all parts of the country save perhaps the Sodoms and Gomorrahs of the Atlantic coast. Inasmuch as everything about America was felt to be on a grand (or "grandiferous") scale, overstatement became the rule. This inflated verbosity was defended, or at least explained, by Daniel Drake (*Discourse on the History, Character, and Prospects of the West*, 1834), who felt that there was a definite connection between the declamatory style, as he called it, and political freedom. Moreover, according to him, "a people who have fresh and lively feelings will always relish oratory." That the flamboyant style was a Western development is evident from the fact that Timothy Flint, writing as late as 1830 in the *Western Monthly Review*, could still characterize the oratory of the East as "sober, passionless, condensed, metaphysical," whereas that of the West was "free, lofty, agitating, grand, impassioned." All the same, the American eagle was often made to scream and the British lion to roar with pain even in staid New England, particularly by Fourth of July orators; one commentator remarked in 1846 that "the bird of America has so often been made to take flight that his shadow may be said to have worn a trail across the basin of the Mississippi." As for the British lion, said the same observer, "the poor lord of the beasts has become so familiar with the point of a hickory pole and of an ash splinter, that he has slunk away to his lair." There can be no doubt that this frontier grandiloquence has lingered on into our own day, particularly in the more backward parts of the country. Lincoln's Gettysburg Address was not an altogether fatal blow to it, nor were F.D.R.'s studiedly informal "fireside chats." Many a citizen remains impressed by an impassioned gush of roaring words. So recently as March 6, 1950, *Time* made reference to "the treasury of the vehement, sonorous and shamelessly corny phrasing which is the tribal language of U.S. politics," by way of illustration quoting a Southern congressman as expressing his disapproval of a certain bill by declaring that it was "conceived in iniquity and nurtured with the milk of corruption," along with other fine flowers of rhetoric. Readers of the *Congressional Record* will not consider the language exceptional, and it is altogether likely that the congressman's constituents consider him to be in the line of Demosthenes, Burke, Clay, and William Jennings Bryan.

The sensibleness of James Fenimore Cooper's comments upon the language of his countrymen has not been sufficiently noted. In his *The American Democrat* (1838) he observed that "the common faults of American language are an ambition of effect, a want of simplicity, and a turgid abuse of terms," also mentioning as characteristically American "a formality of speech, which, while it renders conversation ungraceful, and destroys its playfulness, seriously weakens the power of language, by applying to ordinary ideas, words that are suited only to themes of gravity and dignity." After citing a number of "perversions of signification" (*lady* and *gentleman* for *man* and *woman*, *boss* for *master*, *help* for *servant*) which he regarded as verbal subterfuges unworthy of American citizens, he went on to say: "The love of turgid expressions is gaining ground, and ought to be corrected. One of the most certain evidences of a man of high breeding, is his simplicity of speech; a simplicity that is equally removed from vulgarity and exaggeration. He calls a spade, a 'spade.' His enunciation, while clear, deliberate and dignified, is totally without strut, showing his familiarity with the world, and, in some degree, reflecting the qualities of his mind, which is polished without being addicted to sentimentalism, or any other bloated feeling. He never calls his wife, 'his lady,' but 'his wife,' and he is not afraid of lessening the dignity of the human race, by styling the most elevated and refined of his fellow creatures, 'men and women'."

It should be observed that, although the American no longer refers to his wife as his *lady*, he almost invariably refers to her to all except intimate friends as *Mrs.* plus his own surname—a custom almost as pompous viewed superficially as that of which Cooper complained. It has been explained to me that to refer to one's wife as *my wife* or by her Christian name to a stranger fails to show "proper respect"—a revealing commentary on an American attitude which may well have originated on the frontier, where women were so scarce that they were put upon pedestals. It is perfectly true that books of etiquette, which are almost as unrealistic as handbooks of "good" English, condemn this usage, but it is nevertheless very widespread, and may be heard from men of unquestioned social standing—bishops, senators, university presidents, and prominent business and professional men. It is likely that Winston Churchill was deferring to American custom when he wrote to the late President Roosevelt, in a letter dated March 19, 1943, and sent from 10 Downing Street, that "I have shown the photograph [of a supposed American kinsman which the President had sent him] and Mrs. Harrison's letter to Mrs. Churchill, and we are both much interested in them." A photograph of this letter appeared in the issue of *Life* for November 13, 1950. American women also sometimes use the formal appellation in referring to their husbands, but this is probably because it seems to them "more dignified" (the usage has actually been so explained to me) rather than with any notion of showing "respect."

The American use of *Hon.* (pronounced *honourable*)—in British usage, prefixed by *the*, it is the usual form of address on an envelope for those children of peers who are not entitled to *Lord* or *Lady* as a courtesy designation—has been amusingly discussed by H. L. Mencken in his "Bulletin on 'Hon.',", published in *American Speech* for April, 1946. The title is in America used by legislators, but they lavishly and unselfishly confer it upon others, including their more influential constituents. In the Appendix to the *Congressional Record* for 1945 the designation was given to "former occupants of high office, to the head men of national organizations controlling substantial blocks of votes, to professional politicians of the higher chops, and to newspaper editors supposed to be influential in their dioceses." In the provinces the title is used to designate occupants of high public office, former occupants of high public office, defeated aspirants to high public office, and occasionally even prominent citizens who have never held public office of any sort.

The American attitude towards titles—even phony ones—has frequently been remarked. It is true that calling a man by the title does not in itself make him a colonel, a major, a captain, or a judge; but if enough people confer one or the other of these titles upon a particular man, he ultimately begins to acquire at least some of the honours, rights, and privileges appertaining to the rank which he has attained to, verbally, if in no other way. All these titles have been widely used as mere marks of distinction in American English, and there are still a great many colonels, particularly in Kentucky, who have never heard the roar of cannon fire. Colonel E. M. House, the adviser of President Wilson, was such a colonel—not a real one in the European sense, as he freely and humorously admitted, but a geographical one. His title caused him considerable embarrassment when he went to Potsdam in 1914. In earlier times *colonel* did not imply appointment to the governor's staff (there are now also governor's staff generals and admirals), but might be bestowed upon any prominent citizen. An English writer observed in 1746 (in the *London Magazine* for July) that in Maryland, Virginia, and Carolina the titles *colonel, major,* and *captain* were so frequently used that "the whole country seems at first to you a retreat of heroes," and Alexander Hamilton—not the Secretary of the Treasury, but a Scottish doctor of the same name—declared in 1744 that along the Hudson any man who had killed a rattlesnake was designated *colonel.* In my boyhood railroad conductors were given the title *captain,* but this custom seems to have died out in most parts of the country. In the Middle West and in some of the Southern states an auctioneer is designated *colonel.* George Hamilton Combs reported in his column "It's All New York" on November 24, 1950, that in sophisticated New York City "there are thousands of senators and judges whose actual incumbency of such offices is both vague and remote. . . . Even notary-publics like to be ticketed 'commissioner' and court attendants are punctilious about calling lawyers 'counselor'." This use of the unmerited honorific is distinctly American; an Englishman would probably be somewhat resentful if such a title were bestowed upon him, for he would be likely to infer, not that he was really being honoured, but that his leg was being pulled.

In American usage, not only physicians, but all who in any way minister to the ills of the flesh—osteopaths, naturopaths, optometrists, chiropodists, chiropractors, psychotherapists, etc.—are given the title *Dr.* British usage confers the title upon medical practitioners, but not upon dentists, veterinarians, and surgeons; when an English medical man decides to specialize in surgery, he ceases to be *Dr.* and becomes plain *Mr.* The title is also used before the name of bishops and archbishops of the Church of England, who are Doctors of Divinity, and for holders of other honorary and earned academic doctorates, these latter nonclerical degrees being far fewer in England than here. In America ministers of the gospel, whether or not they are bona fide Doctors of Divinity, are frequently addressed as *Dr.,* which may take precedence of *Reverend;* plain *Mr.* is felt to be inadequate for a man of God. American teachers who have earned the degree Doctor of Philosophy or Doctor of Education, as well as many who have not, are likely to be called *Dr.* in all save the most sophisticated academic circles. Frequently teachers themselves, particularly those who profess the sciences and pedagogy, attach the handle when they must give their names, as, for instance, when answering the telephone. In the Philadelphia and Baltimore areas, and perhaps elsewhere, it was formerly customary to address druggists as *Dr.*, but this usage is now old-fashioned, though still widely current.

A similar linguistic inflation is illustrated by the present use of *engineer*, not, of course, as a title, but as a designation for practitioners of a variety of trades and vocations, for instance, *sanitary engineers, exterminating engineers, equipment engineers, recreation engineers,* and a good many others. The same desire to dignify verbally is seen in the use of the suffix *-tor* in *realtor* and of *-ician* in *mortician, beautician,* and a number of other fine flowerings of the equalitarian spirit as it evinces itself in language. It should be noted also that *profession* has practically lost its older meaning and may now designate practically any trade or vocation: the Governor of Florida, addressing the Florida Barbers' Assocation, informed the assembled practitioners (as reported in the Jacksonville *Florida Times-Union* of August 8, 1950) that "since my older brother stopped cutting my hair with sheep's shears 35 years ago, I have enjoyed knowing members of your profession." On the same occasion the Attorney-General of the State declared, "It's good to know that the barbers are going to form an association that will reflect a credit on the profession." That this was not mere flattery from men in high places, but instead a courteous adoption of the usage of the members of the association, is indicated by a very earnest reference of the chairman to "the standards of our profession."

Turgidity is, of course, by no means confined to American English. Individuals have in all times and places been addicted to the use of high-sounding, inflated language; it is especially likely to occur—it is, in fact, practically an occupational disease—among public officials, politicians, the lesser breeds of business executives, pulpiteers, and pedagogues. In its modern manifestations turgidity need not consist merely in sesquipedalian verbiage; it is a matter of the spirit rather than of the letter. There is even an inverted variety of it, as illustrated by the use (outside of chemical contexts) of *breakdown* for *analysis* and *to break down* for *to analyse:* were it not for its very self-consciousness, *breakdown* might be regarded as a simplification in that it employs an English verb-adverb combination for a word which is ultimately Greek in origin. But the use of *breakdown* in such a phrase as "a breakdown of the entire situation" is frequently more indicative of humourless pomposity than of simplicity, to judge by the sort of people who use the word, and is born of a love of verbal tricksiness and heavy-handed "cuteness." After all, *analysis* has long been completely naturalized and, despite its learned origin, has been well known, even if not widely used, on the popular level of language for a good many years. A genuinely modest and unassuming man is more likely to use *analysis*, for such innovations as *breakdown* do not come from the rank and file; they originate with people who are of considerable importance in our American scheme of things—efficiency experts, "co-ordinators," public relations men, professors of education, and others who live in a more or less rarefied intellectual and spiritual atmosphere.

In our employment of fancy words for plain things and big words for little things, we may sometimes be actuated by humanitarianism, as in *underprivileged* for *poor*, *intellectually underprivileged* for *stupid*, *socially underprivileged* for *ill-mannered*, and *social promotion*, a wondrous phrase recently reported to me as being in use in the public school system to denote the unearned scholastic advancement of an "intellectually underprivileged" pupil in order that his spirit may not be crushed by the mortification of having to go to school with children younger and probably brighter than himself. To put it more baldly, the child who is too dull-witted to learn is nowadays, according to my informant, promoted anyway, just as an earnest of the democratic spirit in American education; the notation *social promotion* is made on his school record, but of course does not reach his parents, who are thus mercifully allowed to think that he is just as smart as anybody else's child.

Usually, however, inflated language reflects the psychology of a people and a period. Only pomposity could have been responsible in the beginning for the use of *to contact* in the senses "to meet, see, talk with," though perhaps euphemism is also involved when the verb means, as it frequently does in the language of business, "to entertain a prospective customer with wine, women, and song for the express purpose of securing from him a handsome order for whatever one happens to be selling." *Philosophy* is likewise a highfalutin word for "mental attitude, point of view," or sometimes simply "plan": "There has been developed in this institution a philosophy of student counselling whereby personality judgments of each student by at least three of his counsellors go into that student's permanent record file in the Dean's office"; "We have adopted the philosophy that only the best in quality and service is good enough for our customers." Similarly, *reaction* has come to be a synonym for *opinion*, *impression*, as in "What is your reaction to this philosophy?" Conceived of the desire to embellish, this sort of thing succeeds in being merely fatuous and windy, but the fact remains that it impresses many worthy people.

The pretentious language of our own day lacks the vigour of that of the backwoods, but it almost certainly springs from the same desire to impress. The "gobbledegook" of bureaucracy—Congressman Maverick's wonderfully apt word might have come straight from the tall timber—the fancy lingoes of psychiatry, pedagogy, welfare, and big business—these are the twentieth-century equivalents of "tall talk," sharing in the windiness of the nineteenth-century variety, but, unlike it, incredibly dull and vapid. The hyperbole, grotesquery, and braggadocio survive only in American slang.

Cheek by jowl with this watered-down and devitalized "tall talk" is a notably uninhibited use of profanity in the American English of our day. It would be amazing indeed if the otherwise violent language of the West had not been freely sprinkled with profanity, but the fact is that, like obscenity, it is no part of the recorded language of that region. This lack is probably due in part to the desire of observers and recorders to idealize the frontiersmen and river boatmen, but in larger part to squeamishness, for the nineteenth century was less tolerant of profanity than the twentieth, and respectable people of that day doubtless made considerably less use of it than people of comparable station today.

It is likely, however, that the free use of profanity in present American English is indeed a survival of frontier usage, in its turn stemming from earlier British fashion which seems to have been reflected even in the hotbeds of Puritanism, for evidence of profanity among the New Englanders is not lacking. The English were, in actual fact, so notoriously given to swearing in the seventeenth and eighteenth centuries that Englishmen were known on the Continent as *goddams*. But fashions in speech, like all other fashions, have a way of changing; and *damn*, with its many combinations and derivatives, is considerably less frequent in England nowadays than in America. *Hell*, which, if not technically profane, has some of the force of profanity (it is still forbidden to children as a "bad word"), is likewise more common in America than overseas: it is used in many ways (*a hell of a mess, like hell you did, the hell you say, what in hell, to raise hell, to give someone hell, hell on wheels,* etc.) and occurs in a good many combinations and derivatives (*hell-raiser, hellbinder, hell-for-leather, hellbent, hellhound, heller, hellion,* etc.), many of them of American origin. Much use is also made of toned-down forms of all the staples of profanity; such minced words as *heck, darn, durn, danged, gosh, golly, doggone, goshdarn, goldarn, gee, gee whiz,* and *jeepers creepers,* to mention only a few, are pretty much confined to American use, though not all are of American origin. One of these softened forms, *darn* (with its variant *durn,* sometimes spelled *dern*), called by the late Professor Krapp "the universal American expletive," is of considerable etymological interest. Noah Webster connected the word, which he knew only as an intensive ("an adverb to qualify an adjective, as *darn sweet,* denoting a great degree of the quality") with Old and Middle English *derne* "secret, obscure," hence "evil, magical," an etymology which was accepted by Krapp in his *English Language in America* and also by the *Dictionary of American English.* This theory leaves out of account any etymological connection with the more profane synonym *damn*—a connection which Webster could not be expected to detect inasmuch as he was apparently not aware of the use of the word in question as an imprecation or an expletive, if indeed it was so used at the time of his reference to it in the *Dissertations* of 1789. Louise Pound has set forth a much more credible explanation of the origin of *darn* in her article "The Etymology of an English Expletive," published in *Language* for June, 1927, and reprinted in the *Selected Writings of Louise Pound* (University of Nebraska Press, 1949), in which she derives the word from *tarnal,* an old-fashioned aphetic form of *eternal* used in the late eighteenth century to express abhorrence or disparagement and, somewhat later, as a mere intensive. Miss Pound goes on to suggest, most plausibly it seems to me, that *tarnal* derived its original force as an expletive from the phrase *eternal* (that is, *etarnal*) *damnation.* The form *tarnation* is, according to her theory, to be explained as a blend of *tarnal* and *damnation.* From the contamination of *tarnation* by *damnation* arose a form *darnation,* whence the verb *to darn* and the participial adjective *darned.*

As has been implied, Americans are probably somewhat more given to profanity than Englishmen of comparable class. Despite Robert Graves's regretful report in his *Lars Porsena, or The Future of Swearing,* of a "notable decline" among his countrymen of both swearing and foul language, it is likely that the Britisher, although less profane—if he is lower-class, the somewhat stodgy *bloody* is likely to be his maid-of-all-work—is more expansive and certainly more imaginative in the matter of verbal indelicacy. This impression may be in part verified merely by leafing through Eric Partridge's *Dictionary of Slang and Unconventional English*, a British production; L. V. Berrey and Melvin Van den Bark's *American Thesaurus of Slang*, although it lists a great many indecencies, presents nothing comparable in lushness of erotic fancy.

Euphemism, the substitution of supposedly milder or more decent language for what is felt to be harsh (*pass away* for *die*) or unseemly (*abdomen, tummy, midriff, breadbasket*, etc., for *stomach*, which is in its turn, except in medical usage, a genteelism for *belly*) is probably almost as ancient as language itself. Many persons suppose that life's harsher realities may be ameliorated, if not indeed dissipated altogether, by the simple expedient of using different words to name them: to call a *spittoon* by the lovely name *cuspidor* somehow lent beauty and dignity to that lowly and now happily archaic receptacle; to call a *coffin* a *casket* (that is, a jewel box) has no doubt confused many a youthful reader of *The Merchant of Venice* when he came to the famous casket scenes, but it seems to lessen considerably the sting of death— for the survivors, at any rate; *to retire* seems to many persons less intimate and hence more seemly in its connotations than *to go to bed*; to call a necessary feminine appurtenance of every well-appointed cocktail lounge a *powder room* is to remove some of the reticence attendant upon the performance of a humble natural function.

In many circles the notion of death seems to be more tolerable to the human consciousness if the verb *to die* is not spoken in reference to this most unpleasant and most unaesthetic of all the phenomena of life. Miss Pound has collected an impressive list of substitutions in her "American Euphemisms for Dying, Death, and Burial," published in *American Speech* for October, 1936, among them such fine growths as "laid down his burden," "the golden cord is severed," "breathed his last," "called to his reward," "gathered to his fathers," "the Angel of Death claimed him," "her frail tabernacle drifted away," "called to Jesus," "he has left a vacant chair," "his clock has run down," "slipped into the great democracy of the dead," "safe in the arms of Jesus," "passed within the pearly gates," "gone to the Great Adventure," "the bell rang and he went," and "at five o'clock in the morning she plumed the wings of her soul and took her flight to glory." Miss Pound concludes that "one of mankind's gravest problems is to avoid a straightforward mention of dying or burial."

In the mid 1930s the crusade of Dr. Thomas Parran, Jr., then health commissioner of New York State, did much to bring the discussion of venereal disease into the light of day, though it met with much opposition at first. Despite the fact that *venereal disease* has largely replaced *social disease*, *vice disease*, and *blood disease*—even names of specific complaints have come to be fairly freely used within the past fifteen years or so—*insanity* recently has been euphemized into *mental illness* and still other softened expressions have been introduced, like *Hansen's disease*, the term now used by the American Medical Association for *leprosy*. An interesting euphemism of comparatively recent origin is *condition* in the sense "ailment," that is, "*bad* condition," as in "He has a heart [or *liver* or *kidney* or *arthritic* or *rheumatic*] condition." Perhaps this usage originated with medical men. "You have a heart condition" is not so specific—and not so alarming to the patient, presumably—as "You have heart trouble." Apparently one can still have ailing eyes, even if a "condition" is all that can affect one's heart, for *Time* has recently reported that Thomas Cardinal Tien, Archbishop of Peking, was in this country for "treatment of an eye ailment and a heart condition." The American Medical Association, as quoted by the same news magazine (January 22, 1951), has declared that "it is difficult to imagine how one could do himself or his profession greater harm from the standpoint of the abuse of the trust of a patient suffering from any condition [than to endorse a certain patent medicine]." The reviewer of a biography of Paul Gauguin in the New York *Herald Tribune* Book Review for July 17, 1949, was less reticent about venereal than about cardiac affliction, for he tells us that Gauguin suffered in Tahiti from "untreated syphilis and a heart condition." When spoken, *condition* in this comparatively new sense is uttered in hushed tones which indicate its ominous nature. *Cancer*, like *syphilis*, has come out into the open recently; so far as I know, there are no euphemisms for it. *Parade*, a syndicated Sunday newspaper supplement, has written frankly of "cancer of the womb" in its issue of February 4, 1951, the article being illustrated with photographs of a personable young woman who recovered from the dread ailment. It is perhaps just as well that Noah Webster has long since joined the Choir Invisible; the very word *womb*, it will be recalled, aroused him to such an extent that he expunged it from his bowdlerized Bible.

Where concepts of decency are involved, American English has tended to be notably euphemistic. What has been called Victorianism in language arose in America even before Victoria came to the throne; Webster's purified Bible just alluded to was published four years before the death of William IV. Captain Marryat noted in his *Diary in America* that in 1837 (the year which marks the beginning of Victoria's reign) a young American lady whom he was escorting at Niagara had the misfortune to slip and graze her shin. Noticing her limp, the Englishman inquired, "Did you hurt your leg much?" As the Captain tells it, "She turned from me, evidently much shocked, or much offended,—and not being aware that I had committed any very heinous offence, I begged to know what was the reason of her displeasure." The fair one proceeded to explain to him that in America the word *leg* was never spoken in the presence of ladies. "I apologized for my want of refinement, which was attributable to having been accustomed only to *English* society," Marryat remarks, italicizing his rather heavy-handed irony. With a daring compatible with his high rank in the Royal Navy, he inquired of the young lady what word he might use to designate "such articles" in the polite circles of America. "Her reply was, that the word *limb* was used." Fortunately for Marryat, this girl was what might be called somewhat "advanced," for she declared that she was "not so particular as some people are"; there were those among her acquaintances, however, who even said *limb* of a table or *limb* of a pianoforte.

A short time later, Marryat visited a young ladies' seminary, where he saw a "square pianoforte with four *limbs*. However, that the ladies who visited their daughters might feel in its full force the extreme delicacy of the mistress of the establishment, and her care to preserve in their utmost purity the ideas of the young ladies under her charge, she had dressed all these four limbs in modest little trousers, with frills at the bottom of them!" There is, I think, a very strong possibility that the Captain is in this anecdote drawing the longbow; coming from a frontiersman instead of an elegantly supercilious Britisher, it might well be labelled a "tall tale."

But, even if we discount the story of the pianoforte with pantalettes, there is yet abundant evidence of the nice-Nellyism of American English in the nineteenth century. Indeed, many of the taboos of those days have survived into our own—nor are they confined to out-of-the-way regions like Appalachia. The ban upon *leg* has been lifted, it is true, though vestiges of it remain in the dinner-table use of *drumstick* and *first joint* for the leg of a fowl—euphemisms precisely parallel to *second joint* and *white meat* for *thigh* and *breast*. But *cock, boar, buck, bitch, ram, jack, stud,* and *stallion* are used without embarrassment only by breeders, and the social status of *bull* is still quite shaky. Perhaps "doggy" people are really unconscious of any impropriety in *bitch*; they use it very freely—so freely, in fact, that the layman may sense a deliberate effort to shock those who are squeamish about the word, which has, incidentally, recently become a verb meaning "to complain," its use pretty much restricted to the younger generation. *Rooster* was early used in American English to replace *cock*, which was carefully avoided—even *haycock* was supplanted by *haystack*—as it still is, particularly by the denizens of our Southern Highlands. In the mountain country one may not even speak of a gun as being *cocked*; instead, "she's ready to go" or "the hammer's back." According to Vance Randolph's "Verbal Modesty in the Ozarks" (*Dialect Notes*, 1928), grown men stammer and blush when in the presence of women at the mere mention of *stopcocks* and *petcocks*; *cockeyed, cocksure,* and *coxcomb* are avoided in general conversation. Even names like *Cox, Leacock,* and *Hitchcock* cause some embarrassment to the mountain folk, whose sensitiveness is pretty much confined to sexuality, for, according to Randolph, they are likely to be quite frank in their reference to excretion. I am informed, incidentally, that the United States Navy has recently dropped the rating "coxswain" in favour of "boatswain's mate third class."

In the West, of all places, side by side with the roistering braggarts who talked "tall," there were in the first half of the nineteenth century a good many very refined people who, according to Bartlett, had "strange ideas regarding the use of certain words, which has led the mock-modest to reject them and substitute others." He goes on to say, in the Introduction to his *Glossary*, that

> the essentially English word bull *is refined beyond the mountains, and perhaps elsewhere, into* cow-creature, male-cow, *and even* gentleman-cow! *A friend who resided many years in the West has told me of an incident where a gray-headed man of sixty doffed his hat reverently and apologized to a clergyman for having used inadvertently in his hearing the plain Saxon term.* Male sheep, male hog, *etc., are of a piece with the preceding, to which we may add* rooster, he biddy, game chicken, *etc.*

This type of verbal delicacy is by no means archaic. According to Kurath's *Word Geography* "in New England, the South, and the South Midland . . . the plain term [*bull*] is not used by older folk of one sex in the presence of the other," and many younger people prefer to avoid the word. *Sire, male animal* (or just *animal*), *critter, seed ox, gentleman cow, gentleman ox*, and *masculine* (rhyming with *fine*) are all used in New England; in the South and the South Midland, *male cow* (or just *male*), *service cow, beast, stock beast, stock brute, male brute, steer, ox, male ox, he animal, Durham, jock*, and *major* are all current, as well as *gentleman cow* (on Chesapeake Bay) and *masculine* (in southern West Virginia). The brutally realistic *top cow, top ox*, and *top steer*, though rare, are used in certain localities in Massachusetts, Vermont, and New Hampshire. Many of these expressions are now used only facetiously, although in the South it is still dangerous to use the plain term in the presence of a lady: in this region *the male, the beast*, and *the brute* are still very much alive.

Unfortunately, language does not always behave as virtuous people would wish it to. Frequently the indecent force of a word is weakened with the passing of time and its original impropriety ultimately lost. What were once verbal indecencies may, without our being aware of the fact, penetrate into ordinary, everyday speech. It is not always easy to demonstrate how this comes about. Often, it is to be suspected, an indelicacy is introduced as a daringly conscious double entendre for the purpose of "getting a laugh" from the knowing, and is repeated and disseminated in all innocence by good, douce people.

The semantic shift of *puss* to "mouth, face" may perhaps be so explained. To decadent middle age the word still calls forth its earlier anatomical connotations, as is evidenced by the sniggers and the howls of ribald laughter which issue from the loudspeaker whenever it is used in the supposedly innocent sense by funny men on the radio. Nevertheless, this word with its altered meaning may be said to have passed into ordinary slang, particularly in the phrase *a sock in the puss*, which, though somewhat crude, is felt to be in no way indecent.

The word *ballock* (Old English *bealluc* "testicle"), with its variant *bollock*, is archaic, in metropolitan usage at least, save in the phrase *to ballocks up*, variously spelled, in which it is employed frequently, not to say usually, with no sense of its original significance and hence with no idea of impropriety. Barnacle Bill the Sailor, a sort of nautical

H

Paul Bunyan, was Ballocky Bill in the original ballad commemorating his adventures, usually amorous and on a scale in keeping with his name. The popular song heard a few years back was presumably a bowdlerized version of this ballad, with toning down of subject matter similar to the toning down of the hero's name, which would have been a bit too bald to fool anybody. No such feeling, however, attaches to *ballocks up*, which not infrequently occurs in print nowadays. In Arthur Kober's "Dilemma in the Bronx," published in the *New Yorker* (September 7, 1946), Mac (*né* Max), who is of the essence of refinement and much given to euphemism—witness his delicacy in referring to his "kidney condition"—writes to Billie (*née* Bella) Gross of his regret that World War II had come along to "bollix" everything up. Conscious that the word is not quite standard English, he primly puts it within quotation marks. The plot of a motion picture widely exhibited in 1951 to the "family trade" was described in the otherwise notably chaste Jacksonville *Florida Times-Union* as "the wildest, wackiest, most hilarious, and completely bollixed-up day you ever heard of." The phraseology was not that of the local exhibitor, for a friend has sent me a copy of the same advertisement from a newspaper in another part of the country; it is apparently a part of the promotional "literature" for the film, circulated nationally, and has doubtless appeared on billboards in letters a foot high. The word *ballock* is not listed in any of its forms in Berry and Van den Bark's *American Thesaurus of Slang*, Harold Wentworth's *American Dialect Dictionary*, or Farmer and Henley's *Slang and Its Analogues, Past and Present*. All "commercial" dictionaries save the *New International* omit it, perhaps because it is felt to be obsolete, perhaps *pudoris causa*. Joseph Wright's great *English Dialect Dictionary* lists the compounds *balack-handed*, *bollocky-'anded* ("left-handed," hence "clumsy") and the derivative *ballocky* (*bollocky*), also meaning "left-handed." *Ballocks up* is recorded in none of the dictionaries consulted. There can be no doubt, however, that *ballocks*, no matter how spelled, has attained to complete respectability in the verb phrase *to ballocks up*, and may be freely (and innocently) used even by persons of unimpeachable modesty.

Much more common than *to ballocks up* is *to ball up*, with the same meaning. The supplement to the *Oxford English Dictionary* labels *to ball up* as of American origin and defines it as "to clog" or "to become clogged," presumably with balls (of snow, clay, etc.) This may be so, but it seems highly likely that *to ball up* and *to ballocks* (*bollocks, bollix*) *up* are merely formal variants. The British *to balls-up*, labelled "low" by Eric Partridge in his *Dictionary of Slang and Unconventional English*, is unquestionably also a variant. Otherwise, the similarity in form and the identity in meaning taken together must be accounted a truly remarkable coincidence.

A similar contempt for the appurtenances of sex—a contempt more apparent than real, and manifesting itself largely in linguistic behaviour—is indicated by the now uninhibited use of *nuts* as an exclamation of disgust or disparagement and in the phrase *nuts to you* (*him, her, it*). (For a while, in the middle 1920s, the word was euphemized to *nerts*, which fooled nobody; but this flimsily disguised form is now quite old-fashioned.) Despite its widespread distribution and apparent respectability, *nuts* may not be used in this sense in the cinema. In 1941 Will Hays, then head of the Motion Picture Producers and Distributors of America, Inc., included it among a list of words to be omitted from all pictures. It may be used, however, in the sense "crazy." Presumably Mr. Hays's successor has not rescinded this order, for, in a long career of movie-going, I do not recollect a single occasion when my ears were sullied with the word in the sense under discussion. It may be heard not infrequently on the radio, and the most respectable newspapers apparently suffered no qualms in reporting General Anthony C. McAuliffe's use of it in reply to a German command to surrender at the time of the Battle of the Bulge. *Balls*, used in exactly the same way, has not fared so well socially: it is distinctly "low" on either side of the Atlantic. Whereas the American co-ed, or even her maiden aunt, may unblushingly hiss "Nuts to you!" taboo continues to operate against its British equivalent.

The fact that the first syllable of *shitepoke* rhymes with *bite* rather than with *bit* has perhaps tended to becloud its scatological origin. At any rate, it is certain that the ladies of our grandmothers' generation had no idea of the significance of the word when they used it jocularly and endearingly to their children and grandchildren as the equivalent of "little rascal." *Bugger*, a highly indecent word in British English —it was actionable until 1934, according to Eric Partridge—was, and doubtless still is, used by unsuspecting souls who would be appalled if they knew its origin and its present meaning in British English (though dialectally it is, as in American English, simply the equivalent of "chap, fellow"). The usual American pronunciation rhymes with *sugar*; the English rhyme it with *slugger*.

Feist (also *fice, fist, phyce, fise, fiste, faust*) has long been a perfectly proper designation for a small, worthless cur in American English, whence the adjective *feisty*, sometimes applied to a restless, troublesome child. The noun, originally meaning "*flatus*," actually denoted a frequent failing of dogs not usually referred to *coram publico*. But this earlier meaning has become quite obsolete, as also in the related *fizz, fizzle,* and *foist*. A similar gastric metaphor is evident in *to peter out* (French *péter*), the equivalent of *to fizzle out*. It is to be wondered how many people who quote Hamlet's "Hoist with his own petard" are aware of the coarse joke in the etymology of *petard*, or, for that matter, whether Shakespeare himself was aware of it. *Pétard* as a military or pyrotechnical term would seem to have no indecent connotations in Modern French. *Pétarade* with its literal meaning is of course low in that language, but, for all I can discover, apparently perfectly proper as a military term for "useless cannonade"; similarly, *pet-de-nonne* "apple fritter" and *pet-en-l'air* "short morning gown"; yet French verbal delicacy prefers *impasse* to *cul-de-sac, vespasienne* to *pissoir*.

But there is really no need of multiplying examples. Enough has been written to demonstrate the unwitting indecency of respectability. Euphemism is not here involved, as it is in such expressions as *horse-feathers, bull* (or *b.s.*), *s.o.b.*, *S.O.L.* (explained as "short of luck"), or the many *-fu* words of army slang (*snafu* was explained to "Mom" as "situation normal—all *fouled* up," but G.I. Joe knew perfectly well what the italicized word really stood for). Instead, the full, unmutilated form is uncompromisingly and unhesitatingly employed, frequently by a class of speakers who are, when they are actually conscious of verbal indelicacy, highly intolerant of it—people who are indignant at any literature which employs words connected with sex or excretion with which they happen to be familiar. They are, as has been said, good, sweet people for the most part, who are sometimes more offended at verbal indecency when they recognize it than at downright immoral conduct, like the old gentleman who objected to Joyce's *Ulysses*, not because of what the people in the story did, but because of certain words they used. There is, as we have seen, a largish class of verbal indelicacies, including those discussed here, which have undergone a toning down or a complete loss of their original content; these are freely and undisguisedly used in all innocence by speakers who, when aware of the slightest hint of verbal impropriety, are careful to avoid it at all costs. The cream of the jest is, that those who would wear fig leaves on their lips should be unintentionally guilty of even a limited use of words and phrases which were as shocking a few generations ago as would be much of the fireside and dinner-table talk at the great houses of Elizabethan England or, for that matter, of colonial Virginia and Maryland, were we privileged miraculously to hear it.

SEVEN

Later American Speech: Coinages and Adaptations

THE War of 1812 and the appearance on the American scene of the frontiersman—both in the flesh and as a national symbol—mark the beginnings of an indigenous *psyche Americana* which is strikingly reflected in the flood of Americanisms originating in the nineteenth century. The gaudy pageant of American history in that era—the standard of living, science, politics, morals, taste, in short America's contribution to civilization such as it has been—emerges from a bare list of such Americanisms. The dates in parentheses in the list which follows are those of the earliest citations for the words in M. M. Mathews's *Dictionary of Americanisms*:

cocktail (1806)
gerrymander (1812)
spoils "political system" (1833)
bowie knife (1836)
gold fever (1847)
bloomers (1851)
coeducation (1852)
filibuster (1853)
pay dirt (1856)
brownstone front (1858)

blockade-runner (1863)
boys in blue (1866)
apartment house (1876)
rustler "cattle thief" (1882)
nickelodeon (1888)
Anti-Saloon League (1892)
basketball (1892)
stogy (1893)
mortician (1895)
gangster (1896)

The America of our own century is similarly mirrored in the next list, which gives the merest sampling of twentieth-century Americanisms, arranged in roughly chronological order. The reader of mature years who is acquainted with the "American way" will have no difficulty supplying an approximate, and in many instances an exact, date for the earliest appearance of the words which follow:

big stick	superhighway
sundae	autocourt
Rotarian	Technicolor
Liberty Bond	G.I.
companionate marriage	bobbysox(er)
Hays Office	Dixiecrat
dust bowl	stratocruiser
studio couch	dianetics

Words as a rule cannot fail to tell us something about the people who use them or have used them, and every one of these randomly chosen Americanisms is redolent of some aspect of American history, American life, or the American character. To tell the story behind them all would require a work of far greater magnitude than the present volume. Here it will be possible to touch upon only a few.

Stogy, for instance, calls to mind the Conestoga wagon and the part it played in the amazing westward push early in the nineteenth century. The vehicle and its name were in use as early as the mid-eighteenth century, but seem not to have been much known outside Pennsylvania until the 1800s. *Conestoga* was the name of an Iroquoian tribe, now long extinct; the tribal designation was applied to a valley in Lancaster County, Pennsylvania, where the large covered wagon which was the principal means of westward transportation before the introduction of railroads seems to have originated. The early Conestoga wagoners rolled long cigars for smoking on their trips, and such a cigar was called a *conestogy* (which is merely the earlier pronunciation of *Conestoga,* like *Iowy* for *Iowa*); this was subsequently clipped to *stogy.* The *prairie schooner* was a later development of the Conestoga wagon, built on a somewhat smaller scale.

Gerrymander is only one of a prodigious number of Americanisms that have grown out of our national politics. The eighteenth century gave us *caucus* and a few others, but it was the nineteenth century which really saw the full flowering of a distinctively American political life. It is an unhappy circumstance that much of the vernacular of American public life is suggestive of chicanery and deception; the historian's lot is far from being a happy one if he also happens to be an idealist.

Gerrymander, originally used as a noun but within a year of its coinage converted into a verb, is a blend of *Gerry* and *salamander*. The *Gerry* comes from the name of Elbridge Gerry, a staunch anti-Federalist who was in the course of a long career in politics a member of the Continental Congress, a delegate to the Constitutional Convention, a member of Congress, Governor of Massachusetts, and Vice-President of the United States. In 1812, while he was Governor of Massachusetts, his party, in an attempt to perpetuate its power, divided the state into electoral districts with more regard for politics than for geography. It happened that a district in Essex County somewhat resembled a salamander. When head, wings, and claws were added by Gilbert Stuart, the celebrated painter, to a map, the result was by a stroke of genius called a *gerrymander*. Within a year this attractive and ingenious linguistic novelty was being used throughout the country to describe what had already become a favourite though nameless device of the party in power. Towards the end of the century the word was adopted by the English, who have used it without much consciousness of its American origin.

The *spoils system* was introduced into our government during Andrew Jackson's administration. Strictly speaking, the term denotes the practice of making political appointments on the basis of party service rather than merit, though it has come to be used more broadly for any improper use of public office for political or even personal purposes. Old Hickory's slogan "to the victors belong the spoils" continued to be the accepted rule of political conduct until the introduction of the present civil service laws put a stop to many of the evils inherent in the spoils system.

Filibuster is old in British English as a modification of Spanish *filibustero*, which had in turn been taken from Dutch *vrijbuiter* "freebooter," but the word acquired a new meaning in the United States around the middle of the nineteenth century, when it came to be applied to those American adventurers and soldiers of fortune who engaged in the expeditions against Cuba under General Narciso López, most of them recruited from Louisiana, Mississippi, and Kentucky and many of them, as the New York *Courier and Enquirer* put it, not free and noble souls, but rather "men whom rascality has outlawed, men whom society . . . kicks out with contempt." *Filibuster* soon came to be used as a verb in the figurative sense "to use delaying or obstructing tactics in a legislature." And thus another political Americanism was born.

The most famous of all Americanisms, *O.K.*, grew out of a presidential race, according to the most widely accepted theory of its origin—if indeed a story so well documented must be called a theory. *O.K.* has gained lodgment in practically all civilized languages as well as in a few uncivilized ones. In the course of its hardy existence it has acquired practically every grammatical function; it may be used as an adjective ("His account was O.K."), a noun ("He got my O.K."), an adverb ("He did the job O.K."), and a verb ("O.K. this for me").

The origin of the expression, which began as a political slogan more than a century ago, seems to have been quickly forgotten in the hubbub which was American politics in the first half of the nineteenth century. Beginning shortly after its introduction, numerous theories of its origin have been advanced, many of them ably testifying to the ingenuity of their proponents and some of them quite engaging indeed. Mencken discusses fully these various theories, so that the account which follows must of necessity seem to lean heavily upon his résumé, as indeed it does.

A story which is both charming and plausible, and which would be altogether acceptable were it not for certain details having to do with chronology, derives *O.K.* from the passionate effusion of a semiliterate sign painter whose political sentiments do him more credit than does his orthography or, for that matter, his grammar. According to the story, this devotee of demos painted in large letters the legend "The People is Oll Korrect" on a streamer which was used in a Whig demonstration on September 15, 1840, in Urbana, Ohio. This was during the famous "Log Cabin Campaign" of General William Henry Harrison, the Whig candidate for the presidency, who was running against the Democratic incumbent, Martin Van Buren. The tale runs that Harrison's supporters were so taken by the sentence that they used it as a political slogan, underscoring the quaintness of *Oll Korrect* by reducing it to *O.K.* Unfortunately for this attractive theory, it was discovered in 1934 that *O.K.* had appeared in the Columbus *Ohio Statesman* on September 11, four days before the Harrison rally in question—and subsequent researches in files of yellowing newspapers have revealed a good many earlier occurrences of the mysterious letters.

Some have identified *O.K.* with a Choctaw word meaning "it is so." President Woodrow Wilson was "sold" on the Choctaw origin to such an extent that he always took the trouble to write out *okeh*, as he thought the Indian word should be written, as his mark of approval, eschewing the more common *O.K.* because, though amply justified by usage, it was not in his opinion correct. The supposed Choctaw spelling is also used as a trade name by the manufacturers of a popular brand of phonograph records.

Other theories which have been advanced from time to time have a certain entertainment value and are given here only for that reason. It has been proposed, for instance, that the *K* stands for *Keokuk*, the name of the Sac Indian chief for whom the city in Iowa was named. According to the story, this aboriginal worthy was affectionately called *Old Keokuk*, and, inasmuch as he had aided the Americans at the time of the Black Hawk War, he was quite definitely "all right"; hence the initials of *Old Keokuk* came to be used in the sense "all right."

Still other proposed etymologies derive *O.K.* from the name of a firm of biscuit manufacturers, the Orrins-Kendall Company, who supplied the War Department with their product during the Civil War and who stamped their boxes with their initials; from the name of one Obadiah Kelly, a freight agent who affixed his initials to bills of lading; from *Aux Cayes*, the name of a Haitian port from which the best rum known to the American colonists used to be shipped; from a signal supposedly used by early telegraphers; from an archaic English word variously spelled *hoacky*, *horkey*, *hawkey*, and *hockey*, apparently a corruption of *hock tide*, a festival marking the end of the harvesting season; and from *aux quais* (in effect, "I'll meet you down at the wharves"), a phrase thought to be used in Revolutionary War times by French sailors making "dates" with American girls. Nor are these all. Other theories set forth Greek (ὅλα καλὰ), Latin (*omnia korrecta*), Norwegian, Danish, and even Finnish etyma—all more or less ingenious, be it said, and all indubitably wrong.

On March 30, 1840, the New York *Herald*, the most prestigious Whig journal of that day, attributed the then strange expression *O.K.* to Andrew Jackson in an effort to cast ridicule upon his cultural attainments. The paper reported that, while he was still President, Jackson had said, after examining some documents purporting to expose the skulduggery of his favourite, Postmaster General Amos Kendall, "Mark on them *O.K.*," which letters he thought to be the initials of *all correct.* It is to this political canard, which was widely accepted as true at the time, particularly by enemies of Jackson and of the Democratic party, that O.K. owes its present meaning of "all right," though, as we shall see shortly, that was not its original meaning at all.

It was Allen Walker Read, of Columbia University, one of the world's most indefatigable readers of old newspapers, who set forth what is evidently the true story of O.K. in an article "The Evidence on O.K.," published in the *Saturday Review of Literature* for July 19, 1941. The evidence Read has discovered shows that the term did indeed grow out of the presidential campaign of 1840, though it had no connection with the Whig rally in Urbana, Ohio, on September 15. Far from it—it was not a Whig slogan at all, but a Democratic one. And a senseless slogan was *all* it was in the beginning; it took the false Jackson story to give it a meaning.

Martin Van Buren, who was Jackson's successor and who was, after the manner of politicians, panting after a second term as president in 1840, was a native of a village in eastern New York called Kinderhook. It seems perfectly clear now that O.K. began its hardy existence as nothing more mysterious than an abbreviation formed from the initial letters of *Old Kinderhook.* Throughout his career Van Buren's name was associated with that of his native village: he had been called the Kinderhook Fox by his enemies in the days of the "Albany regency," and it is not particularly surprising that his partisans should also have seized upon the name of the little village—perhaps in retaliation—and have called him the Magician of Kinderhook, the Sage of Kinderhook, and the Wizard of Kinderhook. In any case, *Old Kinderhook* became in time a sort of rallying cry for the Democrats in the days of Van Buren's power.

Read's evidence is to the effect that O.K. first appeared in print in the New York *New Era* on March 23, 1840 (a week before the libel on Jackson's spelling) as part of the name of an organization—the O.K. Club—made up of supporters of Van Buren in his campaign against General Harrison. Even in the light of Van Buren's well-known connection with Kinderhook, those who were not "in the know" were apparently mystified by the letters. Their true explanation appeared in the same newspaper on May 27th of the same year, when it was pointed out that they were "significant of the birthplace of Martin Van Buren, Old Kinderhook," but it seems to have made little impression at the time. The Jackson story had already appeared in the

Herald and had captured the public fancy; the truth simply could not compete with the more romantic lie.

Beginning, then, as the name of a political organization dedicated to advancing by hook or by crook—such was the deplorable state of American political ethics in those unenlightened days—the political interests of Martin Van Buren of Old Kinderhook, *O.K.* was shortly to be used as a war cry by the Locofocos, as the unwashed members of the radical wing of the Democratic party called themselves. The O.K. Club, like other political clubs of the day, seems to have been composed largely of rowdies and bullies, and, on March 27, a group of these ruffians raided a Whig mass meeting in Masonic Hall. According to the report appearing in the *Herald* on the following day, "about 500 stout, strapping men" marched to the meeting place, where "the word *O.K.* was passed from mouth to mouth, a cheer was given, and they rushed into the hall upstairs, like a torrent." The mysterious battle cry spread rapidly, acquiring a sense quite different from its original one—which, as we have seen, was very little sense at all—as a result of the appearance of the Jackson story in the same paper only three days after the ascent of the gallant 500 upon the Whigs. Before very long *O.K.*, meaning "all right, all correct," had spread all over the country, soon losing all connection with the Democratic party, even though commonly attributed to Jackson. Even the Whigs themselves, by a bitter irony, came to make use of the expression.

Despite the very convincing ring of the case built up by Read, it is yet possible, if only barely so, that there are genuinely earlier occurrences of our *O.K.* than that of March 23, 1840. If so, we should have to set aside the *Old Kinderhook* explanation as given in the *New Era* of May 27th as a newspaper writer's fabrication of an etymology after the fact, or else assume that the O.K. Club was using an earlier expression meaning "all right" with the additional connotation of *Old Kinderhook*. If this should be the case, one wonders where the members of the club dug up the expression, for it was obviously not in general use before 1840.

Improbable as such assumptions are, the annoying fact remains that there is one further bit of evidence which must be taken account of —that of the *Travel Diary* of William Richardson, written in 1815, in which the following entry occurs: "Arrived at Princeton, a handsome little village, 15 miles from N. Brunswick, o k & at Trenton, where we dined at 1 P.M." This has been accepted by some as a genuine pre-1840 occurrence of *O.K.*, but Read suggests, in a note in *American Speech* for April, 1941, that Richardson's apparent *o k* is really two other letters, *a h*. According to Read's explanation, Richardson, who had revised the passage considerably already—the manuscript shows deletions and insertions—started to write "a handsome little village" after "N. Brunswick," but after writing the first two letters (*a h*) discovered that he had used the same phrase in describing Princeton: he went no further but neglected to cross out the two letters he had written.

If this explanation or something similar to it is not correct, then we actually have here an occurrence of *O.K.* twenty-five years before that in the *New Era* of March 23, 1840. It is possible that an *O.K.* of unknown origin was indeed in use before 1840, but it is obvious from the *New Era's* explanation of May 27 to the effect that the term was "significant of . . . Old Kinderhook" that it had all the freshness of a new coinage at that time, and the same is indicated by the Jackson anecdote in the *Herald* which apparently furnished a meaning for it.

This Americanism became naturalized in England a long time ago. Today *O.K.* is used about as freely in England as in America, though it was not until 1935 that the London *Times* admitted the expression as a permanent addition to the English word stock. In the same year the Judicial Committee of the Privy Council ruled that *O.K.* was even permissible on legal documents to indicate that the details therein were correctly given. This was two years after *O.K.* had been included in the Supplement to the great *Oxford English Dictionary*. Lord Beaverbrook's report of the Moscow Conference indicates that the wheel is come full circle: as Stalin's demands were read out item by item, Beaverbrook indicated Britain's agreement by *O.K.* (or *okay*, as he spells it); the American representative, Mr. W. Averell Harriman, rejecting his country's noble contribution to language, contented himself with saying *agreed* if the item concerned the United States.

The familiar *buncombe*—usually spelled *bunkum* nowadays—arose out of American political life. Bartlett (2nd ed., 1859) uses a spelling *buncome* (along with *bunkum*) and quotes Thomas C. Haliburton, the Nova Scotian judge who wrote the once famous Sam Slick books, as defining the word, "which is now as well understood as any in our language," as follows (Haliburton is speaking in the character of Slick, a Yankee clock pedlar):

Our free and enlightened citizens don't appreciate silent members [of Congress]; it don't seem to them as if Squashville, or Punkinsville, or Lumbertown was right represented, unless Squashville, or Punkinsville, or Lumbertown makes itself heard and known, ay, and feared too. So every feller, in bounden duty, talks, and talks big too, and the smaller the State, the louder, bigger, and fiercer its members talk. Well, when a crittur talks for talk sake, just to have a speech in the paper to send to home, and not for any other airthly puppus but electioneering, our folks call it Bunkum.

The phrase *talking for Buncombe*, now obsolete, throws light on the word in question. It is explained in John H. Wheeler's *Historical Sketches of North Carolina* (1851), as quoted by Bartlett. Wheeler relates that "several years ago" (presumably during the Sixteenth Congress, 1819–21) the member from the district of North Carolina which included Buncombe County "arose to address the House, without any extraordinary powers, in manner or matter, to interest the audience. Many members left the hall. Very naïvely he told those who remained that they might go too; he should speak for some time, but 'he was only talking for Buncombe.'"

The term caught on rapidly, in the insane way that such terms frequently capture the public fancy, and by the middle of the century was being used in England as well as in America. It has given birth to *bunk* ("The worst bunk ever written," said the Duke of Windsor of published rumours of a marital rift, as reported by the Associated Press on March 16, 1951), *to debunk*, and *bunco* "a swindle, confidence game, misrepresentation." *Hokum*, according to the supplement to the *Oxford English Dictionary*, is a blend of *hocus-pocus* and *bunkum*.

A detailed treatment of all the Americanisms which in one way or another have application to American political life would require a volume to itself. It must here suffice to make brief mention of a few more and pass on to other areas. It will doubtless surprise many to learn that *New Deal* was not originated by the late F.D.R.—actually it is more than a century old—although he was certainly largely responsible for its popularization and for its identification with the policies and measures he advocated. Nor was *forgotten man* a Rooseveltism; there is an odour of cynicism in Roosevelt's appropriation of it, for it appears in 1883 as the title of a speech by William Graham Sumner, the brilliant American economist and sociologist whose political philosophy was diametrically opposed to all the New Deal stood for. The Roosevelt administration did, however, give birth to a good many new combinations, for instance, *economic royalist, court-packing, good neighbour policy, brain trust,* and to such horrible jargon as *co-ordinator, expediter, directive, "must" legislation, to process, to finalize,* and *bottleneck.* It is saddening to have to report that *graft* as a political term is an Americanism.

The *bowie knife* is always associated with the gallant Colonel James Bowie, who perished in the defence of the Alamo with Davy Crockett, the youthful Colonel William Barret Travis, and a good many others whose names mean little today. The lethal instrument seems, however, to have been devised by James's brother Rezin (or Resin) Pleasant Bowie, who survived him by five years, although James was by far the greater virtuoso in its use. The bowie knife, a long and heavy knife with a blade from ten to fifteen inches long, originally made by grinding a large file to razor sharpness and affixing a guard between blade and handle to protect the operator's hand, was for many years the principal instrument of nonsurgical phlebotomy in the American Southwest. According to one of the American ballads of Bon Gaultier, as cited in Bartlett, the weapon was borne even by congressmen. In a passage which throws light on congressional etiquette in the early years of the nineteenth century, a new member of Congress, observing the entrance into the chamber of a "conspicuous character," inquired of Henry Clay, "What kind of a Locofoco's that?"

"Young man," quoth Clay, "avoid the way of Slick of Tennessee,
Of gougers fierce, the eyes that pierce, the fiercest gouger he;
He chews and spits as there he sits, and whittles at the chairs,
And in his hand, for deadly strife, a bowie-knife he bears."

Colonel Bowie and his weapon are immortalized in the *Bowie State,* a nickname for Arkansas, though neither he nor his brother seems to have practised in that state, and by a Bowie County in Texas.

The Bowies pronounced their name to rhyme with *hooey,* and it is still so pronounced in Maryland as the name of a famous racetrack (named for another branch of the family) and no doubt in the Southwest as well, though speakers in other parts of the country are more likely to rhyme it with *showy.* The grim and occasionally tasteless humour of the frontier gave rise to *Arkansas toothpick* and *California toothpick* as facetious metaphors for *bowie knife*.

Bloomers (and *bloomer costume, dress, trousers, hat,* etc.) are named for Mrs. Amelia Bloomer, who was editor of the magazine in which the garment was first described. According to R. H. Thornton's *American Glossary* (2 vols., Philadelphia, 1912; a third vol. was published serially in *Dialect Notes*, 1931–39), "she did not invent it, was not the first to wear it, and protested against its being called by her name." Nevertheless, the good lady did advocate the hideous costume—loose trousers buttoned around the ankle, worn under a short skirt—so that there is justice of a sort in the fact that it acquired her name (or rather, that of her unfortunate husband), a name which, incidentally, seems most appropriate to the costume—so appropriate, in fact, that it comes as something of a shock to learn that it was originally a proper name. Bloomers survived until well past the first quarter of the present century as part of the gymnasium costume worn by girls, happily supplanted in these unreticent days by shorts, and as a type of women's drawers gathered by elastic at the knee. These last were in England usually called *knickers*, a clipped form of the name of Washington Irving's fictitious Dutch author, *Diedrich Knickerbocker*, which was sometimes further curtailed in British slang usage to *knicks*.

Brownstone, a variety of dark-brown sandstone, acquired a special social and economic significance in American English in the nineteenth century, for it was a particularly popular building material for the houses of affluent citizens. A good many solidly built town houses with *brownstone fronts* are still standing, but the descendants of those who built them now live in *apartment houses* or have moved to the suburbs of our cities. *Brownstone* belongs to an era in American life which has passed. The "genteel life" which the term connoted has given way to the so-called "gracious living" of the twentieth century.

The fact that *nickelodeon, mortician,* and *gangster* occur in the nineteenth century will probably occasion some surprise. *Nickelodeon* meant originally any show making an admission charge of five cents, but by 1908, with the development of cinematography, it had come to mean a motion picture show to which the admission charge was a nickel. With the raising of this charge and the erection of the flamboyant "supercolossal" movie palaces of our own day, *nickelodeon* has come to have only a historical interest as far as the motion picture industry is concerned. The word was revived, however, about fifteen years ago to designate a juke box, for which it is already ceasing to be appropriate: in the classier "joints" one can now hear only three records for a quarter.

Though *mortician* first occurs in the mid-1890s, it was not widely used for more than twenty years thereafter; its resuscitation seems to have occurred when the National Selected Morticians was organized in 1917. The linguistic virtuoso who coined the word did so by taking the first syllable of *mortuary* (ultimately Latin *mort-* "death") and affixing to it *-ician*, obviously suggested by *physician*. May he receive his reward in heaven, for he has deprived the grave of much of its victory. As for the analogy to *physician*, it is interesting to note that for a while, around the time of the Civil War, American undertakers assumed the title *Dr.*, but, strange as it seems when we consider the ease with which that title is borne today by virtually all other practitioners upon the human anatomy, they soon abandoned it. The National Selected Morticians also agitated for other verbal reforms: *coffin* to be supplanted by *casket*, *body* by *patient*, *undertaking establishment* by *reposing room*, *slumber room*, or *chapel*, and *hearse* by *casket coach*.

The beauty parlour operators, not to be outdone, followed the example of the morticians and gave *beautician* to a grateful world; considerably later an association of shoe repairers in Texas adopted the term *shoetrician* in the title of their organization, though it seems not to have caught on in other parts of the country, where *shoe rebuilder* is deemed of sufficient dignity to designate one who keeps shoes in repair. During the mid-Prohibition era H. L. Mencken coined *bootician* as a term for a bootlegger with a high sense of the ethics of his profession. Seeking for a term which would impress upon the public mind the high integrity of all their endeavours, the real estate salesmen were somewhat more original. They withstood the temptation of *realtician* and came up, as everyone knows, with *realtor*.

Although it occurs much earlier, *gangster* did not actually have much of a vogue until the so-called *gangster era*, a concomitant of the thirteen long years of wide-scale immorality which crowned the dedicated efforts of the Anti-Saloon League. *Gangster* has given rise to *gangsterdom* and probably furnished the model for *gagster* "comedian."

One other of the terms listed, *sundae*, calls for some comment. Both the *Oxford English Dictionary* and the *Dictionary of American English* suppose it to be a respelling of *Sunday*. (In its first manifestation, in the New York *Evening Post* of May 21, 1904, it was spelled *sundi*.) This

I

origin for the word cannot be established with any certainty, nor can any other. About all that seems certain is that the term is an Americanism and that it arose in the 1890s. It is highly probable that the connection with *Sunday* made by the dictionaries is valid. Mencken recounts in *Supplement One* a story emanating from the Two Rivers, Wisconsin, *Reporter* to the effect that in the early 1890s one of the local highlifers suggested to Mr. E. C. Berners, the proprietor of the ice cream "parlor" in that city, that he pour some chocolate syrup, previously used only in making sodas, over a plate of ice cream. Mr. Berners, who recounted the story many years after the event to the Two Rivers reporter, was hesitant, according to his own admission, fearing that carrying out the daring suggestion might ruin the flavour of the ice cream. But the town blade, whose name was George Hallauer, was of bolder mettle and with true American pioneer spirit declared that he'd by golly try anything once. The experiment was duly performed, and one of America's major gastronomic contributions was born.

Another stroke of sheer genius was required to give it a name. The fame of the delicious concoction spread rapidly to the nearby metropolis of Manitowoc, where one George Giffy offered it for sale. The demand was apparently terrific. The addition of the syrup naturally increased the cost of the product, but it apparently did not occur to Mr. Giffy to raise his prices. Instead, in regular Alice-in-Wonderland fashion he restricted the sale of the novelty to Sundays. There are further details in Mr. Berners's story, but the upshot of the whole business is that in time a dish of ice cream with syrup came to be known as a *sundae.* When this benefactor of teen-age mankind passed to his eternal reward, the Chicago *Tribune* in its issue of July 2, 1939, headlined his obituary, which it considered front-page news: "Man Who Made the First Ice-Cream Sundae Is Dead."

The fancy spelling with *-ae* need trouble no one. Perhaps it came about as a result of the strict sabbatarianism prevailing in those days; to many, calling anything so frivolous and worldly as ice cream and syrup by the name of the Lord's Day would have smacked of vanity. Although the spelling did not change the pronunciation in the least, the word was made to *look* different, and one could argue that it really wasn't the same word at all.

The Hallauer-to-Berners-to-Giffy story has, however, a good many rivals. The late G. M. Tucker in his *American English* listed the word as "*Sunday*, sometimes misspelled 'sundae,'" and stated that the name was said to have been first used, about 1897, at the Red Cross Pharmacy, an establishment directly opposite to the barroom of the Ithaca Hotel in Ithaca, New York. The Sunday closing of the barroom, according to Tucker, suggested to the enterprising proprietors of the pharmacy to offer a "distinctively Sunday drink" (if a sundae can be called a drink). Another story runs to the effect that, in order to circumvent a Blue Law which prohibited the sale of ice cream sodas on Sunday, a shrewd dealer decided to modify the ice cream soda by leaving out the soda and, in the best national tradition, to give it a new name, *sundae*; the sundae was thus a sort of dry soda. *Soda water* and *soda* in the sense "sweetened drink with syrup and ice cream, doused with carbonated water" are also Americanisms; this perverted use of *soda* may have made a new and less ambiguous term for a whiskey and soda seem especially desirable to liquor drinkers, and thus have encouraged the adoption of *highball* as a designation for the alcoholic drink.

And thereby hangs still another tale—for *highball* is as much of an etymological mystery as *sundae*. It is a puzzling fact that the home of the W.C.T.U. should have made such substantial contributions to the vocabulary of drinking. Certainly the most important of these are *cocktail*, now an international word, and *highball*, although we may also lay claim to such notable contributions as *rickey* (actually named after a Colonel Rickey), *fizz*, *sour*, *smash*, *sherry cobbler*, *eggnog*, *sling*, *horse's neck*, *Tom Collins*, *John Collins*, and *Mamie Taylor*, to name only a few. *Julep* is not an Americanism, but *mint julep* is.

The etymology of *highball*, like that of *cocktail*, is something of a mystery. The theory has been advanced that the word comes from the lingo of bartenders in the '90s, who supposedly called a glass a *ball*. If this could be established as a fact, we should have a plausible etymology, for the *high* is amply explained by the size of the glass, which is necessarily higher than that used for a straight (British *neat*) whiskey.

Professor I. Willis Russell has shown, in *American Speech* for February, 1944, that *highball* is a term used by railroaders to denote a signal to go ahead, to go fast, or to go full speed. It is likely that the use of the term to denote the drink is related to this use in railroading. Professor Leo Spitzer later pointed out in a note appearing in the same journal (February, 1945) a parallel semantic development in French, in which *rapide* "express train" is an argot term for "vin qui saoule [intoxicates] rapidement." *Électrique* and *brutal*, also used to designate fast trains, have been transferred likewise to wine which does its job rapidly: the authority quoted by Spitzer goes on to say, "the fact that a *rapide* train, sometimes *électrique*, is called *brutal* leads one to see the same idea in the same adjectives applied to wine, the idea of speed"— the drink being the vehicle which takes one speedily from reason to unreason in this metaphorical use of the adjectives. Similarly, *train direct* is an argot term both for a litre of wine and for a glass of absinthe, and *wagon* "railway car" for a large glass of wine. Spitzer concludes that "evidently American railroad terms must have had the same radius of expansion as did the French": the American highball speeds up the trip to intoxication just as do the wines called *rapide, brutal, direct,* and *électrique* in French.

About all that we can say with any certainty about *cocktail* is that it is an Americanism which has travelled all over the civilized world and has to some extent revolutionized drinking habits wherever it has gone. Many theories of its origin have been set forth. Christopher Morley once suggested that it originated in an American bar where it was customary to empty the last ounce or so of liquors into a bottle, the cork of which was decorated with a cock's feathers. Whether this etymology came to him by divine afflatus or he had evidence of any sort for it deponent saith not.

A more plausible story is that reprinted by Mencken in *Supplement One* from the house organ of the Roosevelt Hotel in New Orleans, the *Roosevelt Review*. It tells of a hospitable apothecary, Antoine Amédée Peychaud (the inventor of Peychaud bitters), who served a drink to his fellow Masons after lodge meetings consisting of sugar, water, cognac, and his own bitters. The mixture was offered in a *coquetier* (egg cup), pronounced *cocktay* by those of his guests who did not speak French. Folk etymology would account for *cocktay* becoming *cocktail*. This story is so pleasant, so apt, and so circumstantial that one wishes there were better authority for it. Other theories are that *cocktail* is from French *coquetel*, a mixed drink associated with the region of Bordeaux and supposedly introduced into America by French officers at the time of the Revolutionary War, and that it is from *cock-ale*, described by Captain Grose in his *Classical Dictionary of the Vulgar Tongue* as a "provocative drink."

There are other drinking terms of an auxiliary nature of which patriots may be proud: *stick* "a portion of liquor," *pony* "a small glass for liquor or the amount of liquor such a glass will hold," *finger,* *jigger, shot in the neck* (which later became *shot in the arm*), and *snifter.* *Hard liquor* is itself an Americanism; the English still prefer to say *spirits.* Also of American origin are *schooner* "tall glass, usually for beer," *to set 'em up, to rush the growler, bracer, barrel-house, family entrance, eye opener, bender, red-eye,* and *to liquor up. Hooch* and *firewater* are of Indian origin, the latter term being supposedly an English rendering of the Indian term for strong liquor. The use of *rum* to refer generically to all alcoholic drinks is an Americanism, confined nowadays pretty much to the Drys; it dates from the early days before whiskey was widely known in this country, when rum was the colonists' favourite strong drink.

Saloon to designate a place for the sale of alcoholic beverages to be drunk on the premises was originally a euphemism in American English, for the word is ultimately from French *salon* "drawing or reception room." The word in its English modification came in time to have such unsavoury connotations for the virtuous that, with the repeal of Prohibition, it was not revived; *tavern* is probably the most widely used of a number of terms which have supplanted it.

Barroom, bootleg(ger), and *moonshine* "illicit whiskey" are all Americanisms. The second word derives from the practice of concealing flat bottles of illegal liquor in the leg of the boot. *Moonshine,* listed in Grose's *Dictionary* with the meaning "white brandy smuggled on the coasts of Kent and Sussex"—it may also mean gin in Yorkshire —came to us by way of England, but was first applied to whiskey in this country. The fact that the earlier British use was confined to white or colourless liquors suggests a possible origin of the term, though it is more likely that the American extralegal whiskey was so called because it was made, and frequently sold as well, by the light of the moon, that is, at night.

A few other famous Americanisms must receive a necessarily brief treatment. *Blizzard* in its present sense, which seems not to go back farther than 1870, is Iowa's contribution to American English. A variant of dialectal *blizzer* "blaze, flash of lightning," its earlier sense was apparently extended from lightning to storm in the Iowa village of Estherville, where *blizzard* was extensively used to designate a terrific snowstorm which fell upon the town in March of 1870 and which was doubtless a subject of animated conversation for a long time thereafter. Subsequently it came to be used in this sense all over the

Middle West and had reached the rest of the country by 1880, when severe snowstorms furnished ample occasion for its use in the East. The word occurs first in 1829 and is defined as "a violent blow," with an ascription to Kentucky. Thereafter it came to be used in the senses of a rifle shot, a crushing retort, cannon shot, and, during the Civil War, a volley of musketry—meanings which, as Allen Walker Read points out in an article published in *American Speech* for February, 1928, prepared for the wider use of the term in the new sense which it acquired in the '70s. It is thoroughly naturalized in British English.

Ballyhoo, meaning showily obtrusive advertising and, as a verb, to make use of such commercialized eloquence, has been connected with the Irish village of Ballyhooly, though precisely what the connection is, other than phonetic similarity, is not made clear. Professor Atcheson L. Hench has modestly suggested in "A Possible Clue to the Source of 'Ballyhoo' and Some Queries" (*American Speech*, October, 1945) that the word may come from *ballahou* (also occurring as *ballahoo* and *ballyhoo*), the name of a fast-sailing, two-masted vessel with fore-and-aft sails which was formerly much used in the West Indies. According to Hench, "the unusual appearance of the ship, with masts raking in opposite directions, caused speakers to apply the word to any lubberly, untrim, or slovenly ship," a meaning to be found in some of the dictionaries. What is needed to give his suggestion weight as an etymology, Hench admits, is some sort of assurance that in seaman's talk *ballyhoo* was ever applied contemptuously to other things than ships. If we could establish that it was—that, for instance, an unkempt sailor could have been called a "ballyhoo of a sailor," if a "tall tale" could have been called a "ballyhoo of a story," or if wild, extravagant talk could have been called a "ballyhoo of words"—we should "come close to solving the problem of the origin of the present meaning of the word." But thus far we must, it seems, be content with the wise notation of the *American College Dictionary*: "orig. obscure."

Uncle Sam is probably only a jocular extension of the initials *U.S.* Bartlett defines it as the "cant or vulgar name of the United States government . . . used as 'John Bull' is in England" and puts forth an amusing explanation, admittedly not his own, to the effect that there was a flesh-and-blood original, one Samuel Wilson, of Troy, New York. Mr. Wilson, an inspector of foodstuffs during the War of 1812, was apparently a comfortably avuncular sort of man, for, according to the story, he was invariably known as Uncle Sam. He superintended a number of workmen employed to overhaul provisions purchased by an army contractor, one Elbert Anderson, who had caused the casks to be marked *E.A-U.S.*, the latter initials being explained by a waggish employee of Wilson's as standing for *Uncle Sam*. The joke spread rapidly when many of Wilson's workmen followed the recruiting drum. With all its appeal, this story is altogether unacceptable, as the late Albert Matthews has conclusively shown in an article published in 1908 in the *Proceedings of the American Antiquarian Society*. The only thing true about it, aside from the fact that Samuel Wilson was an actual person (he died in 1854), is that the expression does indeed date from the War of 1812, the same time that the now obsolete *Brother Jonathan*, or simply *Jonathan*, came into use meaning either the government of the United States or a typical American. It has been assumed that this appellation has its origin in the Biblical story of David's lamentation for Jonathan: "I am distressed for thee, my brother Jonathan" (2 Samuel i, 26). In the more naïve days of our nation, *Jonathan* may well have been used as a term of address between friends; the Father of Our Country himself is said in all innocence to have called Jonathan Trumbull his Brother Jonathan. *Jonathan* was very common as a man's name in eighteenth-century New England and it may well be that it was at one time thought of as a typically "American" name, like *Elmer* and *Homer* in our own day.

The word stock of American English increases at a dizzying rate of speed. In an attempt to record for lexicographical purposes our rapidly expanding vocabulary, I. Willis Russell, with the aid of enthusiastic assistants, conducts from time to time in *American Speech* a department "Among the New Words." Since 1945 he has recorded such new additions to our vocabulary as the following, to choose at random: *balding, name calling, jampacked, tourist court, bebop, spelunker* "cave crawler," *tape recording, TV, soap opera, VIP* "very important person," *Oscar* "statuette awarded for excellency in the movie industry," *to baby sit, aeropolitics, to double park, free wheeling, giveaway (show, program), radioastronomy, straw hat (theater, circuit), eager beaver, escort carrier, POW, jet* (short for *jet-propelled plane*), *aerosol bomb, atomic age, denazification, genocide, prefab, ruptured duck* "discharge button given G.I.s," *stateside* "relating to the United States," *take-home pay, terminal leave, top secret, to cook with gas (electricity, radar)* "to get somewhere, as in 'Now you're cooking with gas'," *bobbysox(er), hot rod, pyschodrama, spot check, rat race, Republocrat,* and *xerography*—to which the reader may be able to add a good many more from his own observation.

Terms like *bobbysox, bebop,* and *eager beaver* will impress the serious as being somewhat frivolous; *expediter, to process,* and *to implement* will seem "corny" to the cynical and sophisticated; but along with these there are very substantial recent contributions, such as *genocide, radio-astronomy,* and *aeropolitics,* which are altogether worthy to take their place beside such older Americanisms as *linotype, electrocute* (a blend of *electric* and *execute,* this may now be used to mean "to kill accidentally by electric shock," as in "Lineman Electrocuted When He Touches Live Wire"), *anaesthesia, urinalysis, appendicitis, hydrant, gorilla, race suicide, typewriter, automobile, tularaemia, moron, rotogravure, phonograph, telegram,* and *to demoralize.*

To baby sit is formed from *baby sitter,* a compound noun having here been made by back formation into a verb. *Bratting* has made some headway, probably mostly within the "profession," as a synonym for *baby sitting.* But such lighthearted terms to designate an activity which is a sign of the times in which we live would never be deemed appropriate by a government agency, and sure enough, the United States Employment Service office in at least one of our cities (Lincoln, Nebraska) has registered practitioners as *child monitors.*

The Motion Picture Academy Award is said to be called an *Oscar* because it looked to somebody or other connected with the Academy just like his Uncle Oscar. Whatever its origin, *Oscar* started something, though whether it was worth starting is a matter for dispute: the *Gertrude,* a silver kangaroo, given to those authors of Pocket Books editions whose works sell a million copies; the *Edgar,* a small bust of Edgar Allan Poe, for writers of detective stories; the *Barney,* a silver cigarette box with engraved sketches of Barney Google and Snuffy Smith, for cartoonists; the *Apparel Annie,* an eighteen-inch bronze statuette of something or somebody, for "outstanding promotion of the apparel industry"; and the *Winnie,* a female nude in bronze, for fashion design.

A large number of the cited recent additions have first appeared in *Time,* which has also been fecund in its original contributions to the American word stock. It specializes in such creations as *cinemactress, steelionaire, radiorator, stripteuse, millionheiress,* and *socialite.* Of these, the first three are blends (*cinema actress, steel millionaire, radio orator*) and the last three puns (*strip tease, millionairess, social light*). Other recent "makers" of American English are Gelett Burgess (*bromide* "platitude, also a person given to platitudes" and *blurb*), Jack Conway (*yes man*), Walter Winchell (*infanticipate*), Will Irwin (*highbrow* and probably *lowbrow*), Bob Burns (*bazooka*), Philip Wylie (*momism*), Sinclair Lewis (*babbitt, hobohemia, philanthrobber*), and H. L. Mencken (*bootician, booboisie, Bible Belt*, and *ecdysiast* "strip teaser").

Blends such as *motel, twinjector, libratory, radarange, daffynition, skinjury* (from the advertisement of a medication for cuts and burns), *Dixiecrat, Chicagorilla*, and *psychiatricky* (a recent coinage of *Time* to describe the ending of a film) are very frequent nowadays. Many of them are nonce usages, and a bare list might be expanded for pages. The process is, of course, not at all new, and its very lack of subtlety probably accounts for its popularity; moreover, it is very easy to perform.

There has probably never been such fertile creation and wide use of acronyms as at present. *Acronym*, itself a new word formed from Greek *akros* "tip" and *onyma* "name"—probably of American coinage, by the way—means a word made from the initial letters of other words: examples are *radar* (radio detecting and ranging), *Care* or *CARE* (Co-operative for American Remittances to Europe), *Unesco* (United Nations Educational, Scientific, and Cultural Organization), *loran* (long range navigation), and *teleran* (television radar air navigation). It is likely that the colloquial name of the women's branch of the Royal Navy, the *Wrens* (Women's Royal Naval Service) furnished the model for the use of such American acronyms as *Wac* (Women's Army Corps), *Wave* (Women's Appointed Volunteer Emergency Service), *Wasp* (Women's Air Force Service Pilots), and *Spar* (Semper Paratus, the motto of the Coast Guard). In the case of *Wave* (and also probably of *Care* and others as well), it is apparent that the natural process was reversed in that the acronym preceded the full name of the organization, which was made to fit. How otherwise to explain the cumbersome and inept full form of *Wave* or the forced use of *Co-operative* in the expansion of *Care*? A great number of trade names also are acronyms: *Amoco, Sunoco, Socony, Alcoa, Nabisco*, etc.

The use of initial letters to designate governmental agencies became a commonplace during the New Deal, as in *NRA* (originally *NIRA*), *AAA, HOLC, CCC, FERA, NLRB, OPA, RFC, OWI, WLB, ODT*, and others, which gave rise to Al Smith's scornful designation *alphabet soup*. The phenomenon was by no means unknown before, as in *O.K., W.C.T.U., P.D.Q., I.W.W., G.A.R., G.O.P., C.O.D., B.V.D., F.F.V.,* and (*on the*) *Q.T.,* all of which antedate the New Deal by a good many years. Other recent examples are *ASCAP* (also, perhaps usually, an acronym, pronounced *ass cap*), *CIO, AFL, NAACP, TV, FM, IQ, M.C.* (which in the sense "master of ceremonies" may be converted into a verb, usually written *emcee*), and, very recently, *LP* (*long-playing*) and *ACTH* (*adreno-cortico-tropic hormone*). Writers of advertising copy have made *B.O.* a constant dire threat to the social, economic, and erotic advancement of the American people. *P.O.* (*perspiration odour*), a subspecies of *B.O.,* constitutes a relatively minor menace to bourgeois euphoria. *TB* and *PJs* (*pyjamas*) differ from the preceding in that they are abbreviations of single words. *A.W.O.L.* is usually an acronym in military use, pronounced *ay wall*. *V.P.* for *vice-president* has recently given rise to *veep*, originally applied to Alben W. Barkley, but now frequently used to designate any vice-president.

Words have circulated among the various functional categories—an ancient linguistic phenomenon by no means confined to American English, or even to English, though such conversions are especially notable in American English because of the very frequency with which they occur. Thus, nouns become verbs—a mighty flock of them, such as *to audition, to program, to accession, to package, to proposition, to vacation, to park* (also *to double park*), *to date* "to make an appointment with one of the opposite sex" (also *to double-date* "to date in couples"), *to burp* (transitively) "to cause an infant to emit a belch after feeding by holding it over the shoulder and patting its back," (intransitively) "to make the digestive noise suggested by the word," *to contact, to clearance, to wow* (the noun *wow* being formed from the exclamation of enthusiasm), *to solo, to needle* "to give verbal digs," *to thumb* (*a ride*), *to service,* and dozens of others. Intransitive verbs may become transitive, as in *to operate a patient, to sleep two people* (from an advertisement of a studio bed). New verbs may be made from clipped forms of nouns, including back formations: *to razz* (from *raspberry,* slang for a vulgar noise made with tongue and lips to indicate disapproval, also known as a *Bronx cheer*), *to emote, to typewrite, to perk* (*coffee*), *to enthuse* (which is from the nineteenth century and which may not be an Americanism, though it probably is), *to phone,* and such complexities as the previously mentioned *to baby sit,* as well as *to soda jerk* and *to practice teach.*

With equal ease verbs may be converted into nouns: *release* "permission to publish, sell, or exhibit," *cut* "reduction, (colloquially) failure to attend class, (slangily) share," *combine*. Nouns become adjectives, or practically so, in *air tragedy*, *cover girl*, and *armament race*; and adjectives become nouns, as in *lovelies* "show girls," *formals* "formal dresses," *informals* "stationery of less than standard size, usually bearing the user's name, initials, or monogram, and sometimes the address as well," *falsies* (with hypocoristic suffix) "artificial breasts, usually of sponge rubber," *tropicals* "lightweight suits or trousers," *casuals* "shoes for informal wear," *separates* "skirts and shirts worn by girls," *personal* "brief newspaper article about a particular person," *dry* "prohibitionist," *wet* "antiprohibitionist," *commercial* "commercially sponsored radio or television programme or, more usually, sales talk on such a programme," *short* "short moving picture subsidiary to the featured picture," *briefs* "women's skimpily cut underwear," and *scanties*, practically the same as briefs.

A very prominent characteristic of current American English, though the practice is by no means new or American, is the combination of verb and adverb to form a new verbal idea, in effect a new verb: *to call down*, *to check up*, *to scare up*, *to stand for* "to tolerate," *to go for* "to be enthusiastic about," *to try out*, *to make out* "to succeed," *to bawl out*, *to slip up*, *to rope in*. Some of these verb–adverb combinations have made themselves thoroughly at home in British English. Nouns frequently grow out of such verbal combinations: *setup*, *checkup*, *pushover*, *cutback*, *kickback*, *breakdown* "analysis," *drive-in*, *smash-up* "wreck," *slowdown*, *buildup*, *hookup*, *comeback* "snappy answer," *sitdown*, *walk-up* "apartment house without elevator," *pin-up*. The last three of these may be used as adjectives, as in *sit-down strike*, *walk-up apartment*, *pin-up girl*. Some of the combinations cited have been in general English use for a long time (for instance, *breakdown* and *smash-up*), but have acquired new senses, or perhaps have been coined anew, in American English. *Pin-up* has made its way into French (and doubtless other Continental languages as well), according to B. Mathieu, writing in the *New Yorker* of November 4, 1950; it is used of any pretty woman, or one who is in the public eye, pictures of Mistinguett frequently carrying the caption *La vieille pin-up*.

Clipping is an old process; it was old, in fact, when Jonathan Swift inveighed against it, and it has contributed a great many words to the standard language—*mob*, for instance, which the Dean objected to as a clipped form of Latin *mobile vulgus*, and which now may appear in the most formal of contexts. Clipped forms which have arisen in America are *gas* (for *gasoline*), *photo, pep, bike, ad, bunk, auto, prof, taxi, tux, con* (for *confidence*, as in *con man, con game*), *fax* (*facsimile newspaper*), and *Jax* (local for Jacksonville, Florida, also the name of a brand of beer made there). *Movie*, and, by analogy with it, *talkie*, are clipped forms with hypocoristic suffix.

Recent American English has made considerable use of prefixes and suffixes, like *de-* and *-ette*, word elements like *para-* and *-burger* which may be affixed in the manner of true prefixes and suffixes, and compounding elements like *-happy* and *-buster*. All these will be here discussed together for convenience' sake. *Para-* dates from World War II, occurring in *paratroops, paratrooper, parabomb, para-medic*, and *parashot*. These, like the *-burger* combinations (and others as well) may have begun as blends (*parachute troops* becoming *paratroops, cheese* and *hamburger* becoming *cheeseburger*); if so, it did not take long for the *para-, -burger*, etc., to be felt as free word elements capable of being affixed to other words. *De-* occurs in American *debunk*; it may be freely used in both British and American English, and it is difficult to say whether *dewax, defrost*, and the like are Americanisms or not. *Super-* has had a great vogue, occurring in such Hollywoodisms as *superfilm, supercolossal*, in *superhighway* and *super market*, and in *Superman*, the name of the comic strip character, who probably has no connection whatever with Shaw's *Man and Superman* or Goethe's *Übermensch. Super* used alone is slang on a somewhat juvenile level ("Superman's sure super today"), as is the rhyming *super-duper* "extra super." *Anti-* is much more frequent in American usage than in British and has been so since the eighteenth century. The prefix was used alone (with a pun on *Aunty*) as the name of the gaunt, bombazine-clad female prohibitionist depicted by the cartoonists in the days before Repeal. *Semi-* is likewise used more in America than in England: American English prefers the more pompous Latinate *semiannual* to *half-yearly*. H. W. Horwill in *Modern American Usage* says that a jubilee in America always becomes a *semicentennial*, and goes on to point out the looseness of meaning of *semi-* in American usage, in which it is frequently the equivalent of *partly, largely*, or *approximately* rather than *half. Near-*, as in *near-beer, near-silk*, and *near-leather*, came to acquire all the derogatory connotations of *imitation*, for which it was a euphemism in the beginning. It has lost ground in recent years. What used to be called *near-leather* would nowadays be called *simulated leather*.

Among the true suffixes, *-ize* has probably been as prolific as any, particularly in advertising writing and Federalese: *glamorize, sanitize, motorize, vitalize, finalize, personalize* "mark with the buyer's name, initials, or monogram, as *personalized stationery, underwear, luggage, bath towels,* etc.," *winterize* "prepare or equip for the winter, as a car," *sanforize* "preshrink by a special process" (from the name of *Sanford L.* Cluett, inventor), *tenderize, customize, comfortize* ("let us comfortize your shoes"), and a host of other verbs. Also widely used is *-ette*: it may be either diminutive (*kitchenette, dinette, bathinette, superette* "small super market") or feminine (*farmerette, conductorette, usherette, guidette, Rockette* "member of dancing chorus in Rockefeller Center's Radio City Music Hall," *tusslerette* "lady wrestler," *hularette* "hula-dancing chorus girl in girl-show *A Night in Hawaii*," and *drum majorette*). After John Philip Sousa, the booteed, swivel-hipped drum majorette is probably America's greatest contribution to band music; it is likely that only America, its sexual mores conditioned to a large extent by the cinematic convention of almost irresistibly alluring yet untouched femininity, could in all naïveté have insinuated this glamorized symbol of sex into martial music. Nowadays marching bands must have as a rule not merely one drum majorette, but a whole corps of them, flanked (metaphorically speaking) by subsidiary Corybantes called *twirlers*.

Among other suffixes widely used are *-ee* (*donee, returnee, draftee, trainee, selectee, giftee, forgettee, addressee, baby sittee*), *-eer* (*racketeer, blacketeer,* "black market racketeer," *donuteer* "girl who served many doughnuts in a USO canteen in Champaign, Illinois," *fashioneer, junketeer, fountaineer* "soda jerk," *vacationeer, fictioneer, budgeteer, chariteer* "professional beggar for charity," *oilateer* "gas-station attendant," *upper-bracketeer, gadgeteer, sloganeer*), *-orium* (*odditorium, lubritorium* "place where cars are greased," *pantatorium* "place where pants are pressed," *shavatorium, barberatorium, shoetorium, corsetorium, spaghettorium, pastorium*), *-ine* (*dudine* "girl on dude ranch," *chorine* "chorus girl"), *-ster* (*gangster, mobster, roadster, pollster, schoolster* "pupil," *jeepster* "type of sports car"), *-dom* (*gangdom, gangsterdom, mobdom, fandom, moviedom, filmdom*), and *-ery* (*hashery, beanery, shoe-fixery* and, from the eighteenth century, *printery* and *grocery*, with *groggery, bakery,* and *bindery* appearing early in the nineteenth). The suffix *-eer* acquired derogatory connotations from *profiteer* and *patrioteer*, both British coinages of the twentieth century. In many of the Americanisms with this suffix, however, it is notable that there is no such connotation; only *racketeer* and *blacketeer*, perhaps *fictioneer*, have it among the examples cited. Certainly *toileteer* "plumber specializing in the installation and care of water closets" has nothing pejorative about it, nor has its synonym *flushologist*, both of which appeared in the four-column newspaper advertising "spread" of a plumbing supply company in Jacksonville, Florida. *Odditorium* was probably an independent coinage of the late Robert L. ("Believe It or Not") Ripley, with whom the word is invariably associated, though an earlier British use has been unearthed. *Pastorium* is used in all seriousness by members of the Baptist fold for *parsonage*.

Word elements freely used in combinations are *-burger* and *-furter*, both of which, because of their foreign origin, will be discussed in the following chapter. The *-wich* has been taken from *sandwich* and used in much the same way as *-burger* and *-furter*, though not so widely as the former: *duckwich* and *turkeywich* have been cited in the pages of *American Speech* in recent years and *Spamwich* was for a time fairly common, but this is a poor showing indeed compared with the prodigious offspring of *-burger*. *Cavalcade* furnished the popular word element *-cade*: *motorcade*, *autocade*, *musicade*, *aquacade*, and a number of similar combinations have frequently achieved the dignity of print. *Icecapade* "skating show" is doubtless a blend of *ice escapade*, but may well have been suggested by the numerous *-cade* words with which it rhymes. *-Mobile* occurs in *bookmobile* "travelling library," *clubmobile*, *snowmobile*, *skimobile*, *foodmobile*, *bloodmobile* "travelling blood bank," *chowmobile* "canteen type of trailer," *whoopmobile* "bus to pick up New Year's Eve celebrants unable to drive their own cars," *jeepmobile* "bookmobile on a jeep," and *vetmobile* "midget auto constructed for a veteran paralysed from the waist down."

The earliest *-buster* combinations are probably *broncobuster*, *trustbuster*, and *belly buster*, all occurring in the latter years of the nineteenth century. Since then, the following, along with many others, have appeared: *gang-buster*, *racket buster*, *union-buster*, *factory buster* "six-ton missile," *button-buster*, *block-buster*, *atom-buster*, *par-buster* (in golf). Combinations with *-crazy*, *-happy*, *-wise*, *-conscious*, *-struck*, and *-minded* are freely made: *girl-crazy* (and *boy-crazy*), *stir-crazy* "too long in prison," *stage-crazy*; *slap-happy*, *bark-happy* (of watchdogs), *fight-happy*, *stripe-happy* (of a soldier itching for promotion), *trigger-happy*;

marketwise, stylewise, budgetwise, fightwise; social-conscious, class-conscious, race-conscious, profit-conscious; girl-struck (and vice versa), *stage-struck, movie-struck; social-minded, security-minded, federation-minded*—these are the merest sampling.

Most of the processes which have been discussed in this chapter are, as has been pointed out, not new, nor are they exclusively American. But the freedom with which they are employed and the attitude towards life they sometimes mirror may certainly be regarded as characteristic of the America of our times. Along with much that is silly, much that is churlish and tasteless, and much that is nauseatingly arch, we have encountered much that is vigorous and vital and wonderfully apt. That American English has been inventive and resourceful no one who has examined the evidence could ever gainsay, nor is it disputable that it has struck fire more often than it has missed: the amazing number of Americanisms that have been adopted by the mother country—not that we should be too much impressed by this—is merely an indication of the American talent for saying things pungently and expressively. What is fittest in language has a way of surviving, as the admirable *O.K., the real McCoy, highbrow, crook, lengthy, haywire, panhandle, roughneck, Annie Oakley,* and *bawl out*—to mention only a few of the finer linguistic growths to spring from our soil—have done. What is graceless or fraudulent or ponderously "cute"—heaven knows sufficient examples have been cited in the course of this volume—ekes out a banal and colourless existence among the silly, the sentimental, and the addlepated, whose name is legion but whose influence is fortunately small.

In its vocabulary American English has indeed manifested the daring, the boldness, and the initiative which have so often been attributed to it on other, and usually irrelevant, grounds. Here there has been and is a warmth, an enthusiasm, a youthfulness of spirit that all the awesome powers of all the teachers and all the textbooks have failed to blight.

EIGHT

Later American Speech: Adoptions from Foreign Tongues

BEFORE 1800 the Algonquian languages, as we have seen, were the principal sources of Indian loans, with the Muskhogean furnishing a good many place names. During the nineteenth century, as the frontier moved increasingly westward, a few words from the languages of the Western tribes entered American English: *tepee* from the Dakotas, *hogan* from the Navahos, both names of Indian dwellings corresponding to earlier Algonquian *wigwam*. The name of Sequoya, the Cherokee who invented a syllabary for writing his language and thus taught thousands of his people to read and write, is perpetuated in *sequoia*, a genus of coniferous trees, and in Sequoia National Park in California. A trade jargon of the Columbia River country in Oregon, composed of words from Chinook and other Indian languages, as well as from English and French, has been the means of transmission for a few words of Chinook, but these can hardly be said to be widely known outside of the Northwest: *cayuse* "horse," the word *chinook* itself to designate a warm, dry wind which blows intermittently in the region of the Rockies (also a warm, moist wind blowing from the sea to land in Washington and Oregon, called a *wet chinook*) and as the name of a kind of salmon, *potlatch* "a giving of gifts, also a winter celebration," *skookum* "great, powerful," *high muck-a-muck*—these are the only ones which might be known to the country at large, and only the last is really well known. *Hooch* is a clipping of *hoochinoo*, an alteration of the name of a tribe of Alaskan Indians who made liquor; during the days of the Noble Experiment it gained fairly firm footing in all parts of the country. *Chautauqua*, the Senecan Indian name of a county and lake in New York, became towards the end of the nineteenth century a term for a kind of tent show playing the small towns and featuring moral and intellectual uplift (lectures by the late William Jennings Bryan and Dr. Russell H. Conwell) sugar-coated with refined vaudeville (Swiss bell-ringers and conjurers). A few translations of Indian terms (or supposed ones) also came into being in the nineteenth century: *Great White Father*, *Father of Waters*, and *squaw man*.

Along with the many Spanish words which crossed the border when our civilization made contact with that which the Spaniards had established to the south came a good many words ultimately Nahuatl, such as *coyote*, *chicle*, *chili*, *mesquite*, *mescal*, *jalap*, *peyote*, *avocado*, *tamale*, *ocelot*, and, amazing though it seems, *McCarty*, a cowboy's term for a hair rope, a folk etymologizing of Spanish *mecate*, which is in turn a modification of Nahuatl *mecatl*. *Coyote* was known long before in British English, which adopted it from Spanish, but there is every reason to believe that it was reborrowed by Americans. The fact that a word has at some earlier date appeared in British English by no means rules out the possibility of independent borrowing in American English; there is no reason to suppose that our earliest settlers along the Atlantic seaboard would have preserved a word for which they had no use. In the West, however, there was a great deal of use for this particular word to designate a creature who was very much in evidence. Before long the word came to be applied, not only to *Canis Latrans*, but to a despicable, sneaking person as well. Similarly, although *chili* had been used in British English as early as 1662, it seems most likely that it was independently reborrowed in America: the first American evidence for the use of the word occurs precisely at the time of our first contact with the Spanish-speaking people of the Southwest.

Jalap is from the Nahuatl name of a town in Mexico where a purgative drug was manufactured—*Xalapan*. The final *n*-sound of the Nahuatl word was dropped by the Spaniards, who in time came to spell the word with an initial *j* instead of the older *x*. From Spanish, *jalapa* (to use the later spelling) passed into French, losing its final vowel in the process, and from that language was borrowed by the English. But, like *chili* and *coyote*, it seems likely that this word has, as M. M. Mathews puts it in his *Some Sources of Southernisms*, "come

K

into the English language twice—once long ago in Europe and again more recently in our own Southwest."

The same is true of *ocelot* and *avocado*. The latter word in a number of forms appears in English as early as the seventeenth century, but was not used to any extent in this country until the early nineteenth century. The Aztec name for the fruit was too much for the Spanish— it was something like *ahuacatl*, ultimately becoming by folk etymology *avocado* "lawyer," one of the forms in which it was taken into English and the one in which it seems a good many years later to have been reintroduced into American English by our pioneers. The *alligator* in *alligator pear* is another of its English alterations.

In 1921 Dr. Edward Francis of the United States Public Health Service coined the word *tularaemia*, which combines elements from Nahuatl (*tul-*), Spanish (*-ar-*), and Greek (*-aemia*), when he made the brilliant discovery that the plague-like diseases which previously had been called by various names (e.g., *rabbit fever* and *deer-fly fever*) were caused by the organism *Bacterium tularense*, named after Tulare County, California. But behind this story lies another story which links the word to the Nahuatl word *tullin* for a tall bulrush which the Spaniards rendered as *tule*. In Spanish the suffix *-ar* may be added to the name of a plant to denote a region overgrown with that plant. Treating *tule* precisely as if it were a Spanish word, the Spaniards called such regions *tulares;* hence the name of Tulare County in California. It was in this county that bubonic plague broke out after the earthquake in 1906. A few years thereafter, Dr. George W. McCoy, also of the United States Public Health Service, discovered that a great number of ground squirrels were dying in Tulare County of a disease caused by an organism which he and his assistants identified and named *Bacterium tularense*, and which, incidentally, is not the organism which causes bubonic plague; this was an instance of looking for one thing and finding something different but equally important, for McCoy had found the organism responsible for a disease of man as well as of the rabbit. But that disease had to wait a number of years for a name, when Dr. Francis came up with *tularaemia*, a dignified, mouth-filling word which was quite literally "made in America."

The Louisiana Purchase and the settlement of the Mississippi and the Great Lakes region brought into the American vocabulary a number of French words: *butte, chute, coulee, crevasse* (in the sense "a break in a levee"; in its geological sense the word is general English for a crack in the ice of a glacier), *depot* "railroad station," *lagniappe*, *picayune* (which has acquired a figurative meaning as well as an adjectival form in *-ish*), and *shivaree* "noisy serenade for a newly married couple." Other French words are used locally in lower Louisiana, but the only one at all widely known is *praline*, named after the Maréchal du Plessis-*Praslin*, whose chef invented the confection. *Lagniappe* is a Louisiana French modification of American Spanish *la ñapa* "the gift"; the word is ultimately from Kechua, the language spoken by the Incas of Peru. The folk word *shivaree* is an altered form of French *charivari*. The word is common to Canada and to much of the United States away from the eastern seaboard, where the custom is called variously *serenade, tinpanning, bullband(ing), skimmilton* or *skimmerton*—variants of the *skimmington* of British folk custom—*belling, callathump* or *callithump*, and *horning. Shivaree* was in use very early in the nineteenth century and is encountered to this day in the entire Mississippi valley from Minnesota and Wisconsin to the Louisiana Gulf. West of the Mississippi it is the predominant term for the uncouth form of entertainment it designates.

To parlay "to wager an original amount and its winnings," also used as a noun designating such a wager, has been taken from French *paroli* "double stake (at faro, etc.)," but is ultimately Italian, French having borrowed the word from that language. It has acquired a broader use in American English, "to manoeuvre a small asset so as to get a large return," and may also be used figuratively, as in "to parlay a big grin into fame" (a reference to the comedian Joe E. Brown).

Writers on women's fashions have been successful in introducing a few French words, usually euphemistic in nature, such as *brassière* (pronounced *brazéer*), which has in recent years been clipped to *bra*, and *derrière* "backside." Manufacturers of perfumes have made lavish use of French and pseudo-French in naming their supposedly aphrodisiac witches' brews: *Heure Intime, Le Premier Oui, Risque Tout, L'Ardente Nuit, Nuit d'Extase, De'Odo Fleur, Honeysuckle de Paris,* and *Sweet Peas de Printemps* are among the priceless gems culled by Arthur Minton in his "All the Perfumes of America," published in *American Speech*, October, 1946; but these are trade names and only incidentally fall within the scope of the present work.

Spanish looms largest among the foreign influences on American English after the onset of the nineteenth century. It was, as we have seen, the medium of transmission for a great many words from Nahuatl, which thus come to us in Spanish dress. In the first seventy or so years of the century, the following words of Spanish origin made their appearance in American English, their order being roughly chronological: *alcalde, hacienda, mustang, ranch, adobe, señorita, peon, patio, tortilla, lasso, canyon, lariat, plaza, frijole, corral, placer, burro, bonanza, eldorado, fiesta, mesa, serape, siesta, padre, quirt* (probably from Mexican Spanish *cuarta*, a modification of *cuerda* "cord"), *sierra, piñon, stampede, chaparral, sombrero, hombre, adios, hackamore, bronco, pronto, rodeo, vamose* (or *vamoose*), *cinch, buckaroo, pinto, vigilante*. Somewhat later are *sabe* (or *savvy*), *loco, mañana, marihuana, hoosegow*, and *chaps*. *Rumba* is of rather recent introduction; it is probably of African origin, but comes to us by way of Cuban Spanish, just as *samba*, likewise the name of a dance which is Negro in origin, has reached us by way of Brazilian Portuguese.

Some of these words, as will be noted, have undergone English changes. *Adobe*, for instance, is frequently aphetized (clipped of its initial unstressed syllable) to *dobie*. It may be used, in either its full or mutilated form, to mean a building constructed of sun-dried bricks. *Peon* has been assimilated to such an extent that it long ago acquired the suffix *-age*. *Vamo(o)se* was first used in American English as a transitive verb, as in *to vamoose the country;* in 1848 it was used intransitively by the New York *Mirror*, and, only eleven years later, in 1859, made its debut in British English. The word, which is completely naturalized, is simply a modification of Spanish *vamos* "let's go." Pronunciation of Spanish *o* as *oo* in the final syllable is paralleled by *lassoo*, a somewhat old-fashioned pronunciation of *lasso*, by *buckaroo*, from *vaquero* "cowboy," and by *calaboose*, from *calabozo*. *Mustang, ranch, lariat* (*la reata* "the rope"), *quirt, stampede*, and *cinch* have lost final vowels, with *stampede*, from Mexican Spanish *estampido*, suffering loss of its initial syllable as well. *Chaps*, sometimes spelled and pronounced *shaps*, is a clipped form of *chaparejos* (or *chaparajos*); the seatless leather overalls designated by the word were worn originally as a protection against *chaparral*.

Pinto first appears as an adjective, in the writings of Bret Harte. It was somewhat later converted into a noun to designate a spotted horse. The word is a shortened form of the Spanish participle *pintado* "painted." It may also designate a kind of bean having mottled seeds. The usual pronunciation of *frijole* is *free holy*. The word is due to a misunderstanding of the Spanish plural *frijoles*, which looks as if it were the plural of a word *frijole* instead of the actual Spanish singular *frijol*, a form sometimes used by cowboys in the approximately Spanish pronunciation *free hole*. Those who use the *free hole* pronunciation for the singular may form the plural by analogy with English speech habits; thus, the plural of *frijol* is sometimes pronounced *free holes*.

Hoosegow is a rendering of *juzgado*, which in Mexican Spanish means "jail." *D* between vowels is frequently lost in American Spanish; *hoosegow* is thus a fairly good approximation of the Mexican pronunciation of *juzgado*. (The sound of *j* in the pronunciation of most of Spanish America is very similar to English *h*, in contrast to the fricative sound in the standard speech of Spain.) *Hackamore* "halter used in breaking horses" is obviously a modification of *jáquima*. *Cinch* "saddle girth," from Spanish *cincha*, soon acquired the slang meaning of a "sure thing," perhaps from the sense of security felt by the cowboy when the cinch of his saddle was securely fastened. The word is also used as a verb; *to cinch* something is to make sure of it.

It has been suggested by Harold Wentworth in *American Speech* for February, 1942, that the "neo-pseudo-suffix" *-eroo*, of which *-aroo* must be considered a variant, may have been borrowed from *buckaroo*, which is, as we have seen, a Western American alteration of *vaquero*. If his suggestion is true, this rather infrequently used word has had a numerous, if belated, progeny: *flopperoo, switcheroo, stinkeroo, stroperoo* ("a novel shoe-shine cloth. . . . It is hung on a hook and the shoes 'stropped' to a high shine"), *blabberoo* (used by a broadcaster in reference to a Senate filibuster), *Tang-aroo* (probably suggested by *kangaroo*, designating a delicacy made with "slices of tender Tang" [a product of the Cudahy Packing Company]), and a good many others from radio, sports, advertising, and the movies.

When the word *rodeo* first appeared in American English, it meant simply a roundup of cattle. Not until 1914 does it appear to have been used of a travelling show displaying the daring and skill of cowboys. *Sabe* is in Spanish the second or third person singular, present tense, of *saber* "to know." It is used colloquially in much less restricted fashion in American English. "I *sabe*" occurs in *Scribner's Magazine*, where it is labelled as slang, in 1879. The word had been used by Bret Harte in 1870 as a noun meaning "sense," spelled *savey*, and again, with the spelling *sabe*, in 1875. *Savvy* is the usual spelling nowadays. The word is probably reinforced by French *savez(-vous)?*, and it is possible that its use as a noun is partly due to Scots dialectal *savie*, ultimately derived from French *savoir*.

In a note on the G.I.'s use of Italian published in *American Speech*, October, 1945, Major J. B. Costanzo states, in perhaps too unqualified a fashion, that our soldiers in Italy "invariably" employed *señorita* in addressing Italian girls because the Spanish word was so much more familiar to them than Italian *signorina*; even the pimps came in time to use *señorita* in their professional contacts with Americans, according to Costanzo. The usual uneducated American pronunciation of *señorita* makes the first two syllables *senior*, which is a very close approximation of the first two syllables of Italian *signorina*. It is likely that a good deal of confusion prevailed, and that many of those who used the *-ina* ending—the "bulk" of those stationed in Italy according to another correspondent who took issue with Costanzo's statement—were under the impression that they were using an only slightly modified form of the familiar Spanish title.

Efforts have been made to find a Spanish origin for *hubba-hubba*, a cry of enthusiasm which was very widespread in the 1940s. About all that can be said with any degree of certainty about this strange verbal outburst of youthful exuberance is that it seems at first to have been largely restricted to members of the Army Air Corps stationed in Tampa, Florida, and that it was originally connected somehow with athletics, an important part of the training of that branch of the service. There is reason to believe that it was used rather early in the decade by baseball players and coaches as part of their inane "infield chatter." No doubt the spelling *haba haba*, used in the early appearances of the word in print, has suggested to some that it is a modification of Spanish *habla, habla* "speak, speak." This theory of the origin of the word is phonologically very far-fetched, for it is highly unlikely that *habla* would in oral transmission lose its *l* and acquire an initial aspirate (the *h* being silent in Spanish). A. D. Weinberger, who was a member of the Air Corps during the War, believes that it was his group that was responsible for the introduction of the expression into the army as well as for its subsequent spread elsewhere into the speech of teenagers, intellectually immature adults, sports announcers, and radio comics (*American Speech*, February, 1947). In a note on the word prompted by Professor Weinberger's interesting article, J. L. Riordan points out in a later issue of the same journal the extreme unlikelihood of the *habla, habla* etymology and contributes two equally unlikely

ones, both also from Spanish: *hubi!* and *habe*, the latter being assumed
to have originated in the *Habe Usted . . . ?* presumably used on the
shopping tours of soldiers stationed along the Mexican Border.
Reading the phrase from his pocket dictionary, the G.I. ignorant of
Spanish phonology would of course pronounce the *h* in *habe*. Be it
said in fairness to Professor Riordan that these theories are not proposed
with any conviction; the same is true of D. W. Maurer, who suggests
in full consciousness of its improbability that the origin of *hubba-
hubba* may be in Chinese *hao-pu-hao*, translated by a learned Chinese
friend of Maurer's as "it is good under heaven when boy meets girl."
While not actually taking much stock in his proposed etymology,
Professor Maurer points out that it is made "tempting" by the fact that
early in World War II a good many young Chinese fliers were trained
in the Florida camps. The truth is that the origin of this strange exclamation, which seems already to be dying out, is probably irretrievably
lost to us. We may expect many "tempting," fascinating, and false
explanations of *hubba-hubba* for years to come.

    Cafeteria is of Spanish origin—Mexican Spanish, it should be said,
for it is likely that a Castilian would regard it with the same sort of
scorn that Englishmen felt for *lengthy* and *belittle* up to the time that
British English adopted those words. In the sense of an eating place
where one serves oneself, the word is distinctly an Americanism. It
was current in California as early as the 1850s, but it then designated a
drinking rather than an eating place. In its present sense, the word
crops up in the last decade of the nineteenth century. The idea of
speeded-up mass feeding appealed strongly to the American imagination, and today the self-service eating place is a national institution
though no longer confined to this country. A Swiss observer, Dr. J.
Henry Wild, looks with jaundiced eye upon it, and declares, in his
Glimpses of the American Language and Civilization (Bern, 1945), that
"the mania for grasping food from a counter, swallowing it in record
time, and rushing back to work, has not merely ruined the health of
millions of Americans, but has also affected their mentality, humour
and outlook on life." Although "during the past few years enterprising
businessmen have bestowed this blessing also upon the Old World,"
it is likely that most Europeans still share Wild's low opinion of this
American threat to their sanity and health.

    The suffix *-teria*, as it is to all intents and purposes in American
English, has suggested many possibilities to American business enter-

prise: *washateria* or *washerteria* "establishment where one does one's own laundry," *shaveteria* "barber shop without barbers, where shaving materials are furnished for one to shave oneself," *spaghetteria* (discovered, to his everlasting glory, by Mr. Mencken—another star in his crown), *bootblacketeria, bookateria* (a self-help lending library in a Lincoln, Nebraska, grocery store), and *dresseteria.* Professor J. M. Steadman, Jr., has pointed out (*American Speech,* June, 1930) that *-teria* need not any more include the idea of self-service and cites *chocolateria, hatateria, smoketeria, snacketeria,* and a number of other coinages which designate mere places of retail business, along with *valeteria* and *wrecketeria* "place where old cars are wrecked," which name places where certain services are rendered.

Spanish is still spoken in New Mexico by a good many people of Mexican origin who know English only slightly or not at all. Until 1941 the laws of that state were printed in both Spanish and English; this was true of California and Texas as well in the early days. A good many Spanish words are in frequent use by Angios (the term for Americans in New Mexico): in certain parts *portal* is used about as often as *porch, frijole* and *pinto* about as often as *bean.* A good many Spanish words are also in use in other states near the Mexican Border and a good proportion of the place names in this part of the country are of Spanish origin, extending into Colorado, Utah, and Nevada as well.

Newcomers in vast numbers arrived in this country from various parts of Europe in the course of the nineteenth century. The wave of emigration from South Ireland which began as early as the middle of the eighteenth century was vastly accelerated by the failure of the potato crop in Ireland in 1845, a million and a half Catholic Irish arriving in the next ten years or so. The political disorders and the abortive revolution in Germany in 1848 brought Germans in great numbers, many of them settling upon the farm lands of the Middle West and in the large cities of the Middle Atlantic and Middle Western states. Scandinavians, more than a million of them, settled in the upper Mississippi valley during the latter years of the century.

With increasing prosperity in Germany following that country's successful prosecution of the Franco-Prussian War, the flood of emigration from Germany abated considerably. Meanwhile, the harassing of the Jews in Russia in the 1880s sent large numbers of these people to America. Beginning with the 1890s there was a tremendous influx from the southern part of Europe and the Slavic countries.

From 1901 to 1905 almost a million came from Italy; from Russia, more than half a million; from the sprawling empire of Austria-Hungary as it was in those days, almost a million. Just before World War I emigrants from the east and south European countries were making up almost seventy-five per cent of our annual immigration of more than a million.

For the most part these people, or at any rate their children, seem to have been remarkably well assimilated, and their influence on American English cannot be said to be very far-reaching. The greatest ambition of a large part of our immigrants has been "Americanization." Consequently, the languages of the Old World, as well as many of its customs, have been abandoned in a generation or so. Even old names are shed: Czekaj becomes Curtis, Vinciguerra becomes Winwar, Rabinovitch becomes Robbins, Sjöstrand becomes Seashore, Müller becomes Miller—by a variety of processes such as respelling, translation, and phonetic adaptation.

Of the many German loan words in American English, a few, like *semester* and *seminar*, remain on a more or less learned level. Both these words are, of course, ultimately Latin, but they come to us by way of the German university system which provided a model for American postgraduate education for a good many years. *Semester*, originally meaning a term of about six months, is made up of the elements *se-*, a combining form of *sex* "six," and *me(n)stris* "monthly," but, as Professor Kemp Malone has pointed out (*American Speech*, December, 1946), the word does not really fit the American academic year, which is divided by tradition into two four-month, not six-month, terms. Nevertheless, German-trained American scholars and those who were admirers of the German educational system have been responsible for the abandonment of *term* in favour of *semester* in many (probably most) of our colleges and universities. The retention of *semester*, despite its etymological inappropriateness, has been guaranteed by the preference of educational officials for long, pretentious words—a preference which they share with administrators everywhere. Malone has found four lengths not uncommon for the so-called American semester: fifteen, sixteen, seventeen, and eighteen weeks. "In no case, however, does the American semester live up to its name," he states; "it never lasts six months or anything like that length of time." *Semester* has not yet made its way to institutions like Harvard, Yale, and Princeton, or Dartmouth, Amherst, and Williams, but is in the best standing in the

West. It is interesting to note that the Johns Hopkins University, the first institution to be founded in this country as a graduate school and definitely established on the model of the German universities, uses the English rather than the German modification of Latin *seminarium*: there a group of students engaged in advanced study or research under the direction of a professor is known as a *seminary* rather than as a *seminar*.

The larger part of the German element in American English is on a much less rarefied intellectual level, including such homely expressions as *gesundheit*, *bower* (the jack in certain card games), *nix*, and *auf wiedersehen*. Strange as it may seem, an Englishman does not cry *ouch!* when he hits his thumb with a hammer; it is likely that this exclamation of sudden pain has come to us from German. It is highly disputable that *to loaf*, *shyster*, and *bum* (both the noun and the verb) are from German, though origin in that language has frequently been suggested for them. Professor H. B. Woolf has recently unearthed a long-forgotten story of the origin of *shyster* to the effect that it derives from *Scheuster*, the name of a very shady character who practised law in New York around the middle of the nineteenth century. Woolf sets forth the story (*American Speech*, February, 1950) in all modesty merely as "another etymology" of *shyster*. It seems not unlikely that *to loaf* is somehow connected with German *Landläufer* "tramp"; a form *landloafer* occurs in American English in the 1830s, subsequently shortened to *loafer*, of which *to loaf* may be a back formation. *Hinterland* may be responsible, according to Ruth M. Stone, for the very earliest of the *back* compounds in American English. In her Marburg dissertation, *Studien über den deutschen Einfluss auf das amerikanische Englisch* (1934), Dr. Stone suggests that *back lands*, first found in William Penn's writings, may be a translation of this German word, which Penn would have known from his missionary journeys in Germany. It is also possible that American *shoe* for *boot* may have been reinforced by German *Schuh*, and there can be no reasonable doubt that *dumb* in the sense "stupid" is due to German influence, for that is precisely the sense of German *dumm*. The suffix *-fest* comes to American English by way of German, Mencken believes by way of *Sängerfest* and *Turnfest*, both of which he declares were well known in this country as early as the 1850s, though it was not until much later that the suffix was actually tacked on to non-German words, such as *slugfest*, *gabfest*, *songfest*, and a good many others.

Many of the German loans in American English have to do with eating and drinking: *biergarten* (and its translation *beer garden*), *rath-skeller*, *stube* (and the compounds *bierstube* and *weinstube*), *lager*, *bock*, *delicatessen*, *wienerwurst*, *frankfurter*, *hamburger*, *schnitzel*, *liverwurst* (a half-translation of *Leberwurst*), *braunschweiger*, *pumpernickel*, *sauerbraten*, *schweizer*, *pretzel*, *zwieback*. *Wienerwurst* "Vienna sausage" is frequently shortened to *wiener*; the diminutive *wienie* is even more widely used. Similarly, *frankfurter* is reduced to *frank*. *Hamburger* has furnished us with a widely used suffix, *-burger*, which occurs in *cheeseburger*, *chicken-burger*, *turkeyburger*, *nutburger*, *wimpyburger* (from the character in *Popeye*), *onionburger*, *beefburger*, *shrimpburger*, *Spamburger*, and a good many others. The following, though they have won the dignity of print (in *American Speech* and elsewhere), are probably not to be taken too seriously: *bearburger*, *caraburger* (i.e. *carabao burger*), *deerburger*, *huburger* (a hamburger prepared and sold in the Hub Grill, Detroit), *Midgeburger* (in Midge's Grill, Detroit), *steakburger*, *glutenburger*, *radar-burger* (cooked by radar impulses in a *Radarange*), *tinburger* (precooked hamburger, packed in tins), *mooseburger* (served in the mess halls of native schools in Alaska according to an NEA dispatch from Anchor-age), *fishburger*, *wineburger*, *buffaloburger*, *raisinburger*, *potatoburger*, *turtleburger* (encountered in Florida), *wishburger* (sold at a stand located near a "wishing well" in California), *wink-at-the-moon-burger* (featured by a restaurant in Washington, D.C.), and *DiSalleburger* (pictured in *Life*, June 15, 1951). The ultimate horror is undoubtedly the *Truman-burger*, "a layer of mashed baked beans spread between the halves of a bun," the inspiration of a restaurateur in Florida. The *-furter* of *frank-furter* has been considerably less prolific, but it also has progeny in *krautfurter*, *turkeyfurter*, and *shrimpfurter*. In German the suffix in both *hamburger* and *frankfurter* is *-er; -burger* and *-furter* are thus new American English word elements to denote kinds of sandwiches served on rolls or buns. A linguistically enterprising businessman in a Southern university town has gone a step farther in naming his eating establishment, which specializes in such sandwiches, *The Burger House*. *Hot dog* may have been suggested by so-called *hot dachshund* sandwiches which Professor Leo L. Rockwell cites in his "Older German Loan-Words in American English" (*American Speech*, December, 1945) as having been sold to spectators at baseball games in New York. The *Swiss* in *Swiss cheese* is merely a translation of *schweizer*, though I have seen both *Swiss* and *schweizer* cheese sandwiches listed on a single bill of fare. What the difference was (aside from the price, the *schweizer* being no doubt imported and hence more expensive), I was unable to discover. *Sauerkraut, smearcase,* and *noodle* have been treated as earlier loans in Chapter II. Before this gastronomical paragraph is brought to a close, the possibility that American *cookbook* (the British use *cookery book*) is due to the influence of *Kochbuch* should be mentioned.

Yiddish is basically German (the name covers a group of similar High German dialects) with a large number of words from Hebrew and Slavic. It is the native language of a good many Jewish immigrants to this country from countries east of Germany. Its principal contributions to the American vocabulary—in fact, the only ones widely known outside New York City—are *dokus* (or *tochus*) "backside," *kibitzer, kosher, mazuma, shmo* (sometimes written *schmo, smoe*), *shnook, schmalz, schnozzle,* and *phooey. Dokus,* of Hebrew origin, is well known in sections of the country where Yiddish influence is highly unlikely. The word occurs as a Yiddish loan in German, which language might thus have been the medium of transmission in those sections. The same holds true for *mazuma,* whose ultimate origin is quite obscure. *Kosher* "lawful" is Hebrew; it has developed a slang sense "genuine" in American use.

Kibitzer, though almost certainly of Yiddish transmission, is simply German *Kibitz* with the agent suffix -*er. Kibitz,* which means "lapwing" in German, has long been used metaphorically in that language in the sense "meddler." The admirable *schmalz* (or *schmaltz*) for sickeningly sweet music probably comes to us by way of dance-band musicians familiar with Yiddish; the word means "melted fat" in German. There is also an adjectival form *schmalzy* in American English, as in the following report, which appeared recently in *Time,* of the offerings of a certain television station: "For youngsters, there is 'hot' pianist Tommy Sheridan; for oldsters, a schmalzy program of old songs called *Let's Remember.*" Yiddish *schnozzle* "big nose" calls up in most American minds the endearing countenance of the great clown Jimmy Durante, who is of Italian, not Jewish, origin. It is quite likely that *O.K. by me* (instead of the more idiomatic English *with me* or *to me*) is due to Yiddish influence. *Ish kabibble* was widely used as a catch phrase about thirty years ago; it and its supposed translation "I should worry" were popularly regarded as Yiddish. *Phooey (pfui!)* is used in German as an exclamation of disgust or shame, but there can be little doubt of its Yiddish provenance as far as American English is concerned.

Like *phooey, shnook* and its synonym *shmo* (the Kilroy-like Joe Smoe is a derivative) have been popularized fairly recently by radio comedians. It has been suggested that *shnook* may correspond to German *Schnucke* "small sheep," but it is far more likely that these terms of disparagement are merely minced forms of *schmuck* (German *Schmuck* "ornament"), in Yiddish an indecent anatomical term often applied contemptuously to a person. *Shmo* and *shnook* have been freely used by younger-generation speakers of both sexes and all creeds in complete innocence of the phallic suggestiveness which the words have in Yiddish—another instance of what I have elsewhere called innocuous linguistic indecorum.

It is possible that Al Capp's shmoo, the miraculous and lovable little creature who symbolized the earth's productivity, was unconsciously suggested to Mr. Capp by Yiddish *shmo*. It should be pointed out, however, that there is also a *shmoo* (*schmu*) "illicit profit" in Yiddish —a word which is probably of Hebrew origin and which would thus be unrelated etymologically to German *Schmuck* and hence to *shmo*. This word has entered the speech of non-Jewish German businessmen in the phrase *einen Schmu machen* "to make a profit by dishonest means." Although Capp in a radio talk stated that he chose the word *shmoo* only because of the expressivity of its sounds, Leo Spitzer surmises, in *American Speech* for February, 1950, that Yiddish *shmoo* "may have rung in his ears." According to Professor Spitzer, Capp has freed the word from its "ironical connotations . . . and has discovered in it a (secondary) onomatopoeia which made it symbolic of his genuine American optimistic pantheism." It may be so, but it seems at least equally probable that a quite different Yiddishism, the aforementioned *shmo*, may have rung in Mr. Capp's ears without his being aware of the fact.

In addition to *kosher* and *dokus*, a number of less well known words of Hebrew origin are current in American English, in metropolitan areas at any rate: *matzoth* "cakes of unleavened bread," *bar mizvah* "a boy of thirteen, at which age he takes on religious responsibilities; colloquially, the occasion upon which he does so," *goy* "a gentile," *Yehudi* "a Jew" (probably popularized by the catch phrase of a radio comic, "Where's Yehudi?"), and the names of the Jewish holidays *Yom Kippur* and *Rosh Hashana*, though these are probably fairly widely understood in British English also.

Borscht (or *borsch*) "sour beet soup" is Russian, but the word is probably of Yiddish transmission in American English. It occurs in *borscht circuit*, in theatrical parlance a type of show business playing Catskill Mountain summer hotels, where *borscht* is a favourite dish. Another culinary contribution of Yiddish is *gefilte fisch*, but this is actually only a slight alteration of the German past participle *gefüllt* "stuffed" plus *Fisch* "fish."

Although there are many Americans of Scandinavian descent, the Scandinavian languages have contributed little to the American vocabulary. Within the past few years *smörgåsbord* (usually written without the Swedish diacritics) has come to be widely known. Other Swedish terms are in use in Minnesota and neighbouring states where Scandinavians have settled, but these have no general currency; the same is true of Swedish idioms noted in these parts, such as *to cook coffee* and *sour hen* "setting hen" (from Swedish *sura höna*). Dano-Norwegian influence is even slighter, and likewise confined to the Scandinavian settlements in the Middle West.

Americanisms of Italian origin are few and far between. The *Dictionary of American English* lists *macaroni*, with the first citation dated 1802, but the word denoted a strange dish to the writer cited. *Spaghetti* is not listed at all, and it is difficult to determine whether the word has a legitimate claim to be called an Americanism; there can be little doubt, however, that it is much more completely naturalized with us than with the English. The same is probably true of *antipasto*, *ravioli*, *minestrone*, and *pizza*, though these are considerably more exotic to Americans than the very familiar *spaghetti* and, save in Italian restaurants, are seldom encountered by Americans not of Italian descent. Spaghetti has become a staple of the American family's diet; it is thoroughly domesticated and may even be procured ready prepared in cans, its sauce modified, no doubt, according to American taste. *Baloney* "nonsense" is almost certainly from Italian *Bologna*, though its semantic development, unless contamination with *blarney* may be assumed, remains somewhat hazy. It is still categorized as slang, despite its use in public addresses by the late Alfred E. Smith (*baloney dollar*) and Mrs. Clare Boothe Luce (in the blend *globaloney*). The *Mafia* is certainly better known in America than in England. The name of a rival organization, the *Black Hand*, is an Americanism; it is actually a translation of Spanish *mano negra*, having been adopted by the Italians from the name of an anarchistic secret society in Spain.

Though citizens of Irish descent comprise a sizable part of our population, their impact upon American English is probably negligible and certainly difficult to determine. As for individual words, *shanty* may be from Irish (Gaelic) *seantig* "hut," but it is at least equally likely that it is from Canadian French *chantier*, which has the same meaning. It is possible that *slew* "a large number" is from Irish *sluagh*. *Shenanigan* may be Irish, but no phonologically feasible prototype has been adduced for it; its "Irish sound" is probably merely an impression given by the spelling, as Howard Meroney has pointed out (*American Speech*, December, 1947). Professor Spitzer has suggested in the same journal (October–December, 1948), a German etymon in *schinägeln* "to work, especially under strain," a word which may have entered American English by way of lower-class German immigrants; the word is not standard German, but comes from *Rotwelsch*, the argot of pedlars and thieves and other shady characters. It is true that the American word suggests indolence rather than labour, but Spitzer believes that it came in time to denote the tricks employed by the labourer to spare himself exertion, that is, sham activity, "monkey business" indulged in for the purpose of avoiding work. *Phony*, used as either a noun or an adjective, is certainly the noblest contribution of Irish to American English. There seems little reason to doubt that it is a variant of *fawney* (Irish *fáinne* "ring") and grows out of an old confidence game, described thus by Captain Grose in the second edition of his *Classical Dictionary of the Vulgar Tongue* (1788): "A fellow drops a ring, double gilt, which he picks up before the party meant to be cheated, and to whom he disposes of it for less than its supposed, and ten times more than its real, value."

Chow in the slang sense "food" is an Americanism from Chinese Pidgin English *chow-chow*. *Chow mein, chop suey*, and *tong* "a Chinese secret society in the United States" are probably the only other Americanisms of Chinese origin. Japanese has contributed only *hara-kiri* (literally "belly cut"), which appears first in *Harper's Magazine* for March, 1856, *jujitsu*, *Nisei* "a native-born American of Japanese parentage who is loyal to the United States," and the less well known *Issei* and *Kibei*, meaning respectively a Japanese-born resident of the United States who is loyal to his native country and an American-born person of Japanese parentage who goes to Japan for education. These last three words, though doubtless fairly familiar on the West Coast, are not well known in the rest of the country—were hardly known at all, in fact, until the time of World War II. *Ukulele*, taken from

Hawaiian, had a tremendous vogue in the 1920s, when it was frequently clipped to *uke*. The instrument has recently enjoyed a faint revival of popularity.

There is, it should be said, nothing distinctly American in our habit of taking words from other languages, for the English language has in the course of fifteen centuries of development augmented itself tremendously by assimilating into its word stock a mighty host of words from foreign sources. In our own open-door linguistic policy we have simply carried on a common English tradition—a tradition which is in large part responsible for the marvellous richness of the English vocabulary.

NINE

American and British
Word Usages

EXCEPT for the somewhat exaggerated subservience of American speech to the normative influence of the schools, a factor which has given rise to a good many artificialities in pronunciation and syntax in the usage of the self-consciously educated part of the American community, the most notable development of the English language in this country has been in vocabulary. Despite undeniable present differences in all phases of British and American linguistic usage, it is unlikely that there are very many characteristics of American pronunciation and syntax which can be shown to be of American origin or development; there are unquestionably some, but we remain largely in the dark about them for lack of a linguistic atlas of the British Isles.

It is, however, unlikely that there are many features of normal, unaffected American speech which are not traceable to earlier usages in one part or another of Great Britain, a phenomenon clearly demonstrable in the case of a good many American local and regional word usages in the speech of the folk. It is hardly surprising that American developments should be more or less restricted to the rather superficial level of vocabulary when we consider the relatively short time that we have been separated—though never completely isolated—from the mother country. Even Mr. Mencken modified considerably, in the fourth (1936) edition of *The American Language*, the somewhat extreme views which he held in regard to the extent of these differences at the time of the first publication of that work (1919). By the time of the fourth edition he no longer believed that the English of America was diverging so markedly from the English of England as to become a distinct language, though the Anglophobia which is to some extent a humorous literary device with him led him to declare that British

English was becoming so much like American English that in time the Englishman might find himself speaking "a kind of dialect of American."

There is, however, no very convincing evidence for such a belief. It is quite true, of course, that many Americanisms have entered the speech of England, some imperceptibly, some over a great deal of opposition. The transfer, as a matter of fact, began quite early, long before talking films and radio were even thought of. Sir William Craigie states in *The Study of American English* (Oxford, 1927) that although "for some two centuries, roughly down to 1820, the passage of new words or senses across the Atlantic was regularly westwards," practically the only exceptions being words denoting things peculiar to America, "with the nineteenth century . . . the contrary current begins to set in . . . bearing with it many a piece of drift-wood to the shores of Britain." He cites as evidence such importations from America as *backwoods, beeline, blizzard, bluff, logrolling, lumber* "timber," *prairie, shanty, snag, squatter, swamp, bunkum, carpetbagger, caucus, gerrymander, governmental, lynch-law, wire-pulling, bowie knife, cross-cut saw, to strike oil, to make one's pile, ahead of* (in the figurative sense), *at that, to take a back seat, to boom, boss, to catch on, to appreciate* "to rise in value," *balance* "remainder," *to belittle, cloudburst, doughnut, graveyard, loafer, law-abiding,* and *whole-souled.* Even the incomplete material furnished by Thornton's *American Glossary* indicates more than two hundred such borrowings. *To antagonize, to placate, to advocate, lengthy,* and *reliable* all finally found a place in the British word stock despite the terrific lambasting which they had to take from British commentators. It will be noted that many of these words, as well as later borrowings from America like *cafeteria, phonograph,* and *radio* (now about as well known in England as *wireless*) and some of those cited by Craigie, are by no means slangy or colloquial; *whole-souled, law-abiding,* and *to demoralize,* for instance, would occur as a rule only in formal contexts.

There can be no doubt that the enrichment of British English by way of America has been considerably accelerated by such agencies as the movies and radio. Many a Cockney moppet is now able to hiss "Stick 'em up, you mug!" out of the side of his mouth, like Mr. George Raft, or without any perceptible lip-movement, like Mr. Alan Ladd. *The Times* has officially deplored this baleful assault of Hollywood upon the purity of British English, which from a frequently encountered British point of view is "pure" English, all deviations therefrom partaking of the nature of barbarisms. A more liberal English attitude is that of Ernest Weekley, who in his *Adjectives—And Other Words* (New York, 1930) finds it remarkable that his countrymen should have got on so long without *stunt, dope fiend, highbrow*, and *sob stuff*, which last somewhat out-of-date compound, it must be said, most Americans have got on very well without for a number of years. Elsewhere, in his *The English Language* (New York, 1929), Weekley refers to the "eager adoption" by the English of *brass tacks, to cut no ice, live wire* (in the figurative slang sense "alert person"), *to butt in, snag, to pan out, bedrock, to sidetrack, washout, third degree, frame-up*, and *gunman*. H. W. Seaman, another English writer, observed in the *American Mercury* for September, 1933, that *high-hat, hokum, getaway, panties, water-wagon*, and *hangover* are all used in British English, though it should be stated that, with the exception of *panties*, they are by no means common in the daily speech of the man in the street. To these might be added the following, according to H. W. Horwill's *Modern American Usage: filling station, float* "moving platform bearing a display," *to get away with* "to succeed in doing," *fudge* "candy," *to make good* "to succeed," *happening* "event," *jaywalker, layer cake, highbrow, lowbrow, to get a move on, to put over* and *to get over* "to accomplish by shrewdness," *to park, publicity* "advertising," *mass meeting, to rattle* "to unnerve," *to register* (in a hotel), *to round up* and *roundup* (extensions of cowboy lingo), *to shut down* "to close" and *shutdown* "closing (of a factory)," *to turn down* "to refuse," *up against* "confronted with," *up to* "incumbent upon," *wear* in such combinations as *footwear* and *neckwear, to fill the bill, hot air* "windy talk," *to blow in* "to appear," *to feature, fan* "devotee of some game or other form of entertainment," *to cut* "to reduce," *cut* "reduction," and, of course, *O.K.* Somewhat less familiar but still widely known and in fairly wide use in England are *to bank on* "to count on," *bargain counter, begin to* with a negative as in "It does not begin to do justice to . . . ," *to contact, to cover* "to report (journalistic)," *cub* "novice," *to doll up, to step on the gas* "to depress the accelerator" and figuratively "to hurry up," *good and* "thoroughly" (as in "good and hard"), *hard-boiled* "tough," *to hold down* "keep" (as in "to hold down a job"), *to hold up* in the senses "to rob" and "to delay" along with *holdup* as a noun, *horse sense, hot dog, to hustle* "to hurry" (the usual English meaning is "to jostle"), *joy ride, key man, to see the light* "to become convinced," *logrolling* (as a political term), *machine* "party organization," *to soft-pedal, proposition* "affair" (as in "a tough proposition"), *pull* "influence," *punch* "energy," *pep, roughhouse, showdown, to stay put, stung* "cheated," *uplift* "moral exaltation," *to have no use for* "to dislike," and *yes man*.

Horwill furnishes interesting evidence of what Mencken has called "the infiltration of English by Americanisms." During a residence in this country in the early years of the present century he jotted down a good many American linguistic usages that were unfamiliar to him as an Englishman. Many of these expressions were subsequently to become so familiar in England that in 1935 Horwill expressed doubt whether he would have thought of them as originally American had he trusted to his memory alone.

But facts like these—and a good many more might be cited—still do not justify the slightest suspicion that American English will ever supersede British English in England. They simply mean that the British have found a good many American expressions too colourful, useful, or economical to be rejected and have adopted them, frequently with no awareness of their American origin. In far more fundamental respects, such as phonology, intonation, and morphology, it is safe to say that there has been no influence of American on British. It would be difficult to find an Englishman affecting an American accent; there are, on the other hand, a fair number of Americans (they would, of course, constitute only a very insignificant portion of our total population) who try with varying degrees of success to use what they conceive to be a British accent.

In the matter of recent vocabulary, there has indeed been an exchange back and forth, though there can be no question that England has gained more than we have. Obviously, any circumstance that makes for increased communication between the two peoples brings about a wider familiarity with the differentiae of their respective vocabularies. Thus, in the course of two world wars, many of our soldiers found out that *petrol* was the British term for what they had been all their lives calling *gas* (less frequently *gasoline*), and became for the time being almost as familiar with *lorry* as with *truck*, although there was no tendency to adopt the terms. On the other side of the ledger, as reported by *Yank*, the service man's magazine, in its issue of October 7, 1942, "the average Englishman today can tell you without hesitation where the nearest subway station is, where you can find a movie house, whether you can park an automobile here, or how many blocks away the nearest Army gasoline pumps are located." There was a time when the American in England, if he expected to be understood immediately and without condescension, would have had to refer to such things as an *underground station, a cinema, a motorcar* and a *petrol station. Blocks* would probably have been interpreted to mean *blocks of flats* (in America, *apartment houses*). According to *Yank*, it was no longer necessary in 1942 to ask the telephone operator for "Directory enquiry, please": "Information, please" was readily understood, and "Exchange nine-four hundred" did just as well as "Exchange nine-four-double O." "Some quick-witted hello girls even go so far now as to tell a Yank 'Here's your party,' rather than 'You're through, sir.' " The author speculates that "Hi-Yo Silver! Away!" may in time supplant "Tallyho!" in British English, but this seems to be going rather too far.

On the other hand, the American levy upon the British vocabulary has been considerably less extensive. H. W. Seaman, in the *American Mercury* article already alluded to, cites *swank, spoof, to click* "to be successful," *to tell off*, and *to tick off* as Briticisms in American use. There are others, of course, such as *shop, dressing gown,* and *dinner jacket* if they can indeed be called Briticisms. When we come to a listing of differentiae, we shall see that a good many supposed Briticisms are actually in fairly wide use in the United States. It is likely that many of them have been used as variants in American English for so long and to such an extent that they should not be regarded as Briticisms at all, if indeed they ever were so regarded by their users. Expressions thought of as characteristically British—for instance, *jolly* and *bloody* as intensifiers, *cheerio* and *righto*—have certainly had no vogue at any time in American English, and Mencken is fully correct when he declares in *The American Language* that such words would strike "most members of the American Legion as almost as unmanly as *tummy* or *pee-pee*" (p. 265). There are, of course, a good many borderline cases.

The differences in vocabulary and idiom are none the less sufficiently great that few English writers (P. G. Wodehouse is a notable exception) are able to reproduce American speech with any degree of accuracy. These differences usually occur, however, on a comparatively simple level of communication and for the most part consist of names of concrete objects. The more abstract or philosophical the subject matter of speech, the fewer the differences in word choice are likely to be. It is, as a matter of fact, principally in slang and in specialized vocabularies that we notice very striking differences. In the specialized language of motoring, for instance, the folding top of a car is in England called the *hood*; what Americans call the *hood* is in England the *bonnet*. Similarly, British *gear lever* corresponds to American *gearshift*, *first speed* to *low gear*, *dynamo* to *generator*, *accumulator* to *battery*, *sparking plug* to *spark plug*, *windscreen* to *windshield*, *wing* (or *mudguard*) to *fender*, *silencer* to *muffler*, *dickey* to *rumble seat*, *saloon car* (or simply *saloon*) to *sedan*, and *two-seater* to *roadster*. *Carburettor* is so spelled by the British, who pronounce the *e* as in *get*. American spelling usually employs only a single *t*, the last two syllables of the word practically always rhyming with *freighter*. Although *automobile* (with its abbreviation *auto*) is perfectly well known to the English, the word seems to have made little headway among them in actual use, except in the names of the Automobile Association (the A.A.) and the Royal Automobile Club (the R.A.C.). The usual British term is *motor-car*, or simply *car*. *Motor-car* is quite familiar in America, though seldom used; *car*, however, is very common, perhaps even more usual nowadays than *automobile*, which remains the formal term. Horwill is surely in error when he cites *autoist* as the usual American equivalent of British *motorist*, for *motorist* is by far the commoner term in America; *autoist* is rarely if ever heard. Similar differences occur in the vocabulary of sports, of the various trades and professions, of shopping, and of transportation. The two last-named activities, common to American and British travellers, have perhaps given many an exaggerated notion of vocabulary differences in British and American English.

Regrettable as the fact may be to sturdy linguistic patriots in our midst, a group of Briticisms which have connotations of swank for Americans have gained a firm footing in this country. *Dressing gown*, for instance, must be almost as frequent by now as *bathrobe*, particularly since the writers of "slick" advertising copy, aided and abetted by Hollywood, have made of the garment a glamorous appurtenance of masculine attire; the thick, fuzzy, blanket-like "bathrobes" worn for warmth in the days before American women demanded that "their" houses should always be overheated have given way to silk, rayon, or lightweight flannel "dressing gowns." *Tuxedo* has given ground in America to *dinner jacket*, though it should be noted that American clothing salesmen tend to use *dinner jacket* for the white garment worn in the summer and call the more conventional black jacket a *tuxedo*. Perhaps the awful vulgarity of *tux* (or even *tuck*), which was current among the seedier class of collegians in the 1920s and 1930s to designate the cheap, satin-lapelled, ready-made, frequently hired suit has played some part in the change to *dinner jacket*, now felt by many Americans (or at any rate by their wives) to be more refined. *Esquire* has for a long time carried notices of *braces* (suspenders), and in a single advertisement in the *New Yorker* (March 11, 1950) a "master cravatier" offers *cravats* (probably a genteelism rather than a Briticism), *braces*, and *sock suspenders* (men's garters) for sale at impressively high prices. A change in fashion has made the widely publicized distinction between British *boot* and American *shoe* practically obsolete, inasmuch as only policemen, firemen, soldiers, and elderly gentlemen with wobbly ankles wear what the English used to call *boots*, that is, footwear fastening over the ankle. As this type of footwear has gone out of fashion, so has the word denoting it; *shoe*, the ordinary British as well as American term for a low-cut boot, is thus the word used for the footwear now ordinarily worn in towns and cities by men in both countries. With the obsolescence of the foot covering which laced or buttoned above the ankle, if only a little above, the Englishman has few occasions to use *boot* except in the sense in which it is also used by Americans, that is, to designate an article of footwear which reaches at least to within a few inches of the knee, such as a riding boot.

Other differences in word use have received a great deal of attention from British and American commentators, some of them far more than their actual importance seems to justify, so that by now most of us are perfectly well aware that what in America is called an *elevator* is in England called a *lift*, and that, whereas an American, when not using a belt for the purpose, holds up his *pants* with *suspenders*, or even with *galluses* if he is a very old-fashioned man of rural upbringing, an Englishman holds his *trousers* up with *braces* and uses *suspenders* for his socks.

Comparative lists, with British word usages on one side of the page and their American equivalents on the other, are interesting to read, but sometimes misleading in the impression which they give. Such lists can be very impressive, nevertheless, because of their sheer bulk. Sometimes, however, their items may not actually represent general use, though there is a great deal of disagreement among commentators on both sides of the Atlantic as to what constitutes general use. Certainly some of the entries on the American side of most such lists are widely known in England (some are even in fairly wide use there), just as a good many of the expressions labelled *British* are known and used in America. Frequently it is simply a matter of degree—a question of a word or a phrase being somewhat more familiar in one country than in the other. As we have seen, American English has preserved a number of older British usages which have never quite gone out of use in England; some of these have indeed re-entered British English by way of America, to be much more widely used in England than the compilers of differential word lists lead one to suspect. Likewise, regional and local usages vary a good deal in this country, and a good many supposed Briticisms are in wide use in particular sections of the United States, even though they may not be known in Chicago, Omaha, or Los Angeles; as has been pointed out earlier, *sidewalk* is the usual term in most parts of America for that part of a street reserved for pedestrians; yet in the large and culturally important Philadelphia trade area *pavement* is practically the only term used, precisely as in British English. To cite another instance, one must not infer from such a list that *mailman* is always used in America for what the English call a *postman*, for the fact is that many Americans use *postman*. What is true is that *mailman* is more widely used in America than *postman*, not that *postman* is British and *mailman* (or *letter carrier*) American. Many American speakers, however, including the present writer, never use *mailman*, though it is safe to say that few Americans use *post* for *mail* as in British English "Has the post arrived yet?" or as a verb, as in "to post a letter." It should be noted that *postman* is at least sufficiently common in American use that Hollywood did not find it necessary to change the title of James M. Cain's novel *The Postman Always Rings Twice* when it was filmed. Some of the national differences in vocabulary are, indeed, no more striking than local and regional differences existing within the United States.

Lists of equivalents invariably include (the British or supposed British equivalent is given first in the pairs to be cited) *boot/shoe*, *shop/store*, and *flat/apartment*. The status of the first two pairs has been discussed elsewhere; it might be added, however, that *flat*, which is in fairly wide use in American English, frequently denotes living quarters somewhat less spacious than does *apartment*, which usually denotes a suite of rooms among other suites in the same building. Equally questionable as national variants, despite the fact that some of them appear in the Army's *Short Guide to Great Britain* (1942), are *return ticket/round-trip ticket*, *bath/bathtub*, *wallet/billfold*, *funny bone/crazy bone*, *snack/lunch, chest of drawers/bureau* (the commercial term *dresser*, though offensive to many Americans, is also used), *lounge suit/business suit, cupboard/closet, Christian name/given name, nursing home/hospital* (private), *whiskey and soda/highball, rubbish/junk, life-belt/life preserver, timber/ lumber, letter box/mailbox, perhaps/maybe, parcel/package, tie/necktie, puncture/flat, lodger/roomer, timetable/schedule, shoelace/shoestring, kipper/ smoked herring, tap/spigot* (or *faucet*, depending upon the region), *neat* (of drink)/*straight*, and *wastepaper basket/wastebasket*. In every one of these pairs, the first term, usually labelled British, is perfectly well known to Americans; the second term in many, though not in all, is perfectly well known to the British, though it may not be much used by them. In actual fact, some of the supposedly British terms are in fairly wide use in this country. *Wallet* is now about as common as *billfold*; the same is true of *snack, cupboard, whiskey and soda, funny bone, rubbish, perhaps, tie,* and *kipper*. The others occur perhaps only in the usage of a cultivated minority, but they are all understood. Only one calls for comment, *closet*, which is avoided by the English in the sense "cupboard" because it suggests to them *water closet*—a term practically archaic in America, having been supplanted by *toilet* and a good many less polite terms.

There are, of course, a great many expressions used in British English which are never used in America. Some of them, in fact, would not even be generally understood in this country. *Perambulator*, with its contracted form *pram*, is well known to us through our reading of English books, though an American would no more use it for *baby carriage* than he would call a *billboard* a *hoarding* or a *water heater* a *geyser. Chemist's shop* as the British equivalent of *drug store* is a stock Briticism, widely known in America as a "curiosity" but never used even by the most egregious Anglophiles.

Also little known in America, and certainly never used here, are *draughts* (checkers), *leader* and *leading article* (editorial), *cotton wool* (absorbent cotton), *wood wool* (excelsior), *flex* (extension cord), *dustbin* (ash can, garbage can), *dustman* (garbage man), *trunk call* (long-distance call), *treacle* (molasses, syrup for human consumption; the English use *molasses* to designate a syrup used in animal feeds), *white wax* (paraffin), *paraffin* (kerosene, also called *coal oil* in America), *ticket-of-leave* (parole), *kiosk* (newsstand), *potato crisp* (potato chip), *public house* or *pub* (drinking place), *char-à-banc* (sightseeing bus), *ladder* (run in a stocking), *bowler* (derby or derby hat), *boater* (straw hat with hard, flat crown and brim), *sleeping partner* (silent partner), *reel* (spool of thread), *vegetable marrow* (squash), *call box* (telephone booth), and *drawing pin* (thumbtack).

The fact that the same word or phrase may have different senses in America and England may sometimes be attended with embarrassing consequences, as when a demure English girl travelling in this country replied, in answer to a polite query whether she had slept well the night before, that she would have done so had she not been knocked up so early in the morning by one of the young men in her party. *To knock up*, which means "to get with child" in American low colloquial use (the phrase is also well known to most educated males), may mean simply "to arouse from sleep" in British English. (Jos Sedley's declaration in *Vanity Fair* that he would marry Becky Sharp even if he had to "knock up the Archbishop of Canterbury at Lambeth" to do so is always bound to give rise to prurient undergraduate sniggers in American classrooms.) Similarly, the British colloquial use of *screw* "wages" (as in "a poor screw," "a weekly screw") and of *to screw* "to stint" (as in Wyld's illustrative example in the *Universal Dictionary*, "the old curmudgeon had screwed all his life") might meet with a somewhat less than cordial reception in the chaster circles of American society. For reasons which are doubtless equally obvious to the American reader, colloquial *pecker* "courage," frequent in British English, as in "to keep one's pecker up," is not used in most types of American English. The British metaphorical use of *ass* "silly fellow," although well known in this country, has ribald suggestions for most Americans, since in American English *arse* "buttocks" is homophonous with it.

Equally unhappy, from the British point of view, is the American familiar use of *bum* for "tramp" or in any of its derivative senses, inasmuch as the word means "backside" in British English and is hence somewhat inappropriate to the drawing room. To say that a person has "plenty of spunk" or is "full of spunk" would cause some degree of consternation in present-day English society, though the Scots use *spunk* in the same sense which it has in America. No American ever uses *bloody* in the shocking English sense—or rather lack of sense, for no one seems to know precisely what it means: the *Universal Dictionary* defines it as a "low, vulgar, blasphemous epithet; also meaningless adjective much used among very low persons." But for an American in England to refer to an automobile accident which he had witnessed as a "bloody mess" would show a regrettable lack of social and linguistic tact. *Bug*, which in American popular use may name practically any insect, sometimes extending its meaning to include bacilli as well, is defined in a representative dictionary of British usage (Wyld's *Universal*) as "a nasty, flat, ill-smelling, verminous, wingless insect, genus *Cimex*, found in dirty houses and furniture," that is, what is called a *bedbug* in America. The American guest in an English house would therefore be well advised not to refer to flies, gnats, midges, and other comparatively decorous flying creatures as *bugs*, but rather as *insects*, which is also used in American English. But it is obvious that *bug*, long a shibboleth word, has lost much of its disgusting connotation in British English, if we may judge by the headline *The Bug Is Boss* which recently appeared in the London *Daily Express* (quoted by *Time*, February 12, 1951), referring to the "influenza bug."

Practically all literate Americans are quite well aware that the English *public school* corresponds roughly to the American private boarding school, usually called in America a *preparatory* (or *prep*) school; thus, Eton, Rugby, Winchester, and Harrow are public schools, though all are expensive and to a large extent exclusive. The American *public school* corresponds to the English *council school* or *board school*. The English use *preparatory school* to designate what in America is called the *elementary school*; it prepares pupils for the public school (in the British sense), not for the university. Other scholastic terminology differs considerably in the two countries. The term *grade* as used in American elementary schools is an Americanism corresponding roughly in meaning to British *form*, used also in many of our private preparatory schools. Horwill points out that a class (first, second, or third) in Oxford or Cambridge is a division in which one is placed after successfully passing an honours examination. To say that two university men were in the same class means to an Englishman not merely that they graduated in the same year, but that they were placed in the same status (or class) in the same honours examination in the same year. Incidentally, *sophomore, junior*, and *senior* are not in use in England to denote respectively students in the second, third, and fourth year of their university career as in America, where the words have extended their scope to include even high-school pupils. The complicated academic hierarchy of the American college or university, with its assistants, instructors, assistant professors, adjunct professors, associate professors, and full professors, is little known and less understood by the English, to whom *professor* indicates a somewhat more rarefied personage than many American teachers bearing the title either by courtesy or legitimately with one modification or another. The American use of *professor* as a title preceding the name of the principal of a high school (though it was likely to be conferred upon any male pedagogue of mature years) is practically obsolete nowadays save in the more remote sections. It was formerly also a courtesy title of male teachers of music, piano players in the tonier New Orleans brothels (the late, great "Jelly Roll" Morton was once a "professor" in this sense), orchestra leaders, conjurers, and acrobats. The aeronaut who during all the years of my boyhood made a parachute jump from a balloon at the county fair held in my native town was always billed as Professor Mike Jacobson.

It would be possible to pile up many more examples of vocabulary differentiae, but the reader, if he is interested in pursuing the matter further, will find plenty of examples in the books by Mencken and Horwill, though these valuable works must be used with some exercise of judgment based on his own observation. He will most probably conclude that many of the differentiae are quite insignificant, like American *bakery*/British *baker's shop*, Am. *toilet*/Br. *lavatory*, Am. *living room*/Br. *sitting room*, and Am. *stairway*/Br. *staircase*; it is also likely that he will be quite aware of the fact that the second term in the last three of these pairs is indeed in fairly wide use in America, even though the first may be the more common.

To summarize, it is in specialized languages such as those of travel, sports, trades, and professions that we notice the most striking differences in word choice in the two countries. On the level of slang the differences are likewise considerable. But a great deal of the current slang of American teen-agers is incomprehensible to their own elders; and among teen-agers themselves there is considerable variation from section to section, and even from social class to social class. It is thus not particularly surprising that much American slang is incomprehensible to the Englishman, and that British slang is at least equally mystifying to the American. Misunderstanding, real or pretended, of an American interviewer's reference to him as "a regular guy," which would mean in British English "a thoroughly grotesque person," furnished the late G. K. Chesterton with a good anecdote; in educated use, however, genuine occurrences of this type of international ambiguity must be rather rare.

It is on such levels, however, that the "quaint" usages beloved of the lay linguist are most likely to occur, and it is easy to give an exaggerated impression of their importance. There is considerable temptation for writers to play down the essential oneness of American and British English. As a matter of fact, in the intellectual reaches of language the differences are practically nonexistent. It should be obvious that a great deal depends upon who is doing the talking (or writing), what the occasion is, and what is being talked (or written) about.

TEN

American Pronunciation

I. GENERAL CHARACTERISTICS

ALTHOUGH Americans are still conscious of the very apparent differences between British pronunciation and their own manner of speaking, they have grown increasingly tolerant of British speech. Yet many of us can remember a time, no longer than twenty-five or thirty years ago, when standard British English—that type of English pronunciation called variously Received Standard, Received Pronunciation, and Southern British English—was commonly regarded in this country as somewhat affected, not to say downright effeminate. Now, however, we have become so accustomed to it in the talking films and on the radio—both of them agencies which, with all their artistic shortcomings, have certainly mitigated American linguistic provincialism—that we take it very much in our stride. Sometimes we even regard this type of British English with a sort of sneaking admiration, for there is a widespread notion among Americans, many of whom suffer from a sort of national linguistic inferiority complex, that even uneducated English people speak better than we do, whatever "speaking better" means.

Differences between American and British pronunciation are far more subtle and elusive than mere variation in the treatment of certain speech sounds such as the postvocalic *r* or in the pronunciation of individual shibboleth words like *schedule, lieutenant, laboratory,* and *clerk.* More sharply distinctive, if less often noted, is intonation. Actually the English pronunciation of an overwhelming majority of individual words does not differ markedly from the American—a fact frequently overlooked by the lay observer, who is looking only for differences; even the Englishman's supposedly characteristic pronunciation of the sound indicated by *a* in words of the *path, glass, staff* type, his slightly rounded vowels in words like *stop, god, clock*, and his treatment of postvocalic *r* do not differ, as a matter of fact, from the practice of many Americans—for instance, eastern New Englanders, who may have every one of these characteristics. An Iowan or a Nebraskan with a fair ear for speech sounds can learn to pronounce broad *a* in those words in which the speaker of standard British English has this sound in distinction to the flat *a* heard in most varieties of American speech; he can, with assiduous practice, learn to omit *r* before consonant sounds or when it is final; he may even acquire the "flapped" *r* between vowels to be heard in the Englishman's pronunciation of *America, very, sorry*, and the like; he can remember to say *shedule* (for *schedule*), *diction'ry, labórat'ry, leftenant, eevolution*, and to rhyme *mobile* and *fertile* with *mile*; he can, in fact, acquire all the characteristics of British pronunciation so far as individual speech sounds go. But, unless he is sufficiently acute to be able to counterfeit British intonation convincingly, he will deceive no one who has ever listened discerningly to genuine British speech.

For, though the words may be the same, the music is strikingly different. And it is this fact primarily which makes British speech sometimes quite difficult for the American to understand, just as the distinctive intonation of American English sometimes baffles the Englishman. Of course, real unintelligibility is seldom involved any more; it would be more accurate merely to say that the foreign flavour of British speech to the American and of American speech to the Englishman is due largely to these differences in intonation, or pitch variation in speech. In singing, where the stresses and the tune are set by the composer, what is called an "accent" is hardly noticeable, so that to determine whether a singer is English or American is sometimes not possible. Singers in English dance bands sing Tin Pan Alley creations in what often seems to the American listener to be perfectly good American English. Usually they are not trying to do so. Conversely, there is little or nothing that incontrovertibly indicates the American origin of most of our native singers of popular songs of the sentimental or impassioned variety, though their regional and social origins are evident enough when they indulge in supposedly witty chit-chat with masters of ceremonies and announcers. If the singer has learned to omit preconsonantal and final *r*'s and to pronounce broad *a*—tricks which even untrained vocalists often acquire—then the chances of identifying him by nationality become practically infinitesimal.

There are, of course, regional, local, and even social variations in intonation within both American and British English. The speech tune of a Bostonian is different from that of a Chicagoan, even somewhat different from that of a New Yorker; similarly, the intonation patterns of Liverpool or Manchester are not precisely those of London. But these are slight as compared with those intonational variations which unmistakably mark off the speech of the American from that of the Englishman—variations so noticeable as sometimes to cause mutual irritation, though fortunately this is much less frequent nowadays than formerly.

The tempo of speech is more or less an individual matter, depending to a large extent upon the intellectual make-up of the speaker and to some extent upon his familiarity with what he happens to be talking about: a person of a slow, deliberative habit of mind is likely to phrase his thoughts in a slow and deliberative manner; the man of volatile temperament whose mind functions rapidly, though not necessarily profoundly, is likely to speak rapidly. Both probably speak more rapidly than normally when excited either by external circumstances or by keen interest in the subject they are discussing. It is also doubtless true that when a speaker is talking about what he likes to talk about—presumably also what he knows something about—he is likely to speak somewhat more rapidly than when his interest in his subject is only mild and his knowledge of it uncertain. It is, nevertheless, widely believed in this country that Englishmen speak more rapidly (in "clipped tones," of course) than Americans. It is most likely that nationality has nothing to do with the tempo of speech; the Britisher seems to be "rattling away" at a terrific rate because his speech is in some respects—principally in intonation—strange to us. There is also a widespread American belief that Southerners speak more slowly than Yankees: the truth would seem to be that some of them do and some of them don't. Much has been made of the Southern "drawl," but the quality described by the word has been attributed and the word itself applied to the speech of New Englanders, as, for example, when Noah Webster in his *Dissertations* enjoined the New England "yeoman" to improve his "drawling nasal manner of speaking."

Along with the "drawl," which certainly must denote a slow speech tempo, whatever else it may mean, the American "twang" has frequently been commented upon. It is difficult to know precisely what characteristic of American speech this word describes. Probably it originally denoted nasality, but frequently it seems to have a much more inclusive meaning. In any case, it is certain that most Englishmen, and many Americans as well, believe that American speech is excessively nasal—in fact, that Americans "talk through their noses." There is some slight justification for the notion, particularly in Midwestern and Western speech, and there was doubtless even more in former times in all sections of the country. But the meaning of terms like *drawl* and *twang* is sometimes very difficult to pin down.

Similarly, British English is often referred to, usually with approval, as "clipped," which is not much less vague than the American "drawl" and "twang," though it seems clear that "clipping" is sometimes conceived of as the antithesis of "drawling." Sometimes *crisp* is also used as descriptive of British speech; apparently it denotes the same qualities as *clipped*. These terms, unsatisfactory as they are because of their subjectivity, nevertheless do mean something, or at any rate have meant something. Perhaps the "clipped" quality of British speech to American ears is due to the Englishman's pronunciation of *t* between vowels (as in *water, butter, later*) as a voiceless alveolar stop, in contrast to the widespread American pronunciation of this sound as something very like a *d*. It is likely, too, that the "flapped" *r* between vowel sounds used by some speakers of British English plays some part in the American impression of British speech as "clipped" or "crisp." But this is a rather slight justification for so sweeping a description as is implied by the words. Perhaps the Englishman's strong (from an American point of view, frequently excessive) stressing of accented syllables, occasionally at the expense of unaccented syllables, as in his pronunciation of such words as *library* and *medicine* as *lybry* and *medsin*, gives a "clipped" effect to some hearers. It is possible, too, that his preference for a short *ĭ* sound in the second syllable of *telegraph*, *telephone, animal*, and the like, in all of which American English prefers the so-called "murmur" vowel indicated by the symbol ə (schwa) in the alphabet of the International Phonetic Association, has something to do with this impression of "clippedness." But all such subjective terminology, let it be said again, is really quite unsatisfactory for the description of speech.

No one with the ability to hear, however, can doubt that American intonation, as compared with British, tends to be monotonous (the word is of course used here only in the sense "having a narrow pitch range"). It is on the whole more deliberate, and frequently seems intent upon giving to each syllable what is thought to be its proper value, in

M

contrast to British English, with its marked risings and fallings, its stronger stresses, and its consequent scanting (from the American point of view) of unstressed syllables, as in a word like *extraordinary*, in which the Englishman stresses the *-or-* and seems to be taking the rest in a sort of running jump.

This American tendency to give what is apparently felt to be its due regard to each and every syllable may well be a survival of older British usage. It has been suggested, indeed, that the deliberate and measured articulation of American English, as well as the nasalization which is still to some extent characteristic of it, may originally have been a Puritan affectation. There is some reason to believe that, along with speaking "i' the nose," the English Puritans of the seventeenth century cultivated a singsong manner of speaking which was doubtless thought, by themselves at least, to give an impression of superior piety. Nicholas Cresswell, an Englishman who spent some time in this country in the 1770s, referred to an indescribable "whining cadence" which characterized the speech of New Englanders of that day; it was the sole local peculiarity which he observed in American speech and may well have been a survival of older usage among the English Puritans. Webster, who certainly did not in the least disapprove of the development of Puritanism which flourished in his day, must have had no suspicion of any such origin, for he speaks disapprovingly in his *Dissertations* of "that drawling, whining cant that distinguishes a certain class of people." He is obviously referring to a type of pronunciation current in his native western New England.

The Puritan origin of American intonation is an attractive theory, and one wishes that it were capable of proof. It has also been pointed out that our intonation resembles that of the north of England much more closely than that of the more fashionable type of English spoken in the south of England, which is frequently thought of in this country, quite mistakenly, as being the speech of all England. It is not likely that Captain Marryat's explanation of American intonation was ever widely accepted in this country: "the Americans dwell upon their words when they speak—a custom arising, I presume, from their cautious, calculating habits; and they have always more or less of a nasal twang." When the gallant sailor-novelist asked an American lady why she drawled, she replied in a burst of not altogether uncommendable linguistic patriotism, "Well, I'd drawl all the way from Maine to Georgia, rather than clip my words as you English people do."

It was long ago noted that Americans talked "by the book." Perhaps occasional statements in the eighteenth century to the effect that the educated colonists used "better" English than those who stayed at home may indicate nothing more than that American pronunciation even in those days tended to follow spelling. It is likely that most of the commentators were also favourably impressed by the comparative uniformity of American English. Some of them, in fact, mention it. But, aside from this notable uniformity, one wonders what other objective standard they might have had, the state of linguistic knowledge being what it was in their day. Perhaps they were favourably impressed by a type of articulation which seemed to them superior in its clarity because it conformed to written language.

There can be no doubt that to the American school tradition must be attributed some of the dubious credit (dubious from a historical and aesthetic point of view, at any rate) for the deliberate articulation of American English. Unquestionably much of it survives, as has been suggested previously, from earlier British practice, particularly that of the northern part of England and the lowlands of Scotland. Deliberate, monotonous speech may result from factors other than the attempt to follow a written standard: but the consciousness of such a standard may well bring with it an overcareful and overprecise manner of speech which a great many speakers no doubt think of as somehow "purer" and more "correct" than the more volatile, dashing, and devil-may-care usage of a society based upon hereditary aristocracy. And it might indeed be argued that it is more truly democratic to follow a written standard than to imitate in servile fashion the usage of those who speak according to an ancient tradition, for with a written standard "good" speech is within the reach of even the commonest man.

It is likely indeed that the long and widespread use of Noah Webster's *Spelling Book* in its myriad editions, with its emphasis upon syllabication and its injunction to the pupil to give to each syllable its "true value," has tended to check any tendency in America towards such rakish pronunciations as the Englishman's *litracha* (*literature*) and *medsin*. In any event, educated American pronunciation, while lacking tonal and accentual variety, has gained somewhat in clarity and distinctness. The American actually says "How do you do?" not "Howjado?" or "Jado?" He never pronounces *immediate* as *immejit*, as many British speakers do; rather, he seems to be treating each syllable of the word with loving care. He may even scorn to say anything so seemingly careless as *ejacate* (*educate*), and take especial pains to say *ed-you-cate*, as I have heard speakers do.

Nevertheless, pronunciations based upon spelling, when these involve a change in the traditional pronunciation of a word in popular use, are a pretty sure indication not only of a spiritual arrogance which it is difficult to admire in the abstract but also of an ignorance of the relationship between writing and language. Persons who do not understand this relationship are likely to conclude that, inasmuch as *forehead* is so spelled and means "the fore part of the head," it should be spoken as *fore head*—a conclusion which involves the assumption that all previous speakers who have pronounced the word *forid* were speaking incorrectly. Such assumptions must necessarily be common to those who set themselves to speak better than their fellows.

Now when people lack an oral tradition for the pronunciation of a given word, they certainly cannot be blamed if they pronounce that word as the spelling seems to indicate it should be pronounced. In such a case spelling is our only guide. And this is the procedure regularly followed when we come upon learned polysyllables which we mentally pronounce in the course of our reading —words which we never actually speak, but which, if we did, we should pronounce as spelled. There is absolutely no reason why Americans should have an oral tradition governing the pronunciation of such words as *Cholmondeley, Beaulieu,* and *retch* (pronounced in British English *Chumley, Bewley,* and *reech*), since these are not words in common use in America. But consciously to change the pronunciation of a word one has used since first learning to talk—words like *often* and *forehead*—is quite another matter. These are words for which we once possessed a tradition. The abandonment of that tradition, where it has been abandoned, was due in the beginning to a habit of mind which seems to be particularly common in America. This is not of course to suggest that writing has not played a part in the development of all languages which have been reduced to writing; here, as elsewhere, we are concerned with a matter of degree.

Regarding themselves as the rightful custodians of linguistic propriety, and sincerely convinced that "their" language was rapidly deteriorating in America, British observers have for years descanted upon what seemed to them to be the "barbarity" of American English. Although there have been a few outstanding exceptions, most of these commentators have been quite honestly of the opinion that, because on the one hand it has lost some of the older traditions of British English and on the other hand has failed to acquire some of the more recent ones, American English is a corrupt and degenerate language. It should be said that the severest strictures have come from men with little or no consciousness of the fact of linguistic development, men to whom the idea never occurred that American English might be expected to develop somewhat differently from British English.

But there is, as has been observed, another side to the picture. Although we may lack a tradition for the pronunciation of such words as *Glamis* and *Marjoribanks* and *St. John* (as *glahmz*, *marchbanks*, and *sinjun* respectively), we have acquired a tradition of our own—a highly literate tradition inculcated by generations of schoolmasters and schoolmarms, part of whose stock in trade is knowing how the language should be spoken and written. Ironically enough, though the schoolteacher is thought to be in possession of the arcana of linguistic elegance, he is actually little regarded in other lines of endeavour: his opinions in matters of English usage are sought and deferred to as "authoritative" by business and professional men whose attitude towards him in other circumstances would inevitably be patronizing. But the fact remains that the influence of the schools must ever be reckoned with in any examination of the English of America, for the layman has complete and unadulterated confidence in the supposed sources of linguistic information which teachers are thought to be in possession of—sources in which he has infinitely more faith than he has in his own observation of the actual usage of those who speak the language. It is an ironical fact that in this great democratic nation, authority, not usage, has come to be the guiding principle of language for practically all Americans who have ever been to school. Even though he may be deemed a babe in the wood in regard to the affairs of practical life, it is widely, practically universally, held that in the matter of linguistic propriety ("correct English"), "teacher knows best."

Educated American English is thus by no means free and easy-going, daring and independent, as it is flattering to our patriotism to believe; it is if anything overcareful and precise, indeed almost "prissy" in its concern for what are thought of as standards. Such pronunciations as *obey*, *possessed*, and *occasion* with the vowel of the first syllable pronounced as *oh* (instead of the "murmur vowel") and *efficient* and

effective with the first syllable as *ee*, though not unknown in a certain
type of British oratory, indicate what would seem to most speakers
of British English an unnecessary and uncalled-for precision in language. Some American students of speech, it must be said, would
consider such pronunciations instances of semiliterate formal usage.
Nevertheless, a good many pronunciations cited by Professor J. S.
Kenyon in his valuable "Cultural Levels and Functional Varieties of
English" (*College English*, October, 1948) as semiliterate formal—*sun
day* for *Sunday* instead of the *sundy* more usual in cultivated speech,
president with the final syllable clearly pronounced as *dent*, *coalumbia*
for *Columbia*—are by no means unusual in the speech of those who have
gone through college and even graduate school. There can be little
question that the attitude toward language which has given birth to
such artificialities has made considerably more headway in this country
than in England.

Spelling pronunciations must certainly be regarded as, among
other things, clearly indicative of a subservience to the linguistic
attitudes and standards inculcated by the schools. As has been shown
elsewhere, although such pronunciations are gaining ground somewhat in British English, they are of particularly frequent occurrence in
American English. So little is traditional pronunciation regarded when
it seems to depart from what is indicated by spelling that words like
parliament (a fancy spelling for a word of Old French origin, spelled
parlement in that language and in Middle English) and *comptroller* (an
equally flashy Latinized spelling of *controller*) are frequently pronounced as spelled by highly literate and even by distinguished people.
The spelling pronunciation of the latter word is, in fact, so common
that one wonders why it is not recorded in the dictionaries, though
none which I have consulted indicates any other pronunciation than
controller. *Comp-troller* is, however, in no sense an ignorant pronunciation, linguistically naïve though it may be; it is in fact the usual
pronunciation of the title of an important financial officer in many of
our universities.

It is doubtless true that American English lacks a tradition for the
pronunciation of *Anthony*, a name which was not often bestowed
upon American males until the comparatively recent craze for supposedly swank "British" Christian names, like *Stephen*, *Peter*, *Michael*,
etc., in this country. The traditional pronunciation *antony* (whence
the nickname *Tony*), still current in England, is so rare in America

that one wonders why the dictionaries bother to record it as an American pronunciation. Even *Mark Antony* is frequently pronounced by the educated, if not the highly cultivated, with medial *-th-*. Now in the lack of any tradition in regard to the pronunciation of this word, to pronounce it as spelled is a perfectly reasonable and natural thing to do. Both *author* and *anthem* contain the same fancy spelling of *t*, and in both these words the standard pronunciation has had the *th* sound in British and American English for a very long time. A similar misinterpretation of spelling is evidenced in the pronunciation of *Waltham, Eltham, Gotham,* and the like, in which the suffixal force of *-ham* (as in *Buckingham, Birmingham*) was at one time felt; in time, however, the *t* and the *h* were mistakenly regarded as occurring in the same syllable, with the consequence that the words came to be pronounced with the medial consonant sound of *Luther*. The pronunciations *waltum* and *eltum* (with loss of *h* due to lack of stress on the final syllable) survive in British use, though pronunciations with medial *-th-*, originally blunders, are widely current as variants. Only *got 'em* is current for the town of *Gotham* in Nottinghamshire—a pronunciation never heard from Americans when they employ the word as a nickname for New York City.

Pride born of a misguided attitude towards spelling—an attitude most likely to thrive in a period of widespread partial literacy—must be held responsible for changing the pronunciation of common, everyday words like *often*, for which a traditional pronunciation *offen* has long been current. Pronunciation of this word with *-t-* is to be heard in British English, it must be noted, and is presumably in perfectly good standing; it is recorded as a variant in both Daniel Jones's *English Pronouncing Dictionary* and H. C. Wyld's *Universal Dictionary*. Probably it is by now so frequent in both England and America that a long-forgotten novelist's social "typing" of a character by having another character remark of her that "she is the sort of person who pronounces the *t* in often" would have no point for many readers. Although American dictionaries do not record this variant (with one exception, which states it to be "not uncommon among the educated speakers in some sections"), there can be no doubt that it is in fairly wide use all over the country, and that only the conservatism of dictionaries has prevented its being more of a matter of record than it is. When the Duke of Windsor, as Prince of Wales, used the pronunciation in a public address, the London *Times* is said to have attributed it to the influence of the American "set" with which he was consorting, and predicted dolefully that it was only a question of time before he would be wearing a hard straw hat (a "boater"), white flannel trousers, and a blue jacket—a combination considered very natty in America at that time. There can be no doubt, however, that the faction to the extreme linguistic right have fought a losing battle in this instance. *Often* with the *t* sounded is now quite literally the "King's English," if the usage of two kings is a sufficient hallmark; for George VI quite audibly pronounced the *t* in his broadcast speech to the Empire on Christmas Day, 1950.

Another spelling pronunciation already alluded to, *forehead* with -*h*- and evenly distributed stress on both syllables, is listed as a variant in all American dictionaries. It has gained ground at a great rate and is probably more common in current educated American speech, excluding perhaps that of the very highly cultivated and cosmopolitan, than *farid* or *forid*. Daniel Jones did not record the spelling pronunciation of this word until his seventh edition (London, 1945), in which he indicated that it was still rare; Wyld in 1932 called it "vulgar or modern."

Instances of the American faith in spelling as a guide to "correct" pronunciation might be multiplied, but only a few more must suffice. *Worsted* "yarn" is a word so familiar and homely that one would suppose that it would have an excellent chance of retaining its traditional pronunciation *woostid* (the *oo* as in *foot*), as indeed it has among the illiterate and the highly cultivated, whose usage coincides more often than most schoolmasters like to admit. In the great middle ground between these two extremes, however, a spelling pronunciation is widely current which is identical with that of the past tense of *to worst*, with which it has of course no etymological connection. Professor Kenyon in his *American Pronunciation* (10th ed., Ann Arbor, 1950) points out that a good many British place names also occur in America, frequently with pronunciation according to the spelling; he cites such pronunciation for *Greenwich* and *Thames* (British *grinidge* or *grenidge* and *temz*) in Connecticut, *Walthamstow* (British *waltumstow*) and *Edinburgh* (British *edinbruh* or *edinburruh*) in Massachusetts. To these might be added *Windham* as *wind ham* (British *windum*) in Vermont (but *Durham* in North Carolina preserves the traditional pronunciation) and *Delhi* (not English in origin, of course, though of English transmission and pronounced *delly* by the English) in New

York, which residents of that state pronounce *dell high*. The first syllable, and sometimes the second as well, of *Berkshire*, the name of the hills in western Massachusetts, is pronounced in America as the spelling seems to us to indicate; the same is true of the first syllable of *Berkeley*, the name of the city in California. Both these place names are of English origin, and the English use *bark* as the first syllable in both. But the tendency to pronounce according to spelling is by no means confined to America, as we have seen, even though it may have reached extremes here: the English themselves now pronounce the first syllable of *Berkhamsted* (or *Berkhampstead* in a variant spelling) as *burk*, although *bark* is used, according to Daniel Jones, "by some residents, especially members of county families," i.e., the landed gentry. *Worcester* in Massachusetts has retained both its traditional spelling and pronunciation, as has *Worcester* County in Maryland, but the Ohio town of the same name is spelled *Wooster*, which does away with an annoying discrepancy between spelling and pronunciation. *Hartford* in Connecticut shows a similar spelling change with the same motivation; *Harford*, a county in Maryland, has by its respelling preserved another traditional pronunciation of the name of the county seat of *Hertfordshire* in England, the first syllable of which is either *har-* or *hart-*. Other instances of the triumph of traditional pronunciation achieved by respelling are *Barclay*, *Darby*, *Clark*, and *Carr*, from earlier *Berkeley*, *Derby*, *Clerk*, and *Kerr* (or *Ker*).

It is likely that spelling with doubled final consonant has something to do with the American tendency to stress strongly the final syllables of proper names which have initial stress in British English, for instance, *Ríddell*, *Púrcell*, *Párnell*, and *Bárnett*, though *Riddéll* and *Purcéll* occur as variants of the first two. Judging from a close examination of Jones's *English Pronouncing Dictionary*, the same tendency is gaining ground in England. *Littell*, formerly pronounced *little*, is now given final stress by the English, precisely as in American usage (Jones does not even record the older pronunciation as a variant) and *Liddell* is about equally divided between *liddle* and *liddéll*. *Russell* and *Mitchell* have only initial stress in both British and American, despite their spellings.

The usual American pronunciation of *Bernard*, *Gerard*, and *Maurice* with final stress is probably due to modern French influence. *Gerárd* occurs only occasionally in British English; the word is usually stressed on the first syllable, a pronunciation so rare in America, if indeed it is current at all, that the *New Yorker's* theatrical reviewer found it necessary to explain it to his readers: "the hero of this anecdote, Gerard (pronounced 'Jerd'), is a younger brother of the Duke of Bristol" (November 4, 1950). American final stress in *Gerald* would be analogous to *Gerard*, but is never heard. In British English *Maurice* and *Morris* are homophones, but *mo-réece* (or *muh-réece*) is the most usual American pronunciation of *Maurice*, which is thus differentiated from *Morris*. Such pronunciation, which must be comparatively recent in origin, presumably began as a pedantic affectation born of the desire to indicate the speaker's recognition of the French spelling and his superior knowledge of the phonology of the French language, but it is by now so well established in this country as to be heard from comparatively unaffected speakers. For some reason, final stress is judged rather swank in American English, and in many circles to pronounce the cited names in the usual modest British fashion would be considered as somewhat lacking in "tone."

Before passing on to the national and regional characteristics of American pronunciation, we might well consider a few more aspects of that emotional and intellectual attitude toward language which is most widely current in America. It is not surprising that, with our love of authority in such matters, we should revere the dictionary as we do—just "the dictionary," though there are actually a number of dictionaries of varying degrees of reliability. To be sure, the cultured Englishman also uses the dictionary for ascertaining the meanings of words which are strange to him, but inasmuch as he is likely to regard the English language as *his* language, it would probably not occur to him to try to find out from a book how he "ought" to pronounce words he has always pronounced or heard pronounced by people of good standing. On the other hand, the American of comparable economic, cultural, and social status is quite likely to assume, because he has been so well indoctrinated with the belief that teachers, lexicographers, and compilers of lists of words "usually mispronounced" know best, that the chances are against his saying much of anything correctly on his own, and to desire the authority, not of usage, in which he has been taught to have no real faith, but of the dictionary. Even if conscious of the fact that there are a number of dictionaries, he is not likely to have made a comparative investigation, and hence is not aware that there is a certain amount of disagreement among them as to what constitutes "good" pronunciation. In general, it should be said, lexicographers nowadays do not consider themselves linguistic lawgivers. Professor W. Cabell Greet stated an enlightened attitude in his prefatory remarks on pronunciation in the *American College Dictionary* when he wrote, "Without seeking to impair any citizen's right to be his own professor of English, we look for what is national, contemporary, and reputable." Usually the modern lexicographer is content to record what, according to his observation, is "national, contemporary, and reputable" and to recommend only by implication. Even the best of our modern dictionaries are not infallible in the accuracy of their recordings of actual usage; but they are compiled by honest and expertly trained men, and, though it is easy to pick a few flaws, the wonder is really that there are not more, considering the magnitude of the task of preparing such a work. Nevertheless, there is evidence that lexicographers do sometimes turn a deaf ear to "national, contemporary, and reputable usage" and assume a directive function, as when a leading dictionary records *abdómen* and *ay-éerial* as "first choice" or "preferred" pronunciations of *abdomen* and *aerial*. One wonders, also, why curiosities like the practically archaic variant pronunciation of *oboe* as *oh boy* should be allowed to take up precious space. Actually, there is some cause for rejoicing in the fact that the leading modern dictionaries now record first the pronunciation rhyming with *hobo* and that no longer can "holier than thou" speakers claim that *oleomargarine* "must" be pronounced with hard *g* because the much more usual pronunciation with soft *g* is "not in the dictionary." But the popular attitude is still reflected in the opinion of many that these pronunciations were "incorrect" up to the time of their being recorded by "the dictionary."

It may seem contradictory that, with our reverence for "the dictionary," more of us do not use such dictionary pronunciations as have been cited. It is probable that some speakers would like to do so, being convinced that stressing the second syllable of *abdomen* and pronouncing *aerial* with four syllables is "more correct," but simply lack the courage; it is also probable that many do not know that these are "recommended" pronunciations, not having "looked up" the words in question. In addition, many persons have never really learned to interpret accurately the diacritical markings, respellings, and phonetic symbols used by the dictionaries to indicate pronunciation and hence are not aware of some of the discrepancies between recommended and actual usage. Authority cannot, of course, wholly inhibit linguistic change; it can only slow it up, and it has done so with amazing effectiveness.

In one respect, however, the schools have superseded the authority of the dictionary, namely in the treatment of words (including personal and place names) of foreign origin which have been long established in English contexts. The older tradition of Anglicization still followed for the most part by the dictionaries has been almost completely lost in American English. It is not simply, as Professor Greet has said in *World Words* (New York, 1944), a pronouncing dictionary prepared to assist announcers and other speakers of the Columbia Broadcasting System, that "our bright people are more interested in the present international world than in the traditions of English"; quite aside from any world-consciousness, most of our "bright people" have had a smattering—seldom more—of foreign languages at school.

It is fairly obvious that an attitude of mind has developed con-comitantly with the teaching of the modern foreign languages—the teaching of the "reformed" or "classical" pronunciation of Latin, with its un-English vowels, has doubtless contributed—in regard to the pronunciation of words of foreign origin, when that origin is recognized. This attitude expresses itself in the attempt to pronounce such words according to the phonetic system of the language from which they have been borrowed, insofar as that system is known to the speaker. To do so has come, indeed, to be felt as a sort of linguistic obligation. The effect on certain words having behind them a long tradition of Anglicization has been marked in American English to a somewhat greater extent than in British English—though in British English also the tradition of Anglicization exemplified in the older pronunciation of *Calais*, which rhymed with *malice*, is to a large extent lost. Though *Callis* is still used by a few old-fashioned British speakers, the usual British pronunciation now rhymes with *Sal lay* or with *Sally*; in American English, except as the name of Calais, Maine, which is still pronounced in the old way, it invariably rhymes with *allay*—the stress on the final syllable indicating in American English consciousness of French origin, as also in *ballet, café, chagrin*, etc., all usually spoken with initial stress in British English. The notion that French words should be spoken with strong final stress is part of the American school tradition and may, incidentally, be tied up with the tendency, previously treated, to give final stress to English names in *-ell* and *-ett* like Purcell and Barnett, which resemble French feminines in *-elle* and *-ette*, for instance *pucelle* and *lunette*.

By now every American who ever went to high school is aware of the fact that in languages other than English the letter *a* has the approximate value that it has in *father*. This is an elementary fact that almost any linguistic booby, who may of course be quite bright in other departments, is able to master and, moreover, to remember. A good many new pronunciations are attributable to this notion that *a* whenever it occurs in any word of recognizable foreign origin, no matter how long it has been a part of the English word stock, ought to be pronounced as *ah*. In any case, pronunciation of such words as *dilettante* and *Dante* with broad *a* is certainly due to the influence of the schools, though such a modification of older English speech habits would probably not have made quite so much headway as it has without the abetment of that overweening desire to be "correct" which is so prominent a characteristic of educated American English.

This new broad *a* (new as far as English is concerned) occurs principally in words whose foreign origin is plainly recognizable—not as a rule in the more familiar Renaissance borrowings like *balcony*, *cameo*, *stanza*—and is frequently to be heard from speakers who take pride in their linguistic Americanism and who would never affect the broad vowel in such words as *bath*, *master*, and *staff*. It is of increasingly frequent occurrence in words which have entered English by way of the modern foreign languages, but which have nevertheless a long tradition of Anglicization behind them. It is quite true that current fashion prescribes for foreign words of more recent adoption, like *ersatz* and *camouflage*, and particularly proper names, like *Goethe* and *Clemenceau*, pronunciation according to the sound system of the language of origin; consequently people are much concerned to know how such words "ought" to be pronounced. When the exact foreign pronunciation of such words is not known to the speaker, it is deemed sufficient to pronounce in a markedly un-English fashion. Thus, a radio commentator confronted with the name (or *nom de guerre*) *Stalin* may choose, if he has "had" a little German, to pronounce the first syllable *shtah-*, as in German, and heavily stress the last syllable as in American school-French.

The phenomenon with which we are here concerned is essentially a confusion of the older tradition, exemplified in *Cicero, Montaigne,* and *Cervantes* (though *Cervantes* is coming increasingly to have a Spanish or at any rate a pseudo-Spanish pronunciation), with the newer tendency—a confusion which frequently results in new pronunciations for foreign words of long standing in English. Such words as a general rule are rather more likely to lose their Anglicized pronunciations in American usage than in British: this is true of *Marseilles*, *Versailles*, and *Lyons*, previously pronounced *marsails*, *versails*, and *lions*, but now given the supposed French pronunciations *marsáy* or *marsáyuh*, *vairsígh* or *vairsíghuh*, and *lee-ón* (the last frequently with nasalized vowel). *Prague* (for Czech *Praha*) formerly rhymed with *Craig*, but this pronunciation has been supplanted by *prahg*. For a while during World War II, radio speakers took considerable pride in saying *Praha*, but the more sensible of them eventually gave it up. Italian proper names are likely to undergo a sort of Italianization even when their English forms differ from the Italian—for instance *Milan* (Italian *Milano*), which in a very frequent American pronunciation has a strongly accented final syllable with broad (or "Italian") *a*. It is true that the dictionaries without exception fail to record this pronunciation, but it is nevertheless in wide use among educated speakers and is no doubt considered rather elegant. The first pronunciation recorded by dictionaries, with the second syllable accented but rhyming with *fan*, is probably somewhat less frequent than the pseudo-foreign one—in fact, in many educated, if not sophisticated, circles it would be considered somewhat lacking in polish. The other recorded pronunciation, which rhymes with *Dillon*, is probably as rare in American usage as the pronunciation of *Seville* with initial accent (thus rhyming with *devil*)— a pronunciation which is, incidentally, recorded as American by the dictionaries, though I have never heard it from any American speaker. *Milan* as the name of towns in Michigan, Missouri, and Tennessee is quite unpretentiously pronounced to rhyme with *smilin'*.

One familiar with the older tradition but unacquainted with the current American trend might well suppose that a name so well established in educated usage as that of the foremost Italian poet would rhyme with *panty*. This pronunciation of *Dante* is indeed the only one recorded in British usage by Daniel Jones; it is likely, therefore, that it is heavily predominant in England. As for American usage, the fancier pronunciation with "Italian" *a* is certainly just as heavily predominant. The distinction between English *-y* and Italian *-e* is too subtle for most American ears, and hardly worth bothering with, inasmuch as the speaker may so easily experience a warm glow of satisfaction in his supposed linguistic *savoir faire* by pronouncing *Dante* as *dahnty*; he has made it abundantly clear that he jolly well knows his way around in the Italian language, having met all practical requirements by the mere substitution of the Italian vowel in the first syllable. It should be noted, however, that the use of Italian *a* in *Dante* as well as in other words from Italian, such as *dilettante* (frequently pronounced without final *-e*, probably under the impression that the word is French and analogical with *debutante*), *andante*, *canto*, and *regatta*, is a conscious elaboration of natural English speech, born of a desire to speak "correctly" which in America has taken precedence of a long tradition of cultivated English usage. To pronounce these obviously un-English words and those which follow as if they were English seems somehow amateurish to us; and it is noteworthy that in speech as in sports the amateur approach has little appeal for Americans, who desire above all to be experts.

The traditional English pronunciation of *Don Quixote* as *don quicksoat* or *quicksut* is about as archaic in American English as the pronunciation of *Don Juan* which rhymes with *new one* (used in American English, usually somewhat apologetically, only as the title of Byron's poem). To say *don quicksoat* is to give occasion for winces of pain at one's crudeness in most American circles; the "educated" pronunciation is predominatingly *keehóty* (sometimes *keehótay*), which is thought to be purest Castilian. It is perhaps just as well that there is no general awareness of the fact that when Cervantes composed his masterpiece the Spanish value of *x* was the sound usually indicated in English by *sh*; otherwise many "correct" speakers would undoubtedly try very hard to say *keeshóty*.

In a large group of words and phrases of Latin origin, American English has probably gone somewhat farther than British English in what R. W. Chapman in his note "Latin in English" has called "the attempt to foist 'correct' B.C. pronunciation of . . . Latin on a modern vernacular" (*Notes and Queries*, December 13, 1947). As Dr. Chapman points out, the absurdity reaches a climax in the reversal of the final vowels in *alumni* and *alumnae*; "for the faction of the Left call the girls *aloomnigh* or *alumnigh*, and the faction of the Right call the boys just that (or *alumny*), so that a vital distinction is blurred or obliterated." As a result of the teaching of the "reformed" (or "classical" or "Roman") pronunciation of Latin, with seldom a word of instruction in the traditional English method, there prevails in America, and to a lesser extent in England, which has a somewhat better established tradition for the English pronunciation of Latin than we have, an uncertainty in the pronunciation of Latin learned words, phrases, and proper names. The thing has in fact gone so far that many speakers hesitate to employ such words or phrases for fear that their pronunciation will not be understood or that it will invite suspicion of their learning. For a while there was a period of transition, during which one was practically forced to have two pronunciations of Latin, one— the "classical"—for the partially educated and academically hidebound, and one—the traditional English—for the truly cultured and sophisticated. It is evident, however, from the number of "classical" pronunciations current in British English as recorded by Daniel Jones— and he is recording a type of speech which is from the American point of view highly sophisticated—that even on this level there is now considerable wavering. But, as far as American usage is concerned, the speaker is always safer to use the "waynee, weedee, weekee" type of Latin pronunciation taught in the schools; for this supposed "correct" pronunciation has, in this country at least, almost completely superseded the traditions of the past still embalmed in the dictionaries. *Sigh-ny quay non* (the "dictionary pronunciation" of *sine qua non*) is quite as archaic in American English nowadays as *don quicksoat* for *Don Quixote*. Even the familiar *per se* is nowadays more often *pur say* (or even *pair say*) than traditional *pur see*. The old tradition has gone down in ignominious defeat at the hands of a supposedly more proper standard of pronunciation taught in the schools, and it may be only a question of time before *Julius Caesar* will be *Yulius Kysar*. As a consequence, Latin has become for the first time in a good many centuries a dead language even among the learned. The fact that the English tradition has been only incompletely lost in some words has resulted in hybrid pronunciations like *ultimatum* with the unrounded English *u* of *but* in the first syllable and Latin *ah* instead of the traditional English *ay* in the third syllable. *Alma mater* is now usually "Latinized," that is, pronounced *ahlma mahter*, though the hybrid pronunciation *alma mahter* is very frequent. Of the dictionaries of British English, none records any pronunciation save the traditional English (*alma mayter*), a pronunciation which is also, quite misleadingly, given first place in practically all American dictionaries. The phrase is, of course, of much less frequent occurrence in England than in America.

To summarize, then, we are hardly justified in characterizing educated American pronunciation, the speech of our average "effective citizens," excluding the few who have given up in despair of ever achieving the very high standard set by those whom we have chosen to be our authorities, as bold, daring, and independent. Although its traditions are not invariably those of the mother country, it has acquired very real traditions of its own, based not upon usage, but upon authority—the authority of the written word as this is interpreted by the schools. Nothing could be less true of present American English than Captain Marryat's sneer of more than a century ago, when he declared that "every one appears to be independent, and pronounces just as he pleases." American pronunciation has become a carefully schooled and regimented type of pronunciation, sometimes even over-careful from the British point of view; it is on the whole as true to its standards, based as these are upon theoretic and academic criteria, as British English is to its older traditions of usage based upon social custom. The notion that American English is "sloppy" has little basis in fact, particularly on the educated level; and uneducated American speech is certainly no sloppier than uneducated British speech. Except for the American propensity for "tall talk," which is stylistic rather than linguistic in nature, admiration for frontiersmen and cowboys has probably had little or no effect upon the speech of Americans beyond their teens.

II. AMERICAN AND BRITISH DIFFERENCES

Some of the phonetic differentiae of British and American English remaining to be discussed are on the whole less significant as national characteristics than those attitudes toward language which have been discussed previously; for, as has been pointed out, the "American accent" and the "British accent" cannot be explained merely by pointing out variations in the pronunciation of words—that is, differences in syllable stress and the articulation of individual speech sounds. These are as a rule what the observer first notices: they are obvious and more or less superficial.

In the treatment of postvocalic r, and of a in words of the *after, answer, path, grass* type, the usage of the great majority of Americans stands in sharp contrast to that of speakers of standard British English.

N

The use of broad *a* by Americans who do not have it by tradition is fraught with dangers for the unwary, for it is not invariable in standard British English in words of the type under discussion: it occurs, for instance, in *dance* but not in *romance*; in *plaster* but not in *plastic*; in *class* but not in *crass*; in *can't* but not in *cant*; in *master* but not in *mascot*. The British reduction or loss of the penultimate syllable of words in *-ary*, *-ery*, *-ory* is not to be heard in any normal American speech save occasionally in *stationery* (perhaps to distinguish it from the adjective *stationary*), *primary*, *cemetery*, and *confectionery*; it may be heard in *dictionary* as an affectation, but those who affect it do not say *ordin'ry*, *territ'ry*, *necess'ry*, etc. British and eastern New England speech are alike in their use of a rounded or partially rounded vowel for short *ŏ* in words of the *got, odd, stop, clock* type. British English pronounces the *-ile* ending in *agile, docile, reptile, servile, tactile*, and the like to rhyme with *file*. American English usually preserves an older pronunciation of these words with reduced vowel or syllabic *l. Mobile* "movable" has two pronunciations in American English: it may rhyme with *noble* or it may be pronounced *mobeel* exactly like the totally unrelated Choctaw word which is the name of the city and the river in Alabama. Both these pronunciations of *mobile*, incidentally, are current in British English as variants of the somewhat more frequent pronunciation with *ī* in the final syllable. The American pronunciation of *fragile* occurs very occasionally as a British variant. The so-called long *ī* occurs in American English in *crocodile* and *gentile*, usually in *infantile*, and often in *juvenile, mercantile*, and *textile*.

There are other differences less sweeping in nature. Standard British English usually stresses the second syllable in *doctrinal, laboratory*, and *centenary*, these syllables being pronounced *try, bore*, and *tee* or *ten*, though *dóctrinal, láboratory*, and *céntenary* (the last two with characteristic British loss or reduction of the vowel in the penultimate syllable) occur as variants. *Advertisement* is always stressed on the second syllable in standard British English, but this stressing is also widely current in educated American English nowadays.

There are actually very few supposedly American pronunciations of individual words which do not occur as variants in British English. Daniel Jones, who in his *English Pronouncing Dictionary* is concerned only with what he calls Received Pronunciation, that is, standard British English, records as occurring in this type of speech a good many pronunciations usually thought of as characteristic of American

English. The British, it is true, usually pronounce the past tense of the verb *to eat* as *et* (current but substandard in American English); however, the only pronunciation current in educated American use, rhyming with *late*, does occur in standard British English as a variant. *Been, either, neither, again,* and *against* are usually *bean, eyether, nyether, agayn,* and *agaynst* in standard British English; but Jones lists *bin, eether, neether, agen,* and *agenst,* the usual American pronunciations, as variants. *Trait* is in England usually pronounced *tray,* but the American pronunciation without suppression of the *-t* is also current; *nephew* with medial *-f-* is somewhat less usual than with *-v-,* but it is perfectly "standard." *Progress* (noun) and *process* usually have long *ō* in their first syllables, but Jones lists pronunciation with short *ŏ* as occurring, though rarely. Some American speakers use the long vowel in *process,* but not in *progress.*

Many, perhaps most, British speakers use long *ē* (as in *eve*) in the first syllable of *evolution, economic, equable, epoch,* and *predecessor,* but short *ĕ* as in *get* is also to be heard in all these words save the two last named. Of these words, *equable* frequently has *ē* in American English, and so has *economic,* but never *evolution.* Long *ē* in *epoch* and *predecessor* would be decidedly unusual in American English, but such pronunciations are occasionally heard; probably they are affected. *Patriot* and its derivatives *patriotic* and *patriotism* usually have *pat-* for their first syllable in British English, though pronunciations with *pate-* occur as variants; only the latter are current in normal American English. British English has *pate-* in *patron* and *patroness,* with *pat-* as a variant, but only *pat-* in *patronage* and *patronize*; American English usually has *pate-* in all these words, though *pat-* occurs as a variant in *patroness* and *patronage.*

Much, undoubtedly too much, has been made of supposed distinctively British pronunciations of such words as *profile* (rhyming with *no feel*), *tryst* (rhyming with *iced*), *zenith* (rhyming with *Kenneth*), *primer* "book" (rhyming with *timer*), *venison* (as *venzn*), *quandary* (with penultimate stress), *marital* (with stressed *ī* in the penultimate, as in *recital*), and *aristocrat* (with stress on the first syllable, as also occasionally in American English). These words occur in most lists purporting to set forth differences between British and American pronunciation. It is quite true that the British pronunciations indicated within the parentheses are, except for *aristocrat,* never heard from American speakers. It is even more striking, however, that every one of these words—and a number of similar instances might be cited—has in British English a variant pronunciation identical with that most widely current in American English. The possibility must be admitted that some of the variants recorded by Daniel Jones are somewhat rarer in British English than he seems to indicate, for he specifically disclaims including any forms which can be considered rare without the use of some qualifying term such as *rarely* or *old-fashioned*. Not one of the variants cited above is so labelled, however, and Jones's observation and judgment are usually to be trusted in such matters. The usual American pronunciations of *quinine, corollary, tomato, figure, frontier, premier, squirrel, dynasty, chagrin, suave, miscellany, clerk, vase,* and *schedule* are not current in standard British English, in which they are pronounced respectively *quinéen* (with short, unstressed *ĭ* in the first syllable), *coróllary, tomahto, figger, fróntyer, prémyer* (with short *ĕ* in the first syllable), *squearel, dinnasty, shágrin* or *shagréen, swayve, miscéllany, clark* (so pronounced also in our Southern Highlands), *vahz,* and *shedule. Leisure* rhymes with *pleasure* in British English, a pronunciation recorded in American dictionaries but seldom heard, the usual American pronunciation rhyming with *seizure.* But except for such general tendencies as have been discussed earlier, sporadic differences between British and American pronunciation are on the whole insignificant. The list of words having strikingly different pronunciations in the two great English-speaking nations might have been expanded somewhat, but not really very much.

III. AMERICAN REGIONAL TYPES

The diversity of "socially acceptable" pronunciation in America—a diversity in details within the larger pattern of uniformity characteristic of our speech—has already been discussed in the third chapter of this book. Scientific study of American linguistic geography in the past fifteen years or so has made it perfectly clear that the old assumption of a homogeneous "General American" pronunciation, spoken everywhere save in the South and eastern New England, must be once and for all discarded. This assumption, based upon the supposed existence of a linguistic Mason and Dixon's Line separating Northern from Southern speech, is, as Kurath has well pointed out in his *Word Geography of the Eastern United States,* "simply due to an erroneous inference from an oversimplified version of the political history of the nineteenth century." Instead, as we have seen in Chapter III, there is a well-defined Midland area lying between the traditionally recognized Northern and Southern areas. All types of American speech stem ultimately from the three basic types, Northern, Midland, and Southern, each of these having rather clearly defined subareas, such as New York City in the North and the Charleston-Savannah areas in the South.

The speech of western New England is derivative from that of eastern New England and probably represents an older type of Northern speech less influenced by eighteenth-century changes in British English than that heard east of the Connecticut River, as, for instance, in its treatment of postvocalic *r* and of the *a* sound in words of the *pass, staff, ask* type. The speech of the northern United States, as far as it has been investigated, extends westward in an area bounded on the south by a line beginning a little below Sandy Hook in New Jersey, veering somewhat to the north and running along the northern tier of counties in Pennsylvania—settled from New England and New York—and from there pursuing a slightly southerly course through Ohio, Indiana, and Illinois. Its divagations west of the Great Lakes Basin cannot at present be determined with any degree of certainty, complete evidence being unavailable, though Professor H. B. Allen of the University of Minnesota is directing studies of the speech of the Northern Plains States. It is perfectly clear, however, from the investigations of Professor A. H. Marckwardt of the University of Michigan that the boundary separating Northern from Midland extends through the Great Lakes region and the upper Ohio Valley, for, in addition to a good many word uses which are regionally distinctive, such as Northern *white-bread, wishbone,* and *poison ivy,* heard north of this boundary and corresponding to Midland *light-bread, pully bone, poison vine,* heard south of it, there are a number of pronunciations which are equally distinctive. The isogloss (a line on a linguistic map to indicate the boundary of some distinctive feature of speech) for *greasy,* which in Northern rhymes with *fleecy* but which in the speech of the Midland as well as in much of the South rhymes with *cheesy,* bisects Ohio, Indiana, and Illinois. The vowel sound of *hog, fog, frog, on* is generally unrounded (like that of *father* cut short) north of this line, rounded (like that of *law* cut short) south of it.

Northern (excluding eastern New England) and Midland speech

coincide in a good many respects, so that it is not surprising that they were not recognized as distinct dialect areas until comparatively recently. Typical speakers of both regions (1) pronounce preconsonantal and final *r*, as in *card, form, word, beard, for*, and *butter*; (2) pronounce the *u* sound in such words as *duty, tube, Tuesday, news*, and *student* as simple *oo*; (3) pronounce an unrounded vowel sound like the *a* of *father* but of shorter duration, in such words as *hot, god, stop*, and *folly*; (4) pronounce flat *a* in such words as *after, ask, grass, path*, and *half*. The divergences between Northern and Midland pronunciations are much less apparent than their points of contact—and, for that matter, less generalized.

Despite differences so apparent that no one would ever mistake a speaker from eastern New England for a coastal Southerner, these two areas are similar in their treatment of final and preconsonantal *r*, which, as we have seen, survives in the speech of western New England and its western settlement area, as in the Midland with its western and southwestern settlement areas including the southern hills; in eastern New England and the coastal South it is usually lost or vocalized (becomes a vowel sound). Eastern New England, however, regularly retains *r* at the end of a word when the following word begins with a vowel, as in *far off*. In coastal Southern this linking *r* may also be heard; many speakers in the region, however, lack it, as in *fah off*, and sometimes even lose intervocalic *r* within a word, as in *Ca'olina*, *ba'el (barrel)*, and *eve'ybody*. The eastern New England treatment of *r* which has been described is precisely that of standard British English.

Many eastern New England speakers, as well as many in the New York City area, also use what is known as "hiatus *r*," that is, an intrusive *r* sound between a word ending with a vowel and another word beginning with a vowel, as in *idea(r) of it* and *raw(r) egg*. As a rule, only speakers who use the linking *r* discussed in the preceding paragraph use *r* as a hiatus filler; consequently, this intrusive sound is less common in the South. It is fairly frequent in England. George Bernard Shaw was quite in error when, in his Preface to Richard Wilson's *The Miraculous Birth of Language*, he attributed the tendency to confuse *Maria ran* and *Maria Ann* to the man in the street, for "a considerable proportion" of the speakers of standard British English would do the same, according to Daniel Jones.

In New York City, as in parts of the deep South, the *r* of *bird, girl, certain, murky, word, earth*, and the like is by many speakers pronounced *i*, the resultant diphthong being represented in dialect writing by *oi* (i.e. *boid*, *goil*, etc.). Contrary to a widely held belief, fostered to some extent by dialect comedians who resort to such tricks as reversing the usual standard pronunciations of *oil* and *earl*, the use of this regionally distinctive diphthong is by no means substandard.

In its treatment of the vowel sound in such words as *duty*, *tube*, and *news*, Southern American is fairly consistent in its use of a *y* sound before the *u*: *dyuty*, *tyube*, etc.—a characteristic which it shares with the British Standard. Eastern New England and New York City sometimes have this sound; Northern and Midland seldom have it except for those speakers who affect it as supposedly more correct.

The low-back vowel written *o* or *a* before *r* (which may also be spelled *rr*) followed by another vowel, as in *foreign*, *horrible*, *orange*, *Dorothy*, *quarry*, *warrant*, tends to be pronounced *ah* all along the east coast; the *aw* sound predominates in the West. Both vowels are to be heard in the southern hills, which have a mixed type of speech Midland in origin, but rather heavily influenced by Southern.

A frequently noted characteristic of eastern New England speech has been alluded to elsewhere in this chapter and in Chapter III—its employment of the broad *a* or, more usually, a vowel sound approaching it, which has been described as intermediate between flat and broad *a*. One or the other of these variants of older flat *a* also occurs in the speech of cultivated eastern Virginians and Charlestonians of the older generation. Because of its supposed social prestige, certain individuals in all parts of the country affect broad *a* or the compromise vowel described above, seldom very convincingly.

It is impossible to give here anything like a complete picture of so complex a matter as the pronunciation of American English. The reader who is observant of speech will no doubt be able to supply details not treated here, such as the distinctive Southern treatment of intervocalic *l* (frequently spelled *ll*) in such words as *hilly* and *fellow*— the so-called "clear" *l*—and frequent complete loss of *l* (sometimes replaced by a "murmur" vowel) in such words as *help*, *self*, and in the third syllable of *Philadelphia*. Many non-Southerners find cause to comment on an eastern Virginia treatment of the diphthong of such words as *house* and *about*, the first element of which is or resembles the vowel of *but*. This pronunciation is also to be heard in northern New York, northern New England, and Canada. The so-called "ingliding" diphthong in such words as *bait* and *boat* is a notable characteristic of the speech of the Charleston area (thus, *bay-ut* and *bo-ut*), though it extends considerably farther south. Many Southern speakers pronounce initial *shr-* as *sr-* in such words as *shrimp, shrub*, and *shred*; this pronunciation is by no means confined to the folk, as is sometimes supposed, but is to be heard frequently in educated speech. Pairs like *horse/hoarse, morning/ mourning*, and *for/four* are differentiated in eastern New England and the South, the first member of each pair having the vowel sound of *aw*; the second, *ō*. This distinction, which is historical and which is recorded in most of our dictionaries, is also made in the speech of the southern hills, which in so many of its other characteristics is Midland. The British use *aw* in all such words.

But these are, after all, details which would require at the least another volume to treat of systematically and with any degree of completeness. The various regional and local differences which have been cited cause occasional annoyance to the linguistically unsophisticated person, who is likely to believe that only sheer perversity causes the speech of persons from other regions to be different from his own— which is, of course, "correct" speech. The truth is that it is just as natural and right for the Philadelphian and the Chicagoan to pronounce *r* when it occurs before a consonant or before a pause as it is for the Bostonian and the Charlestonian not to do so. Even if it were possible to get all people to talk exactly alike by setting up some sort of artificial standard, it would be pretty silly to attempt to do so, for the fact remains that there are no regional types of American pronunciation— and, for that matter, very few local types—which are not readily intelligible in any part of the country.

ELEVEN

Purity by Prescription

IT IS a great pity that the adjective *liberal* has been applied to the point of view of the objective, scientific observer of language habits and that an exposition of that point of view is so frequently met with the angry question, "Well, how would you like *your* child to go about using double negatives?" In the first place, there is nothing liberal in the current sense of that much-abused word in the linguist's attitude towards language. To the contrary, it is actually conservative, even aristocratic in its recognition of fashion as a more authoritative standard than the fiat of the schoolmarm. Although he is fully conscious of the tremendous influence of the schools upon the development of the English language in the modern period, and more particularly upon the development of American English, the linguist is likely to offend many good, sweet people by his inability to take very seriously so-called rules which stem from analogies, particularly from false analogies, or which merely reflect the aesthetic predilections of the rule-maker (such as the widespread prejudice against the "split infinitive"), or indeed any other rules which have not been induced from the usage of distinguished speakers and writers.

The linguist is also cognizant of the fact that standards of usage are likely to vary a good deal from region to region, from city to city, and from town to town—that the "good English" of Oshkosh is not identical with the "good English" of Boston. But he is likely not to see any reason why absolute uniformity, the desideratum of the prescriptivist, should be any particular concern of the student of language even if it were possible of attainment. He may have no objection to prescription as such; he merely objects, and sometimes rather bitterly, to prescriptions which have no basis in the facts of language, such as the prescription of most American books on "correct" English that *got* should be preferred to *gotten* as the past participle of *get*. It seems to him that anyone with ears and eyes ought to know perfectly well that in American English *gotten* is very much alive on all social and cultural levels and that, as a matter of fact, there must be many fairly cultured circles in America where "I wish I could have got here sooner" would seem somewhat questionable usage, though *got* would, of course, be the usual form in British English.

But because he insists upon the validity of his own observations, supplemented by the painstaking researches of other students of language, it is frequently charged that the linguist has no standards. Now it is perfectly true that he makes no pretence of knowing better how the English language should be spoken and written than those who have actually spoken and written it effectively, powerfully, beautifully; who have wielded it to great purposes with sincerity, clarity, lucidity. But this is not the same as having no standards. If he concerns himself with rules at all, he is content to draw them from the actual usage of these speakers and writers; usually, however, he is content merely to observe and record. And as an observer and recorder of linguistic facts, he is bound to observe and record the fact that American English has to a large extent been moulded by schoolmasters and 'marms, by lexicographers, and by writers of prescriptive text-books, all of whom have tremendous linguistic authority in America. Although he may question their right to be considered authoritative, the linguist is bound to recognize their influence; he is bound by his concern for facts to admit that in their efforts we may see the flowering of a new, or comparatively new, tradition in American English, a tradition based upon slavish acceptance of authority rather than upon the cultivated usage of the past. In fairness it must be said that some masters and 'marms are very well informed about linguistic development and that practically all of them are worthy, self-sacrificing people who doubtless deserve the satisfaction of being regarded as authorities on language to compensate for their ridiculously inadequate material rewards; that our excellent American dictionaries suffer from misuse by linguistically ignorant and gullible people who do not bother to read the prefatory and introductory matter; and that there are at least two thoroughly reliable American handbooks of English usage, both written by men who, because they are highly trained students of language, make no attempt to dictate usage but are content to record the facts.

As for the question about one's child using double negatives, the answer is that it would of course be grossly unfair to any child not to teach him to eschew the vigorous "I didn't do nothing about it" for the decidedly less emphatic "I didn't do anything about it." For here as elsewhere the prescriptivists won the day long ago; they succeeded in outlawing a construction which is of frequent occurrence in the writings of our earlier writers and was presumably so in their speech as well. Today such a multiple negative construction as Chaucer's "He nevere yet no vileynye ne sayde/In all his lyf unto no maner wight" is, and has been for a great many years, low. Though it is not true that "I didn't do nothing" means "I did do something," as was laboriously explained to me many years ago in school, it is certainly true that, because of the general acceptance of a false application of mathematical logic to language, no recent writer has used the construction in what was intended to be standard English, nor does it occur, so far as I know, in any variety of educated speech. The fact that it is of frequent occurrence in the language of the "common man" is no recommendation for its use unless one wants always to associate with common men. The linguist is, of course, vitally interested in the speech of the folk, which shows the natural, untrammelled development of language better than that of the educated; but he does not himself speak folk speech, nor does he recommend that others should speak it. He is quite conscious of the fact that among the folk there are many exceptionally able people who will always be deprived of intellectual and spiritual companionship so long as they speak a nonstandard form of language. George Bernard Shaw has stated the essential justification for the prescriptive teaching of language, though many teachers will disapprove of his using *their* and *them* to refer to *person*: "People know very well that certain sorts of speech cut off a person for ever from getting more than three or four pounds a week all their life long— sorts of speech which make them entirely impossible in certain professions."

Because no one, so far as I know, questions that the double (or multiple) negative with negative intent is substandard, I should of course insist that a child under my tutelage avoid it; but I should certainly want that child to know that there is nothing inherently "bad" about the construction, that its outlawing was due in the beginning to a mistaken notion, and that its use is quite *de rigueur* on certain social levels which are commonly and no doubt accurately thought of as low, though no moral disapprobation need be implied by the adjective. Robert A. Hall, Jr., in his *Leave Your Language Alone!*

(Ithaca, 1950) tells of a friend who, when he went to work in a ship-
yard during the war, was regarded as a snob until he substituted *them
things* for *those things* in his speech; in the circles in which he temporarily
found himself, *those things* was definitely not "good" usage. But it is
to be doubted that an educated person would want to remain for a
lifetime in those circles. I should endeavour to make clear, even to a
very young child, that avoidance of such constructions as the double
negative and *them things* has become a hallmark of social respectability
and that he could not hope to be accepted by the sort of people it is
presumed he would wish to associate with if he used the locutions in
question. They are eschewed even by Hopalong Cassidy, Roy Rogers,
and the Lone Ranger; furthermore, according to an Associated Press
dispatch of December 18, 1949, "an uproar from parents and teachers
about kids of today absorbing so much bad grammar" has been
responsible for the fact that even such old standbys as *podner, plumb,
shore,* and *yore* "are becoming conspicuously absent from the current
crop [of Western films]," and presumably from radio as well.

But many of the usages condemned in the schools are not really
substandard at all; for example, the use of *like* as a conjunction, as in
Dickens's "Nobody will miss her like I shall" (*Letters*), Gissing's "He
can't write like he used to" (*New Grub Street*), and Shaw's "I do not
need beautiful armour made to my measure like you wear" (*Saint Joan*).
This locution has either been flatly condemned or labelled "colloquial,"
which latter in the opinion of most prescriptive authorities is somehow
inferior to "formal." Now the ordinary speech of persons of assured
social position, of sophistication, of culture is certainly the most
pleasant type of speech one could hope to listen to. The fact that this
easygoing familiar language of the truly cultured differs very little if
at all from their platform and pulpit speech or, for that matter, from
their written language would hardly be suspected from the ex cathedra
pronouncements of our unofficial but none the less potent linguistic
dictators. Such speech, and such writing as well, is likely to be sprinkled
with "ungrammatical" constructions which would be taboo in
American classrooms.

When Winston Churchill said "This is me" in a recorded speech
made at New Haven in 1946, our custodians of linguistic propriety
went into a dither, even though it is true that most of them now
grudgingly "allow" this locution, hallowed as it is by centuries of
cultivated usage. The label *colloquial* is, however, practically always

affixed to it, a qualification which, when it is not confused with *local*, is frequently interpreted to mean "incorrect." In any event, Sir Winston's usage would certainly be considered eccentric, not to say substandard, in many academic circles with which I am acquainted.

Of the examples cited in the following paragraphs, those from Wells, Stephens, Kipling, Meredith, Byron, and Bentley unquestionably represent informal usage; most are taken from works of fiction and are intended by the authors to represent the speech of educated persons, that is, colloquial standard English. The examples will doubtless be regarded by prescriptive grammarians as exceptional, an attitude which reveals both the conventional disapproval of what deviates from a set standard and a belief in the desirability of uniformity; but for the most part they are not really so, as any student of Otto Jespersen's monumental *Modern English Grammar* will know perfectly well. On the contrary, they represent normal, natural English usage and should be regarded as altogether acceptable variants of the occasionally stilted forms recommended in the classroom and the handbook. This is of course not to say that the academically prescribed forms do not also occur, sometimes side by side with the proscribed ones, in the work of one and the same author; many forms recommended in the textbooks are actually those most often used by writers and speakers of repute, though variant usages are not necessarily "bad," as the textbooks so frequently imply. Unfortunately no statistical studies have been made to establish the relative frequency of such divided usage as is represented by *everyone . . . they* and *everyone . . . he*. Such a survey would probably indicate that since the seventeenth century the so-called indefinite pronouns *everyone, everybody, each, anyone, anybody, no one, nobody, someone, somebody*, are in British English followed somewhat more frequently by *they, them, their* than by a singular form of the third personal pronoun: the plural is used by Shakespeare, Sidney, Fielding, Richardson, Defoe, Swift, Johnson, Goldsmith, Jane Austen, Scott, Byron, Shelley, Thackeray, Dickens, Kingsley, George Eliot, Trollope, Newman, Arnold, Ruskin, Wilde, Leslie Stephen, Kipling, Bennett, Wells, and Shaw, to name only the most distinguished writers who have committed what is held to be an "error" by most American prescriptive grammarians.

H. G. Wells's "The real reason I am out of place here is because I like men" (*Ann Veronica*) and John Ruskin's "The false, unnatural, and destructive system is when the bad workman is allowed to offer . . ." (*Unto This Last*) fail to stand up against the categorical statement of a very recent textbook for college use that it is a violation of consistency to use a *when* clause or a *because* clause as a predicate nominative after the verb *to be*. Even stronger language is applied a few sentences later when the term "error" is used for such "violations of consistency." Wells and Ruskin, it is obvious, would not be able to do well in Freshman English in most American universities, assuming that they could get through high school. In the light of this fact, it would seem to some jaded observers of the workings of the human mind to be a "violation of consistency" to hold Ruskin's prose style up to students as a model of excellence.

The distinction between *who* and *whom* so beloved of teachers apparently makes little impression upon many cultured speakers and writers. The *Oxford English Dictionary* boldly records that *whom* is "no longer current in natural colloquial speech," a type of speech which is apparently considerably rarer in America than in England. Many of us have learned laboriously to make the distinction; some of us have no doubt wondered whether the game was worth the candle, particularly when we come upon such results of overzealous learning as Hugh Walpole's "She did not know whom this strange young man might be" (*Fortitude*). James Stephens's "Who are you talking about?" (*The Crock of Gold*), Kipling's "Who are they likely to send down to examine us?" (*Debits and Credits*), and Meredith's "Who has he come for?" (*The Ordeal of Richard Feverel*) all fall considerably short of the standards set by American prescriptive grammarians.

Similarly, Hazlitt's "these sort of critical verdicts" (*On Patronage and Puffery*) would not have got him very far in the American school system, for, according to a representative recent textbook, "formal usage" requires *this* or *that* with *sort* (and *kind*). The authors cite the following as an example of a formal sentence: "You know that sort of shoe which scoops up sand and pebbles." It is, of course, a bit difficult to conceive of a situation in which one would need to speak formally of open-toed shoes. Apparently the difference between formal and informal usage is governed not by style, subject matter, or occasion, but only by whether one uses the singular or the plural demonstrative, inasmuch as the same sentence with "those sort of shoes which scoop up . . ." substituted for "that sort of shoe which scoops up . . ." is labelled *informal*. But be that as it may, one cannot help wondering whether Hazlitt knew that he was writing informally. The locution which he used has behind it a long tradition. Sir Philip Sidney's "those kind of objections" (*Defence of Poesie*), Dryden's "These kind of thoughts" (Dedication of *Dramatic Poesie*), Swift's "these kind of feats" (*Gulliver's Travels*), and Jane Austen's "these kind," "these sort" (*Pride and Prejudice* and elsewhere) are only a few instances of its use by the most reputable authors. Dean Alford in his *The Queen's English* (1864) stated that *those kind of things* is "now almost become idiomatic," but it is to be observed that twentieth-century Americans conscious of their schooling take pride in substituting for it *that kind of thing* or the queer *those kinds of things*. The rejection of the natural construction seems to give many of them a feeling of great satisfaction; perhaps it is a sort of linguistic catharsis.

Lord Byron's frequent use of *don't* as a contraction of *does not* in his letters ("If it don't take, I will leave it off where it is"; "She will come round—mind if she don't"; "If it don't take it will be discontinued") must be almost as distressing to those who wish to shackle the English language as his "there let him lay" in the fourth canto of *Childe Harold's Pilgrimage*. Both usages are, however, not infrequent in the colloquial language of the well-bred and the educated. Dean Alford testified that in his day the intransitive use of *lay, laid* was quite usual among Eton men and hence must have had some of the prestige value of the old school tie; but that fact hardly excuses Lytton Strachey, the distinguished scion of a distinguished writing clan, for writing in our own day of those "manuscripts which had long laid hidden." William Morris, George Moore, Charles Dickens, and Joseph Conrad have made the same "error." Eminent authors like these can hardly be said to be "playing the game" with those who make up the rules of the English language. American authors are, on the whole, more sporting. Of *don't* as a variant of *doesn't*, Kemp Malone has recently called attention to the patent fact—patent, that is, to anyone willing to trust the evidence of his eyes and ears, but not to those who prescribe what is "good"—that this form is "well established in English colloquial speech, and has been for many years." He testifies to having heard it "innumerable times from persons of good breeding and high cultivation" and declares that "no reasonable objection to it can be made, and it is high time for the teachers of English to give up their silly agitation against it" (*English Journal*, February, 1950). "Persons of good breeding and high cultivation" will doubtless go on using the form; those who are apprehensive about their social and intellectual status will doubtless go on inveighing against it because they regard it only as a contraction of *do not*, hence "incorrect" and "illogical" when used with a pronoun in the third person singular.

John Galsworthy ought to have been aware that "the subject of a gerund should be in the possessive case," but unfortunately an expensively genteel British education failed to apprise him of this fact, for he wrote, "She would never get stout, as there was every danger of Clara doing" (*The Freelands*). E. C. Bentley, in *Trent's Last Case*, made an even more egregious "blunder" when he wrote, "I was prepared for it happening," for the possessive form of the pronoun with the gerund is considered even more essential to grammatical elegance than that of the noun. Galsworthy and Bentley, along with a good many more distinguished writers, would not come up to our American standards of linguistic immaculacy. "Do not use a perfect infinitive instead of a present infinitive," warns a representative textbook—which is to say that Lord Dunsany, who is both a peer and a professional author of high repute, ought to have written, "Yet I should have liked to go a hundred miles or so . . ." instead of what he actually did write: "Yet I should have liked to have gone a hundred miles or so . . ." (*The Travel Tales of Mr. Joseph Jorkens*). But there is really no need of multiplying examples of this sort. Enough have been cited to indicate that the English have retained considerably more freedom in the use of our common tongue than we have, though they too have lost to some extent the older courtly tradition—a loss which has, indeed, been an important factor in the development of the English language since the latter part of the seventeenth century. Linguistic attitudes have changed considerably since William Caxton, an educated man according to the standards of his day, submitted his manuscripts for correction to the Duchess of Burgundy, an English lady.

American writers have on the whole been quite docile to rule. Lacking an aristocratic tradition in speech, we have supposed it necessary to depend wholly upon the schoolmarm's fiat. Occasionally "blunders" do occur, like that of John Livingston Lowes, professor of English at Harvard from 1918 until his death in 1945, author of *The Road to Xanadu*, and one of the glories of American scholarship, who wrote in his *Geoffrey Chaucer and the Development of His Genius* of "the lady's request for a respite of a year in which she may make up her mind between the three." From practically any schoolmarm or her textbook we may learn that *two* things or units are present or implied in the object of *between*, although use of the word may be "allowed" with an object implying three or more *if* one intends a relationship of each with all the others. Now it is very doubtful to me that Professor Lowes had any such subtle implication in mind. He was writing a book, and he chose to write "make up her mind between the three" simply because "make up her mind among the three" is, despite all the injunctions of all the teachers and all their textbooks, not idiomatic English. And when Miss Katherine Anne Porter wrote that "Any one of these writers I have named have had more influence on their time . . . than Willa Cather" (New York *Times* Book Review, September 25, 1949), she added grammatical insult to injury, from the point of view of the prescriptive grammarian, by her use of the plural verb *have had* in addition to *their* in a sentence the subject of which, as any bright high-school student should know, is *one*.

But few educated Americans have been so recalcitrant to the teachings of their school days. The cavalier attitude towards speech survives mainly in our South, where there are still persons of culture and breeding who use *don't* as a contraction of *does not* and *ain't* as a contraction of *am not*. The South Carolina field records for the *Linguistic Atlas* disclose that the natural, normal, and historically quite respectable contraction *ain't* is actually of frequent occurrence in the conversational speech of the most cultured speakers, though it has long been under the schoolmarm's ban. Raven I. McDavid, Jr., of the *Atlas* staff, has pointed out in *American Speech* (May, 1950) that in the South the prejudice against this form is strongest among those who have recently risen from humble circumstances and that reluctance to use it is to some extent an indication of social insecurity. The British variant *an't*, frequently written *aren't* in the question "Aren't I?"—a perfectly good way of writing it for those speakers who, like the British, have no preconsonantal *r*—is sometimes used by naïve American speakers who have seen it in British novels, but who would never think of saying *ain't*.

It is obvious from what has been said about the beginnings of American English that even without much effort on our part we should have achieved a relatively homogeneous form of speech in this country. Some mysterious constituent of the ideological atmosphere of our land has, however, proved especially salubrious to those persons —they have undoubtedly existed in all times and places—who desire above all to regulate and uniformize. Consequently, even before the

O

beginning of our national period efforts were made, as we have seen, to ensure the regularity and uniformity of American English. Usually the hoary delusion of linguistic "purity" is brought into the picture, for the desire to regulate language has for a corollary the idea of preserving what is thought of as its purity.

In our own day the concept of linguistic purity is very much alive, and we frequently read in the newspapers that the "purest" or "most perfect" English is spoken in one city or another—the locale varies with the "expert" who is opinionating. In February, 1947, the United Press reported that the Linguaphone Institute of America, "authority on American speech," had awarded the palm for "the most perfect speech," which I assume would be the "purest," to Dallas, Texas, with New York ranking only thirtieth. Cities other than Dallas which won the Institute's accolade were Los Angeles, Chicago, and Mason City, Iowa—the last because it is "the least influenced by outside speech habits."

What does it all mean? I haven't the faintest idea. In fact, in my opinion it does not even make a good news story, though I am no judge of such matters. But, because of the authority which the newspaper has come to acquire, such notions are accepted without question —those experts ought to know what they're talking about. Sometimes it is to be suspected that nowadays "pure English" means simply clearly or carefully articulated English, as when the claim is made—and George Bernard Shaw would seem to have believed something of the sort—that the English of Dublin is "purer" than the English of London. It would, incidentally, be difficult to demonstrate that there is anything either pure or impure about precise articulation.

In any case, this absurd notion is still with us, though it has undergone considerable change through the centuries, growing progressively vaguer with the passing of time. It is no doubt an outgrowth of the equally absurd idea of linguistic corruption—that is, the widely held theory that language is going steadily downhill, some vestiges of its pristine purity surviving from year to year in Dublin, Boston, Charleston, Baltimore, Keokuk, or Mason City, Iowa, depending upon the experts who do the talking for the reporters. Carrying to its logical conclusion the point of view of the schoolmarm (for convenience' sake, the term is used bisexually), who officially as well as by temperament objects to all linguistic change, we really ought to speak the reconstructed Indo-European language.

It is of course flattering to our philosophico-political notion of ourselves as libertarians to think of American English as "free and easy," untrammelled by rule and tradition; but there is actually little truth in the notion save on the lowest social levels. The speech of educated Americans—that is, those who have been to school, which has come to mean much the same—is anything but free and easy. Nor does it, heaven knows, lack tradition of a sort, though that tradition is of the schools rather than of a royal court and an aristocracy. It is much—some would say overmuch—concerned with the proper choice between *it is me* and *it is I*, *shall* and *will*, *he don't* and *he doesn't*, *can* and *may*, *mad* and *angry*, and, for *ration*, the pronunciations *rayshun* and *rashun*. And if the American does sometimes fail to make what are thought of as the proper distinctions or is unable to understand them (for some, such as the *shall-will* business, are quite fine-drawn), he is at any rate conscious of his linguistic deficiency and either apologizes for it or pretends to glory in his crudity as something characteristically American—as it were, a sort of inverted linguistic snobbery.

The teaching of English in our American schools, which are certainly among the most potent influences shaping American English, has fostered a normative attitude, the principal postulate of which is that there is a certain standard which is "correct"; a corollary is that any divergence from this standard is "incorrect." Thus was born the feeling, particularly common among speakers of American English, that they have two strikes against them whenever they open their mouths to make the simplest statement, for the mastery of a language set off in a linguistic stratosphere, a language which nobody is likely to speak correctly save those who teach its ineffable mysteries—and even they slip up occasionally—is too much for most people. Despite unquestioning faith in a linguistic norm, many of our citizens simply give up the whole job and just talk as they please—a quite sensible procedure, as a matter of fact. Many more, however, try very hard to realize the counsels of perfection disseminated by the schools, and frequently topple over backwards; thus are born such "hypercorrect" monstrosities as "between you and I," "lunching was served," and "there has been some confusion . . . as to whom is and whom is not a reservist," this last specimen having appeared in the Dallas (Texas) *Morning News*, as quoted by the *New Yorker* for February 24, 1951. The *New Yorker's* comment is "Oh, confusion schmooshun!"

The triumph of the tribe of rule-makers as arbiters of linguistic

elegance has indeed been overwhelming in our country. The consequence is that most Americans belonging to that segment of our
society whose social milieu is somewhere between that of the late
George Apley and Jeeter Lester—which is to say, the great mass of our
people—go through life believing that those whom they have themselves set up as linguistic dictators are in possession of secret information
about the use of language which is not vouchsafed to ordinary mortals.
Overzealous warnings in the classroom against such crudities as "he
sang bad" have resulted in "he felt badly," "the milk smells badly,"
so that teachers and texts must now warn against *badly* after the verbs
feel, taste, look, sound, and *smell.* The children of the culturally underprivileged (to use an elegant euphemism for "poor, lowly, and un-
schooled," quite in accord with the spirit of our enlightened times)
now say "She gave the party for he and I" instead of "Me and him
went to the party." These are but a sampling of the great victories of
the prescriptive teaching of English in America. Some cynical observers
will probably think them Pyrrhic victories.

It is an amusing irony that the development of an idiomatic,
colloquial form of language on the educated level has been less free in
democratic, freedom-loving America (to accept at their face value the
labels which in moments of patriotic ardour we apply to ourselves) than
in the supposedly more conservative, tradition-bound England. We
are proud to believe that the salient qualities of American English are
its daring and independence. Although he has modified his opinions
somewhat in his *Supplement Two,* H. L. Mencken has referred in *The
American Language* to its restlessness and impatience, its lack of both
restraint and conformity. These are qualities difficult to discover in the
speech of the educated, whose very uncertainty about the perplexities
with which they have been told language is fraught indicates their
consciousness of the lessons imperfectly learned in school and college.
Mr. Mencken has dealt at length with the vulgar tongue, "the daily
speech of nearly 100,000,000 Americans," a form of English which
despite the imposing number of its users has not been a principal
concern of the present work. Their speech, rewarding as the study of
it may be, is in many of its details not standard American English,
though in its main outlines it is not radically different from the speech
of the educated, certainly not to the degree that the speech of a Cockney
is different from that of an Oxford don.

Standard American English has been defined as the speech of those more or less average citizens who carry on the effective business of our so-called "American way of life." Although it may vary somewhat, as we have noted, from community to community, there are few places in our country where it can be described as being free and easy in its pronunciation, its morphology, or its syntax. On the contrary, it is predominantly a highly self-conscious and rigorously regimented form of expression, and it has been so since at least the middle of the nineteenth century, by which time it is safe to assume that the standards set up by the schools had come to apply to the community at large. What was thought of as "good" speech was by this time regarded as a criterion of respectability. People in general were quite conscious of the standards promulgated and disseminated by the schools; otherwise, deviations from those standards such as may be encountered in the writings of Artemus Ward (Charles Farrar Browne), Josh Billings (Henry Wheeler Shaw), and Petroleum V. Nasby (David Ross Locke) would never have seemed funny. The amusement which these humorists excited (*mirabile dictu*) was of an indulgent sort, not unmixed perhaps with a sneaking admiration of their linguistic independence. In our own day many have found cause for amusement in the supposed cowboy lingo in which was couched the cracker-barrel philosophy of Will Rogers, the Oklahoma pundit. But despite the widespread adulation of Rogers as a "great American" and even a "typical American," it is very doubtful that any educated adult American, except for an occasional politician addressing his rural constituency, ever tried to talk like him.

The rip-snorting, hell-for-leather turgidity and hyperbole of our western frontier in the last century have frequently been supposed to mirror the boldness and admirable self-confidence which we are pleased to think of as typical of us. This sort of language is, however, no more typically American than the bombast and fustian and the "inkhorn terms" of Elizabethan English are typically English. Nevertheless, it continues to connote in the American imagination the virgin wilderness, the covered wagon, the great open spaces, the manly fortitude of the pioneer—in all, a way of life which most of us have never really known and which is certainly more interesting when viewed through the shimmer of romance than ever it actually was.

The stiffly formal diction of educated characters in American fiction is frequently in striking contrast to the easygoing colloquialism of speakers of comparable social station in English novels, as has been noted by G. H. McKnight in an article published in the brilliant maiden issue of *American Speech*. The language of the people in Henry James's later novels, though more obscure, is at the same time more colloquial than that usually encountered in American novels, including James's own earlier works, for James had literally to cross the Atlantic before he was to learn how to write natural, colloquial dialogue. The supposed solecisms by which Howells attempted in *The Rise of Silas Lapham* to indicate Lapham's lack of formal schooling and which stand out in sharp contrast to the speech of educated American speakers in the novel are for the most part forms of speech sanctioned by the best British usage.

Writers of the generation before James and Howells were notably conservative in their use of language. Few characters in British society novels of the day speak more formally, more elegantly, more parsably than Cooper's noble savages, and there is little or nothing in Irving, Poe, Emerson, Longfellow, Hawthorne, Lowell (except for the Yankee dialect of the *Biglow Papers*), or Bryant which deviates from the most formal British English, save perhaps that the American writers seem to have achieved a somewhat greater degree of formality than their British contemporaries. Bryant seriously believed that the language of America had been "undergoing a process of corruption for the last quarter of a century," and as editor of the New York *Evening Post* did his part to arrest that process by preparing a list of words—many of them Americanisms like *lengthy, presidential, to locate, to advocate,* and *to legislate*—which writers for his paper were to eschew because to the venerable poet-editor they represented the decay of the English language.

Our eighteenth-century writers were altogether colonial in their linguistic attitudes. Franklin, who despite his stalwart republicanism loved to hobnob with European aristocrats, tells us in his *Autobiography* that it was one of the greatest objects of his ambition to write English well and that he had therefore as a young man formed his style upon that of Addison. He was quite pernickety in his attitude towards the English of America and was never really in sympathy with Noah Webster's linguistic patriotism.

It is a notable and rather sobering fact that Americans, regardless of their political leanings, threw off the shackles of linguistic subservience to England only when they could be assured that there was an even "safer" standard—that of the schoolmaster and, later, his female counterpart. Except for vocabulary, the boldness, the independence, the impatience with tradition upon which we pride ourselves in matters of language have in actual fact been so efficiently kept in check by the birch of authority that, to modify Hamlet's phrase but a trifle, they are more honoured in the breech than the observance.

Our respect for linguistic authoritarians has been just as great as that which we have shown for the political, economic, and moral overseers who play so conspicuous a role in our national life. What with all our loving toleration of boards of censors, watch and ward societies, organizations for the suppression of practically everything that nonmembers enjoy, and groups devoted to the minding of other people's business, it is indeed remarkable that the various attempts to set up an academy for the purpose of regulating the use of our language have come to nothing. But we have never really been without direction in such matters, and perhaps the reason we have no academy is that those who have functioned as linguistic dictators have disciplined the language so thoroughly that an academy would have been altogether supererogatory. As a result of their dedicated efforts, the speech of educated Americans is frequently dry, dull, tedious, overprecise, and halting as compared with the speech of Englishmen of the same class. What Dryden called the "language of well-bred ease" has been of our own free choice rejected for language governed by the rules and regulations of the dictionary, the textbook, and the classroom. Perhaps the appropriate inference is that well-bred ease has no place in democratic life.

To many this will doubtless seem a gruesome note to end on; others will be convinced that it is altogether meet and right that America, ever in the vanguard of progress, should have evolved an attitude towards language and a norm of speech not rooted in social caste but attainable by any man or woman capable of following certain prescriptions. In any case, it can hardly be denied in the light of the evidence that the higher linguistic morality which has been the subject of this concluding chapter is a prominent development of American English, whether linguistic antinomians like it or not. The other, and to some the more attractive side of the picture, that which displays the altogether pleasing American genius for word-making, has already been presented. But equally revealing of a quite different aspect of the national character is the willingness, even eagerness, which we have always shown in our surrender of small, individual liberties for the sake of an ideal—in this instance a potential linguistic equalitarianism similar to the potential opportunity of the humblest lad to sit in the seats of the mighty provided that he guides his career by the proper set of precepts. In this aspect of our linguistic behaviour more than in any other is reflected that moral earnestness which has ever characterized the American people. The fact that we sometimes fail to act in accordance with our ideal is quite irrelevant.